Praise for the first edition of *In the Wake of the Butcher*

"This is a well-researched book on a subject that remains a haunting mystery in Cleveland to this day."—*Library Journal*

"This work is an astonishing piece of localized history; sometimes you feel as though you are actually being stalked by the mysterious, unknown killer; at other times you are hot on the killer's trail."—*Sunday Salem News*

"James Jessen Badal is the first to give the torso murderer of Kingsbury Run the scrutiny these notorious crimes merit. . . . The crimes mesmerized Cleveland, stupefied local law enforcement, and captured national attention."—*Northeast Ohio Journal of History*

"Despite being the most carefully researched version of the infamous torso killings yet, *In the Wake of the Butcher* reads like a suspense novel. Fascinating stuff for history and true-crime buffs."—Les Roberts, author of the Milan Jacovich Mysteries, including *The Dutch, The Indian Sign, The Best Kept Secret,* and *A Shoot in Cleveland*

"The photos and details will bathe your eyes and brains in bloodshed."
—*Akron Beacon Journal*

"Jim Badal takes readers along as he investigates the 'Mad Butcher' murders more thoroughly, objectively and professionally than any previous researcher or author. To those of us who have studied this case and longed for more details, this is the book we've been waiting for. Complete with exclusive interviews and investigation reports never before seen, Badal's authoritative work on the serial killer adds a new dimension to the fascination and the mystery that will forever surround the case. . . . While others have gone to press with the regurgitation of stale and sometimes inaccurate reports, . . . Jim Badal waited until he had it right, and for all the right reasons."—Paul W. Heimel, author of *Eliot Ness: The Real Story*

"[Badal] attempts to clarify popular misunderstandings about the murders and provide the first clear, detailed historical narrative of the case. . . . The result is a fine contribution to the history of this gruesome chapter in the history of Cleveland. . . . *In the Wake of the Butcher* also includes fascinating glimpses of Eliot Ness and the role of the press in the ...
—*Northwest Ohio Quarterly*

D1273070

In the Wake of the
BUTCHER

In the Wake of the
BUTCHER
CLEVELAND'S TORSO MURDERS

Authoritative Edition, Revised and Expanded

James Jessen Badal

THE KENT STATE UNIVERSITY PRESS ❧ KENT, OHIO

This book was made possible through the generous cooperation
of the Cleveland Police Historical Society.

© 2014 by The Kent State University Press, Kent, Ohio 44242
ALL RIGHTS RESERVED
Library of Congress Catalog Card Number 2013048858
ISBN 978-1-60635-213-7
Manufactured in the United States of America

Frontispiece: A police photograph of victim no. 4's head as it was found
in Kingsbury Run on June 5, 1936. Cleveland Police Historical Society.

LIBRARY OF CONGRESS CATALOGING-IN-PUBLICATION DATA
Badal, James Jessen, 1943–
In the wake of the butcher : Cleveland's torso murders /
James Jessen Badal.—Authoritative edition, revised and expanded.
pages cm
Includes bibliographical references and index.
ISBN 978-1-60635-213-7 (pbk.) ∞
1. Serial murders—Ohio—Cleveland. 2. Homicide investigation—
Ohio—Cleveland. 3. Ness, Eliot. I. Title.
HV6534.C55 B35 2014
364.152'320977132—dc23
2013048858

22 21 20   5 4 3

To the memory of Robert E. Scherl
Friend! Friend! Good!

CONTENTS

This mass murder mystery parallels any of the famous mass murder cases known to history in interest, gruesomeness, and ingenuity on the part of the murderer. If he is ever caught, it will most certainly be by accident.

—Dr. Samuel R. Gerber, coroner for Cuyahoga County, 1936–86

Preface and Acknowledgments to the Authoritative Edition

"It's your destiny," laughed my longtime collaborator and research partner Mark Wade Stone when I told him the Kent State University Press had asked about the possibility of a revised and expanded edition of my 2001 book *In the Wake of the Butcher: Cleveland's Torso Murders*. And so it would seem! After three books, three TV documentaries, and an endless series of talks devoted to Cleveland's notorious butcheries from the mid-1930s, it would appear I was not done with Kingsbury Run—or, perhaps more accurately, Kingsbury Run wasn't finished with me. Frankly, I've always regarded "updated" and "revised" editions with a fair degree of suspicion; was there really anything new and significant here to justify a new book, or was this simply a vaguely unethical ploy to entice those who had already invested in the original publication to fork over the cash for a "new" edition? Primarily for this reason, I have resisted suggestions over the years that a new edition of *Butcher* might be in order.

I have served on the board of trustees of the Cleveland Police Historical Society for a dozen years, a position that allows me to keep track of the memorabilia that constantly trickles in to the Cleveland Police Museum from a variety of sources—usually retired officers or the families of a deceased former officer. Naturally enough, this stream of material often contained something related to Kingsbury Run and the torso murders; but none of it—interesting and enlightening as some of it may have been—seemed sufficiently significant to warrant a new edition of *In the Wake of the Butcher*. Stray bits of new information that were coming forward may add a touch of color or a tad more detail to the history of the murders, but they changed nothing! That is until August 2012 when Ted Krejsa attended one of my "torso talks" and handed me an incredible photograph—something that could only be described as the proverbial jaw-dropper.

When I began serious research into the Kingsbury Run murders in the mid-1990s, the information available on the case tended to be an utterly bewildering tangle of fact, fancy, and outright fiction. Some of the treatments of the murder-dismemberments in massive true crime anthologies or encyclopedias were seriously off base in a number of different ways and as fanciful as a Disney cartoon. One of the murkier issues of the case has always revolved around Eliot Ness's assertion twenty years after the murders that he had a "secret suspect"—a man he graced with the rather odd pseudonym of Gaylord Sundheim. According to Cleveland's one-time safety director, his suspicions about this individual had been growing steadily; so in May 1938 operatives pulled "Gaylord" off the streets and spirited him away to a downtown hotel room where a lie detector test firmly established his guilt. With no proof that could be taken to court to back up the polygraph results, however, Ness was forced to let his quarry go. Unfortunately, there was no hard evidence to back up any of the details of this incredible story. The conspiratorially minded found it all intriguing and embraced it; the more cynical rejected it for a variety of perfectly understandable reasons: "Who had administered the test? Where had the lie detector come from (the East Cleveland police owned the only machine in the area, and there was no record of it ever having been loaned out)? Who was present? How could anything so elaborate be planned and carried out behind the scenes and kept secret for so long?" Ness's account left too many significant details unaddressed. Benjamin Franklin had once wryly quipped that three people could keep a secret if two of them were dead. In this case, how could so many keep such a vital secret for so long? Was this really a true story that could be verified, or was this simply a famous lawmen—a hero in many people's minds—attempting to polish his sagging reputation by rewriting history? When I wrote *In the Wake of the Butcher,* I felt there were three vital questions associated with Ness's story of his secret suspect that needed answering: 1) Could it be established that the hotel room interrogation really took place? 2) Could the person so questioned be positively identified? And 3) Was that individual the elusive

Mad Butcher of Kingsbury Run? In *Butcher* I was able to answer the first two questions in the affirmative. Now, thanks to Ted Krejsa's photograph, I was well on my way to answering that final question: was the man Eliot Ness called Gaylord Sundheim actually the Butcher?

The yellowed photograph that Ted handed me that evening showed six rather serious-looking gentlemen all nattily dressed in white suits. One of them was Dr. Edward Peterka, Krejsa's great uncle. The other five men were doctors with whom he shared a thriving medical practice at 5026 Broadway, just west of St. Alexis Hospital where, presumably, all six were employed. Among them sat Dr. Francis Edward Sweeney—the man Marilyn Bardsley first identified in the 1970s as Eliot Ness's prime suspect in the murder-dismemberments—expressionless, staring vacantly into space, seemingly focused on nothing. I knew about the Peterka-Sweeney medical partnership, but I did not realize that it was a relatively major enterprise involving four additional physicians. Once a vital and thriving Central European neighborhood, today the Broadway-East 55th area struggles against decay and blight. Virtually all the buildings that had once lined the south side of Broadway between East 55th and Pershing have been demolished, leaving nothing behind but vacant land; so there was no way of determining what the building that housed that practice looked like. In 1938 a one-time vagrant named Emil Fronek had shared a lurid tale with Cleveland police about having escaped from the clutches of a "doctor" who had apparently tried unsuccessfully to drug him for some reason; but when police took him to the Broadway-East 55th area where Fronek insisted this had happened, he was unable to find the office. What was the problem? What did this so-called "office" look like? Was it a small neighborhood office building, or was it something else? There was no way to tell for sure; Platt maps from the period merely showed there was some sort of building on that piece of land.

Shortly after the talk, Ted sent me a second photograph of the structure that once had stood at 5026 Broadway along with floor plans drawn by his father who often visited his Uncle Edward's office and clearly remembered the layout. It was not an office building in the accepted sense of the term at all; it was a large, two-story house, a former residential structure whose first floor had been remodeled to serve as a small medical facility complete with waiting room, examination room, even a room for minor surgery. The second floor, however, could still serve as a living space. Directly behind the house stood an old stable, long since fallen into disuse save as a catchall storage area. Part of the Raus Funeral Home that occupied the land directly east of the one-time residence at 5040 Broadway was clearly visible on the left side of the photograph. Surprisingly, the photograph showed that there was a much newer structure housing a small delicatessen to the west of the "office" on the corner of Broadway and Pershing Avenue. It had been built virtually up against the medical facility; and the front of the building extended out toward Broadway much farther than the house. These revelations as to the exact nature of the building that served as a medical office, its interior layout, and both the types and locations of the structures that surrounded it were crucial; suddenly the most perplexing mysteries that have been associated with the torso murders since they began in the mid-1930s had been solved. It was now clear where and how the killer incapacitated his victims; it was now possible to pinpoint the exact location of the Butcher's long-sought-for "secret laboratory." Thanks to Ted Krejsa, this new edition of *In the Wake of the Butcher* became possible; there was a new, vitally important story to tell.

The section dealing with Eliot Ness's suspect Dr. Francis Edward Sweeney has been substanitially rewritten and greatly expanded into an entirely separate chapter; I have also fleshed out somewhat the sections dealing with Frank Dolezal's death—a subject I explored at length in *Though Murder Has No Tongue: The Lost Victim of Cleveland's Mad Butcher* (Kent State University Press, 2010)—and seemingly similar murders committed outside of Cleveland are covered in depth in *Hell's Wasteland: The Pennsylvania Torso Murders.* Other than that, little has changed. I have corrected a few minor factual errors, as well as some spelling slipups and other grammatical goofs that had somehow managed to survive multiple readings from several different sets of eyes before the book's original publication in 2001.

Acknowledgments to the First Edition

My book *Recording the Classics: Maestros, Music and Technology* had hardly made it to the shelves when I approached John Hubbell and Julia Morton of The Kent State University Press in the summer of 1996 with a proposal for a book on the Kingsbury Run murders. At the time, I doubted there was enough information available to justify a full-length book only on the killings, and I felt that a chronicle stitched together solely from contemporary newspaper and magazine accounts would be of little interest or value. All I had at the time was some significant information about the crimes known to few others. Would the Press be interested in the possibility of such a project without my making a formal proposal? With their encouragement I dug for more information, tracked people down, and worked to fashion a detailed and coherent narrative over the next three years. Through it all, people at the Press offered their interest and encouragement, sharing in—sometimes enduring—my excitement as people came forward to tell their stories and previously undiscovered major sources of information suddenly opened up. My thanks to them for that continuous, enthusiastic support. My thanks also to my editor Joanna Hildebrand Craig for her skill, sensitivity, and patience.

In late winter of 1999, Anne Kmieck, then curator of the Cleveland Police Historical Society Museum, phoned me with the news that she had obtained the address of Marjorie Merylo Dentz, daughter of the chief investigator on the case. Mrs. Dentz's father, Detective Peter Merylo, had been assigned to the murders full-time in the summer of 1936, and he worked on them almost exclusively until his retirement from the police department in 1943. He was the cop the press and the public most closely associated with the case. At the time of his departure from the force, the press suggested that the indefatigable detective had taken his personal files with him. Students of the Kingsbury Run killings, therefore, have been taunted for nearly sixty years by the possibility that Peter Merylo's papers still existed, and his daughter confirmed that her father's files were, indeed, in her family's possession. Mrs. Dentz graciously made all of her father's papers available to me and diligently manned a copy machine for over nine straight hours duplicating the fragile documents. A year later she found another box of material stored in her garage, the existence of which she had been previously unaware. Without hesitation, she returned to the copier and sent me a second formidable pile of documents. Many of the photographs that appear in this book are also from her father's files and her family's private collection.

In the spring of 2000, an article about the publication of this book appeared in the *Plain Dealer*. The Sunday it ran, I received a phone call from writer/brewmaster Dave Satula, who, after introducing himself, lamented, "You beat me to it!" How could two people in the same city delve into the same subject for so long without ever encountering or even hearing of the other? He willingly shared his research, and his generous cooperation allowed me to flesh out pertinent details of the case. Thanks to our conversations, I also was forced to revisit some of my basic assumptions about the crimes that resulted in subtle but important changes in the manuscript.

My thanks to the administration of Cuyahoga Community College for allowing me time off from teaching to do some of the major research necessary and to the Board of Trustees of the Cleveland Police Historical Society for its generous cooperation.

I owe a considerable debt to some people who, by their own requests, will remain anonymous. My sincerest thanks to the following for their assistance: Brian E. Albrecht (staff writer for the *Plain Dealer*), members of Edward W. Andrassy's family, Dr. Daniel W. Badal, William Becker (archivist, Cleveland State University *Press* Collection), David Bernatowicz, Louis Bodnar (funeral director), Marilyn Bardsley, Commander Robert Cermak (Cleveland Police Department, retired, and chairman of the Board of Trustees, Cleveland Police Historical Society), Judith Cetina (manager of the Cuyahoga County Archives), Nikhil Chand (Technology Learning Center representative, Cuyahoga Community College, Eastern Campus), Dr. Thurston Cosner, Anne Louise Dolezal, Mary Joan Dolezal, Kathy Fana (office supervisor at the morgue), Dr. Marge Geiger, Paul W. Heimel (author of *Eliot Ness: The Untold Story*), David Holcombe (curator and director of the

Cleveland Police Historical Society Museum), Marilyn Jeck, Steve Jerziorski, Tomi Johnson, Richard Karberg, Anne T. Kmieck (former curator of the Cleveland Police Historical Society Museum), John Kostura, Anne Krupa, Richard Wallace LaGassie, Mary Lucak, Robert Mancini, Rebecca McFarland (vice president of the Cleveland Police Historical Society), Thomas Mullady, Michael Nevin, Delmar O'Hare (volunteer at the Cleveland Police Historical Society Museum), Paul F. Perhacs, Allen P. Pinell, Walter Piszczek, Cynthia Quinlan, Bill Redmond, Tim and Barbara Riley, Arnold Sagalyn (former special assistant to Eliot Ness), Andrew R. Schug (member of the Board of Trustees, Cleveland Police Historical Society—good friend, skilled and fanatical researcher), Ann Sindelar (Western Reserve Historical Society Library), James L. Singler (former registrar at the Ohio Veterans Home, Sandusky), Jan Skaar (Medical Records, the Ohio Veterans Home), Noel A. Slagle (retired assistant professor of Health Education, Cuyahoga Community College), Bob Smith (Holy Cross Cemetery), Don Stragisher, Mark Stueve (Old Erie Street Bookstore), Mary M. Suva (Cuyahoga Community College copy center), Carolyn Svetz (records management officer, Cuyahoga County Archives), Ed Vance, Linda Walker (Brooklyn Police Department), Joanne S. Witbeck, Michael Zaverton (attorney at law), Michael Zemba, and Kenneth A. Zirm (attorney at law, Walter and Haverfield). Thanks also to the staffs of the Cleveland Public Library, the Cleveland State University Library, and the Western Reserve Historical Society Library.

INTRODUCTION

When I took American history in the eighth grade, our teacher rounded off the academic year by reading us John Bartlow Martin's 1949 *Harper's Magazine* article "Butcher's Dozen: The Cleveland Torso Murders" over a two-day period. Just why he thought twelve decapitation murders from the mid-1930s were fit company for the Civil War, Thomas Jefferson, and the Great Depression, I never knew. It was history, I suppose—local history that he, perhaps, felt we should know something about. Maybe he had just been bitten by the same bug that infects Jack the Ripper fans and devotees of other horrendous but unsolved crimes.

Then as now, murder in Cleveland meant the Sheppard case—not just for city residents but for the entire country as well. But the story in that old issue of *Harper's* released a dark, frightening shadow from the city's past, a tale so mysterious, so gruesome and compelling that it effectively obscured Dr. Sam and his brutally murdered wife, Marilyn. To a group of eighth graders just hitting their early teens, the battle between good and evil that emerged from Martin's recounting of those long-ago crimes immediately assumed epic, indeed mythological proportions—a classic confrontation worthy to stand with Beowulf and Grendel, God and Satan. On one side stood Cleveland's safety director, Eliot Ness, the man who finally got Capone and had since added to his legendary status by cleaning up a city crippled by corruption and labor racketeering; on the other side roamed an unknown psychopath who littered the inner city with a dozen decapitated and otherwise mutilated bodies over a three-year period and vanished as mysteriously as he appeared, leaving virtually no clues to his identity. It was a case that placed the city in an embarrassing national spotlight as it struggled to climb out of the Great Depression and handed the seemingly invincible Ness a humiliating defeat from which his law enforcement career never fully recovered. It was also the story of a city—how its people, press, and social institutions reacted to a situation virtually without precedent in modern American history and how they ultimately responded when the forces of good seemed inexplicably unable to prevail.

Rather than having our seats lined up in traditional rows, our teacher favored a horseshoe arrangement with his desk standing between the two legs; as he read the lengthy article, I could look around the incomplete circle and wonder if the details of those terrible murders were burning as deeply into the imaginations of my classmates as they were in mine. Edward Andrassy. Flo Polillo. Frank Dolezal. Those names have haunted the niches of my memory ever since.

There were, however, some flashes of black humor to lighten the somber classroom atmosphere. A popular song of the day had a first line that ran, "I found my thrill on Blueberry Hill"; and in a sly burst of creativity, our teacher had adapted it to fit the present circumstances: "I found my thrill on Jackass Hill" and "I found my fun in Kingsbury Run." It seemed to me that he had actually composed some wicked little ditty about the crimes— his own personal version of "Lizzie Borden took an ax," but I had to check with some of my contemporaries to make sure my memory was accurate. "Floating down the river, chunk by chunk by chunk; / Arms and legs and torsos, hunk by hunk by hunk!"

Years later, I bought Donald Rumbelow's book *The Complete Jack the Ripper.* I was hooked. His murders possessed those two qualities guaranteed to compel enduring fascination: they were unspeakably horrible, and they remained unsolved. Mary Ann Nichols, Annie Chapman, Liz Stride, Catherine Eddows, Mary Jane Kelly—these brutally slashed women joined their butchered Cleveland counterparts in my imagination. The antiquity of the case actually became part of its appeal; the gulf of years created a dense fog that I was always trying to penetrate. Clues could only be traced so far before the century-old mists obscured the threads. The truth always lay just out of reach behind the faded and grainy photographs of murder sites, investigators, victims, and suspects.

I envied those amateur sleuths who lived near the scenes of those infamous crimes or had the time and money to travel there simply to soak up the atmosphere of Buck's Row, Miller's Court, Hanbury Street, and Mitre Square. Then the distant, grim echoes from those last two days in eighth grade American history began to grow louder. Why should I be jealous? Cleveland could boast its own series of sensational, unsolved killings— nearly as old and just as horrible as anything that had happened in that dingy London slum over a century ago. To a native Clevelander, especially someone alive at the time, no murder case ever gripped the public imagination more fiercely than those infamous butcheries. Older city residents remembered those murders clearly; most of their younger counterparts at least knew of them. It seemed impossible to be a Clevelander and not know something about the savage slayings of Kingsbury Run.

The killings also enjoyed notoriety among crime buffs outside the city. The case had been novelized at least twice and had formed an integral part of several true crime anthologies. It had been the focus of one previous book-length treatment, the subject of at least two segments of NBC's *Unsolved Mysteries,* and the impetus behind—of all things—a musical dealing with Eliot Ness's years in Cleveland. Interest in the unspeakably gruesome case has never waned, especially in Cleveland, where the elderly still remember, where local TV news stories, as well as articles in area newspapers and magazines, continue to appear at irregular intervals.

Surely, I thought, there must be all sorts of old, musty local documents—everything from newspapers to police files—to work through and others waiting to be discovered! I could visit those desolate murder sites that sixty years of progress and city growth had not obliterated, where unsuspecting neighborhood residents, an astonishing number of them children, had stumbled across a decapitated, naked corpse or decomposing body parts; I could walk through Kingsbury Run in the footsteps of the investigators, stand along the shores of the Cuyahoga River where pieces of dismembered victims had floated by, prowl through the decaying neighborhoods where the unhappy lives of Edward Andrassy and Flo Polillo had played themselves out. Eventually I put together a slide lecture on the killings that I delivered frequently to local clubs and organizations. The idea for this book ultimately grew out of that presentation.

The oddly disturbing masks immediately grab the visitor's attention. Time-worn, even dilapidated, they hang on the wall behind protective plastic shields at the Cleveland Police Historical Society Museum in the Justice Center—stark, sixty-year-old memorials to four of the Butcher's victims: Edward W. Andrassy, forever to be known as victim no. 1, the mask probably based on a photograph considering the ravaged condition of his head when police recovered it; Florence Polillo, victim no. 3, the mask no doubt modeled on her mug shot since her head was never recovered; victim no. 8, the petite African American woman tentatively identified as Rose Wallace, the mask probably a fanciful reconstruction based on her photograph since she had been dead a year when her disarticulated partial skeletal remains were discovered; victim no. 4, perhaps the most enigmatic and mysterious of all, the still unidentified tattooed man, his death mask alone a direct casting from his head. Above them hang a series of official police photos of dismembered victims before which the unwary inevitably gasp or momentarily avert their eyes. It remains the largest display devoted to a single case in the entire museum.

Anne T. Kmieck served as museum curator from 1988 until 1999. She, perhaps more than anyone else in Cleveland, can testify to the fascination the seventy-five-year-old murders continue to generate. Besides fielding a barrage of casual questions from museum visitors intrigued by the display, she judges she received a dozen inquiries a year of a more serious nature. One woman called seeking information about the tattooed victim no. 4 because her similarly adorned grandfather had mysteriously vanished in the summer of 1936, about the same time two boys found no. 4's severed head wrapped in a pair of pants under a tree in Kingsbury Run. I gave the museum a diagram from the *Press* files showing the nature and location of the tattoos to aid the identification process, but the woman's search ended abruptly in disappointment. There was a twenty-year age difference between the unidentified tattooed man and her missing grandfather.

Kmieck received a more personal call from Edward Andrassy's granddaughter Tomi Johnson. Since Andrassy, the first official victim, remained one of only two who were positively identified, the police and the press dug relentlessly into his background uncovering tales of drinking and gambling, evidence of petty crimes, and hints of sexual deviance. "Everything is so negative," she lamented. In a reference to one article that branded him a homosexual and unequivocally declared he died having never married or fathered children, she asked somewhat wistfully and jokingly, "Didn't you know Edward Andrassy didn't have a granddaughter?" Though Andrassy was murdered well over a decade before she was born, she has tried to at least leaven posterity's distasteful image by putting together a more rounded, more balanced picture of her infamous grandfather. Her melancholy quest inevitably brought her to the police museum and Anne Kmieck who, perhaps somewhat ironically, supplied her with copies of her grandfather's police mug shots.

Kmieck also patiently listened to theories as to the identity of the killer that ranged from the intriguing to the bizarre, such as the assertion that the murderer was actually Cuyahoga County's legendary coroner Dr. Samuel Gerber. According to this wildly improbable scenario, the police were so in need of his exceptional forensic skills, that when his guilt was uncovered, authorities let him off with the proverbial slap on the wrist so long as he promised to keep his troublesome, murderous impulses under control.

Inevitably Kmieck dealt with inquiries about the case files, records that have vanished in the sixty years since the murders occurred. Their disappearance would seem virtually inexplicable since, according to Cleveland reporter Howard Beaufait, who wrote extensively about the killings during the 1930s, the authorities interrogated approximately 9,100 people during what became the most massive police investigation in the city's history. The sheer volume of paperwork would have been enormous; and although homicide records are never destroyed, sloppy procedures in the past and a couple of moves from one building to another since the 1930s may have banished them into bureaucratic oblivion. Apparently, according to Kmieck, it was also once standard practice for retiring investigators to take their case files with them—rather as departing London policemen routinely lifted bits of the Jack the Ripper files as souvenirs. Occasionally, she got interesting phone tips from "informants" professing to know either the location of the missing documents or the identity of whomever took them in the first place. Whatever the reasons for their disappearance or misplacement may be, the fact remains that there is little surviving official documentation of the most notorious murders in Cleveland history.

Plain Dealer staff reporter Brian E. Albrecht has also experienced first-hand the fascination which the case still compels. He has written a half dozen extensive articles about the Kingsbury Run murders beginning in January 1989, and every story has generated a flurry of calls and letters, mostly from people who were children at the time and need to share their still-vivid memories about the killings. Others want to bounce around ideas as to the perpetrator's identity, while some, mostly the young or those new to the city, simply want to express their amazement that something so shocking could have happened in Cleveland so long ago. What he terms serial killer groupies and mass murder fans also contact him for a variety of strange reasons. "People came out of the woodwork," he reflected. Some of the inquiries were simply bizarre, such as one from an astrologer who requested information on an unnamed suspect with medical training and drinking problems because, according to the inquiry, some signs are specifically tied to surgery, nursing, and alcoholism.

† † †

In 1930, the city's population stood at 900,429. Cleveland was the nation's sixth largest city and a jumble of contrasting faces. The 1920s had been a period of tremendous industrial and economic expansion. Major institutions such as the Cleveland Public Library and Public Auditorium had opened. By the 1930s, the unique assemblage of arts and educational institutions in University Circle on the city's near east side was already flourishing. The art museum ranked as a major force in the cultural world; and in Severance Hall, Artur Rodzinski was molding the superb orchestra that George Szell would inherit a decade later.

But the Depression hit the city hard, blunting the industrial vigor that had propelled it economically since the nineteenth century. In 1930 Cleveland ranked second only to Detroit in the percentage of workers employed in industry (41 percent of 394,898), and by January 1931, over 100,000 of them were out of work. Throughout the decade monthly unemployment figures fluctuated wildly between 46,000 and 219,000. Like other major population centers struggling with the economic collapse, Cleveland was totally unprepared for such massive numbers of the unemployed and the destitute. In 1931, a one-mill levy for county relief passed, and one million dollars were slashed from city operating expenses and channeled into various relief services. In 1932, the newly elected Democratic mayor Ray T. Miller adopted strict municipal spending policies and successfully goaded utility companies into lowering their rates. But such draconian measures were never enough, and both local and federal governments struggled to keep up with the city's skyrocketing need. Throughout the decade, the numbers of unemployed receiving welfare or work relief rose alarmingly: 3,499 in 1928, 52,995 in 1933, 77,565 in 1936. By 1936, 10,075 Cleveland workers received aid under the Federal Emergency Relief Administration; by March 1938, the Civil Works Administration and the Work Projects Administration provided 54,849 county residents with work relief.

The inner city was crumbling into a crime-ridden, poverty-stricken collection of tenements, bars, and brothels. Those segments of the population that could escape the rot pushed outward to the borders of the metropolitan area, leaving behind a sprawl of appalling firetraps without toilets or running water. At the very core of the decaying inner city, the most destitute congregated in the shantytowns of the Flats and Kingsbury Run. At the height of the Depression as many as six separate colonies of varying permanence sprawled from the foot of the Terminal Tower into the railroad yards and the city's industrial area. The largest camp—a maze of makeshift hovels fashioned from wood, corrugated metal, and cardboard—spread from the base of the Eagle Street ramp to the hill at Commercial and Canal Roads. It sheltered a mix of drunks, hoboes, the unemployed, and what we would call today the working poor—men who held steady jobs but did not earn enough to live anywhere else. The unfortunate residents scavenged for discarded vegetables at the East Side Market on East 4th and snatched dead chickens tossed in the allies off Carnegie Avenue by poultry farmers. The very poorest, those virtually without hope, gathered just east of the East 34th Street Bridge where they slept in the tall grass or in the bushes. Some camped on the ledges under the railroad bridge at East 36th; the lucky ones had cardboard boxes in which to sleep.

In stark contrast, affluent suburbs were spreading both to the east and west. Thanks to the foresight of the Van Sweringen brothers, the developers of Shaker Heights, the residents of the posh eastern suburb enjoyed a link to the central business district of the city through a rapid transit line, which, ironically, passes through Kingsbury Run on the final leg of its journey downtown.

Prohibition had brought the mob to Cleveland, just as it had to other major cities; so crime, even violent crime, was hardly unknown. Labor

The face of the Great Depression in a Cleveland shantytown. Courtesy of Marjorie Merylo Dentz.

Part of the sprawling shantytown complex in the Flats and Kingsbury Run. *Cleveland Press* Archives, Cleveland State University.

racketeering, then in its infancy, was developing into a major problem, and mob-controlled illegal gambling became so entrenched that it survived the repeal of Prohibition. In 1931, the city fought back by making George J. Matowitz chief of police and appointing David L. Cowles to the newly created Scientific Investigation Bureau—a modern transformation of the old Bertillon Department. Matowitz was a tough, highly competent professional who moved up the ranks and earned his appointment through simple diligence and hard work; he remained in office until 1950, becoming one of the most respected chiefs in departmental history. David Cowles was a largely self-taught scientific genius who would become one of Ness's most trusted associates and revolutionize crime-solving techniques through emphasis on science and technology. The hunt for the Butcher would be their baptisms by fire, testing the professional skills of both men to the limit.

Eliot Ness, still a federal agent, arrived in Cleveland in August 1934, one month before Lake Erie yielded up a grisly piece of what was probably the Butcher's first victim. The level of crime in Cleveland had earned it an unenviable reputation as the most dangerous city in the country; so in December 1935, the newly elected Republican mayor, Harold Burton—a respected and capable public servant who would win reelection for two additional terms—offered Ness the job as Cleveland's safety director. Three months earlier, a couple of young boys had discovered two decapitated corpses, the first of the killer's "official" victims, in the bushes at the base of Jackass Hill in Kingsbury Run. Even though gangland executions were commonplace, they at least proceeded from understandable causes. The Kingsbury Run murders were something different—gruesome killings in which the motives remained obscure.

Certainly no murder investigation in Cleveland history ever turned up a larger, more varied list of suspects. In the early phases of the case, police focused on revenge, either from mobsters or outraged lovers, as the most likely motive. As dismembered bodies began to accumulate, however, it became clear that something far more sinister was at work; and authorities cast their nets into brothels, dark alleys, flophouses, and sleazy bars, snaring an incredible array of the down-and-out, the sexually deviant, and the insane—men such as the "Chicken Gardener," who decapitated the live birds and ejaculated on their bloody necks. Because of the supposed medical expertise of the killer, police eventually turned their attention to the city's doctors. Any medical man about whom there was the slightest suspicion became the object of official attention and scrutiny.

At times ugly tinges of prejudice and racism crept into the investigation, as many of the unfortunates questioned or checked out were either foreign born, of foreign extraction, or black: a mad Mexican, a mad Russian with a machete who hung around Calvary Cemetery, a bowlegged Asian who lived in a condemned building and carried a long, curved knife. Panic also exacerbated the city's racial tensions. Ness received an anonymous, particularly vicious tip letter suggesting he watch "colored hoboes" whom the writer characterized as probable "man-eaters" who "kill each other when they get hungry enough."

As the investigation ground into its third year, turning up few meaningful clues and no viable suspects, pressure for a solution increased dramatically. The public grew more jittery; newspaper editorials grew more shrill; and the political enemies of Republican mayor Harold Burton used the crimes to batter his administration, especially his hand-chosen safety director, Eliot Ness. The later phases of the search were, therefore, marked by an unfortunate desperation which culminated in Ness's order to round up the vagrants and burn the shantytowns of Kingsbury Run in the early morning hours of August 18, 1938.

An astonishing number of people came under suspicion. Because of the hysteria, some of the suspects became as much victims as those who had

The grim reality of life in a Cleveland shantytown. Courtesy of Marjorie Merylo Dentz.

been murdered; because of the continuing notoriety of the killings and the absence of a clearly identified perpetrator, at least one area family lived with a private, dark shadow of suspicion and shame for more than sixty years.

Crime buffs have often compared the Kingsbury Run Butcher to Jack the Ripper. Their grisly activities created a climate of fear in Cleveland and London respectively, and both eluded capture as well as identification principally because law enforcement officials imperfectly understood the psychological dynamics of a serial killer. In both cases, police simply did not know what they were looking for. Both selected their victims from among the ranks of society's downtrodden: the Ripper preyed on women forced into prostitution to support a drinking habit or simply to earn enough money to get a bed in a doss house for the night; Cleveland's Butcher apparently moved among the anonymous dispossessed of the Great Depression—hoboes, transients, and men out of work and too proud to accept relief who crowded in the shantytowns that grew up around the Terminal Tower and spilled into the darkness of the Flats and Kingsbury Run. Of the twelve official victims, only two were ever positively identified.

Though Ripperologists vary both in their body counts and the length of time they believe he was active, conventional wisdom holds the London slasher responsible for the deaths of five prostitutes between late August and early November 1888. In slightly more than two months, he fomented a growing sense of dread and horror throughout the grimy slums of Whitechapel. How much greater the panic in Cleveland as the city confronted a phantom killer who baffled police while committing a series of brutal murders over a period of at least three to four years! Well into the 1950s, parents in the Broadway-East 55th area, close to where some of the victims were found, controlled unruly children with threats of the terrible head hunter of Kingsbury Run.

As with the Ripper, the time span of the Butcher's activities and the exact number of murders that can be definitely attributed to him are both open to conjecture. Tradition says the cycle of Kingsbury Run murders began officially in September 1935 and eventually totaled a dozen victims before ending in August 1938. At least one of those canonical twelve, however, may not belong on the Butcher's tally; indeed, the woman may not even have been a murder victim. It is also probable he claimed his first victim in March 1934, and his activities may not have ceased until July 1950.

Unlike the Ripper, who confined himself to London's East End, the geographical area in which the Kingsbury Run murderer operated remains open to dispute. At the same time dismembered corpses were being discovered in Cleveland, similar grisly finds were turning up in New Castle and Pittsburgh, Pennsylvania; Sandusky and Youngstown, Ohio; and Selkirk, New York. Though hysterical press coverage combined with public panic to assign many of these additional victims to the Cleveland Butcher, commentators have been, and continue to be, divided on this point. At least one of the main investigators on the case, however, was inclined to believe the same perpetrator was responsible for all the disarticulated remains found across Ohio, New York, and western Pennsylvania.

The squalid living conditions in the hobo jungles of Kingsbury Run. Not all residents were "bums"; many held jobs but could not afford to live anywhere else. Courtesy of Marjorie Merylo Dentz.

In the seventy-five years since the murders occurred, understanding the case has been like looking at the Golden Gate Bridge in a morning fog. One could be reasonably sure where it started and ended, and since the tops of the supports towered out of the mists, the overall shape was apparent. But the details remained obscure. Thanks to several thousand pages of previously unexamined documents, a couple of dozen personal interviews, a lot of determined digging into public records, and the active cooperation of scores of individuals, I have been able to clear away much of the fog and render an accurate accounting of this dark chapter in Cleveland history, far more complex but also more coherent and detailed than any in the past. This book explores in greater depth than before the backgrounds and personalities of the main investigators, the identified victims, and the major suspects. Some of the intriguing legends that have grown around and haunted the case for decades can be established as fact. I also offer a detailed list of the major suspects and the evidence against them. Unfortunately, the identity of the murderer, established beyond any reasonable doubt, still remains just out of reach; this is not a final solution book. I can, however, exonerate one suspect, add a new one to the mix, and tie another closely to the case.

The practical problems in researching this book were enormous. Any notorious historical event that continues to excite the public imagination remains prey to various kinds of distortion. In *The Complete History of Jack the Ripper,* one of the most recent treatments of the case by a reputable scholar, Philip Sudgen, devotes considerable space simply to correcting the misinformation that has crept into the accounts of the crimes and erroneously become part of the Ripper legend. Though the Kingsbury Run murders do not enjoy the same international status as the Ripper slayings, errors in fact have similarly colored the official record. There are a number of details, some of them admittedly rather small, that I try to correct in these pages. I once complained to *Plain Dealer* staff writer Brian Albrecht about the sheer amount of digging sometimes required to nail down relatively minor facts. I could work for days hunting information that would yield only half a sentence of finished text. "You're writing a book of record," he remarked casually—his way of reminding me such frustrations went with the territory.

By far the biggest obstacle I faced was those missing police reports. Without them it was difficult to establish exactly what happened and when. The largest single, surviving collection of official Kingsbury Run material in the city is in the coroner's office. The autopsy protocols contain everything from the preliminary coroner's view slip, through notes taken during the examination, to the final official report. These already voluminous files are supplemented by photographs taken by both the police and the coroner's staff, various pieces of official correspondence, huge scrapbooks of newspaper and magazine clippings, and—most important—police reports dealing with the discoveries of bodies or body parts and chronicling the early steps in the investigations. Apparently, the police department routinely sent carbon copies of their original reports to the morgue to provide the coroner and his staff with necessary background information, and they make it possible to construct an extremely accurate picture of the initial phases of the investigations.

The coroner's records, however, are not readily available for public scrutiny, and once a determined researcher does gain access to them, he will be shocked to discover extremely poor, sometimes unreadable rolls of microfilm. (The problem is particularly acute with the police reports that are part of the coroner's files because the original papers were blurred carbon copies.) The original documents simply are not there.

In research, many significant discoveries are inevitably serendipitous; and while gathering the information for this book, I inadvertently discovered over two hundred pages of original material from the morgue files at the Cuyahoga County Archives. Apparently in response to a flood or some other natural disaster well over a decade ago, the coroner's office sent some files judged historically important to the archive building on the near west side for safe keeping; and, in true bureaucratic fashion, everyone promptly forgot where they were. Unfortunately, not all of the files are complete. While most do contain the complete autopsy protocols, as well as the coroner's notes, in a couple of instances—victim no. 9, for example—only a few pages of material have survived. In those cases, all that remain are the imperfect microfilm copies at the coroner's office.

By far the largest and most significant collection of Kingsbury Run material is the files of Detective Peter Merylo, which are in his family's possession. This massive, voluminous assemblage of documents—amounting to over 2,500 pages—consists of daily police reports by Merylo and others from 1930 until 1943, the vast majority dealing with the Kingsbury Run murders; the typed manuscript of his memoirs covering the killings (155 legal-sized pages); a second manuscript on the case written by *Cleveland News* reporter Frank Otwell in collaboration with Merylo (107 typed legal-sized pages); a couple of dozen "tip" letters; clippings from magazines and newspapers, some out of state; pieces of correspondence among official agencies, including the FBI and Scotland Yard; and more than one hundred photographs, most of them never published.

The Frank Otwell-Peter Merylo manuscript is an interesting document. Merylo's daughter Marjorie Merylo Dentz states that it reads just as her father talked, as if Otwell had strung together a series of the detective's oral accounts. (Having read hundreds of Merylo's daily reports and his memoirs, I can attest to this.) It is, however, sometimes difficult to tell where Merylo leaves off and Otwell begins, because the reporter has obviously spiced the formality of the detective's language with a colorful phraseology borrowed from crime novels and Humphrey Bogart movies. There is no way to establish which Merylo manuscript came first—his personal memoirs or the collaboration with Otwell. What is so fascinating is that the two manuscripts complement each other almost perfectly. Merylo discusses aspects of the case with Otwell that he leaves virtually untouched in his own memoirs—almost as if the two manuscripts were to be published as a unit.

It is now possible to track in minute detail the day-to-day progress of the investigation, its ups and downs, from Peter Merylo's point of view. Granted, he and his partner, Martin Zalewski, could not follow every lead personally, and it would be nice to flesh out the picture with reports from others who spent time on the case. But no one worked on the Kingsbury Run murders longer or knew more about them than Peter Merylo; the press relied on him for information more than anyone else with the possible exceptions of Sergeant James Hogan, head of homicide, and Eliot Ness himself. The continuity of Peter Merylo's perspective is, therefore, invaluable. In the absence of the vast majority of police files, however, it is extremely difficult to be precise about all the details or even to establish exactly what happened because the primary sources of information remain the city's newspapers. Daily press reports do not make particularly good historical records. Although Cleveland could boast of three daily papers during the 1930s—the *Plain Dealer,* the *Cleveland Press,* and the *Cleveland News*—their respective stories frequently focus on different details, sometimes contradicting each other. Their published accounts sometimes move from one investigative scene to another without clarifying the time element or supplying the necessary connective tissue to construct a seamless narrative. Errors in the press accounts also began to accumulate rapidly in the summer of 1936, when both police and public realized that the city confronted a series of killings by a single lone murderer rather than a collection of isolated crimes; the papers responded by running inadequately researched recaps of the previous butcheries in the series. Newspaper stories also invariably contain all kinds of errors, some of them wonderfully creative. In one instance, a befuddled reporter or an overzealous editor confused a person's age with the street address of his house. In another, someone reversed the names of the man who discovered the first piece of a corpse and the neighbor from whose house he called the police.

Many of these inaccuracies have subsequently been accepted as fact. Kingsbury lore states, for example, that the first two officially recognized victims were discovered feet together, arms at their sides. Exactly where this notion came from is unclear; it certainly was not mentioned in the existing reports dealing with these murders, nor is it a part of the original newspaper coverage. Commentators, however, continue to repeat this bit of erroneous intelligence as if it were fact. "One detective remembers, 'They had been laid out,' that is neatly positioned as though by an undertaker, arms along their sides, heels together," wrote John Bartlow Martin in 1949. Newspaperman Howard Beaufait, who covered the case directly, made the same error in 1955. "In a tangle of burdoc and sumac two cadavers were laid out at attention, heels together, arms and hands extended stiffly at their sides." And Steven Nickel dutifully repeated the assertion in 1989. "He [Detective Orley May] noted how the bodies were laid out, arranged with arms tucked at the sides and legs and heels together." Yet May's official police report makes no mention of the bodies being found in such a manner, and a look at the Scientific Investigation Bureau's photograph of Edward Andrassy's naked, decapitated corpse shows him lying on his side, one leg partially drawn up, his right arm stretched out perpendicular to the body, his left hand raised to where his head would have been—almost as if he were sleeping. Television has also created and then perpetuated its own inaccuracies. One of NBC's *Unsolved Mysteries* segments dealing with the case portrayed the killer as a small, neurotic weakling. The police and the medical examiners, however, agreed that evidence from the killings themselves and certain details related to the disposal of the bodies made it clear the Butcher was a large, very powerful man.

The only way I have been able to correct such bits of misinformation, if they could be corrected at all, is through comparing the various contemporary newspaper stories and subsequent printed accounts, checking official documents such as autopsy protocols and police reports, and relying on the memories of the direct descendants of those who participated in the case. The surviving police reports are extremely detailed and precise documents, written, of course, by men on the scene or involved in subsequent phases of investigation. So when factual discrepancies arose between a newspaper story and an official report, I regarded the latter as the more reliable. Disagreements between the coroner's records and police reports or, even more troublesome, between two separate police reports were far more difficult to resolve, and when such invariably minor sticking points arose, I made a judgment call based on whose observations were either firsthand or the most detailed. (Preliminary conclusions about remains, either by the police or the coroner's office, reached at the scene were often modified after the formal autopsy.) Though rare, small problems in chronology and exact dating sometimes occur between Peter Merylo's memoirs, written in the early 1950s, and his own reports. Invariably, I resolved those contradictions by relying on the report because Merylo wrote it immediately after the events described. When similar contradictions arose between Merylo's memoirs and the Otwell collaboration, I regarded the former as the more reliable since they are entirely Peter Merylo's work. I was extremely careful when quoting from the Otwell manuscript to limit myself only to those passages that have an authentic Merylo ring. In a few cases, I could resolve inaccuracies in the written record, such as the position of Edward Andrassy's body when found, only by tracking down police or press photographs of the crime scenes.

John Bartlow Martin's article "Butcher's Dozen: The Cleveland Torso Murders" appeared in the November 1949 issue of *Harper's Magazine* as part of a series devoted to unsolved crimes. In the absence of most of the police files, his piece assumes enormous importance since he obviously had access to records that have subsequently vanished and may have even interviewed some of the investigators involved, most of whom had retired but were still alive in the late 1940s. The only other major piece written reasonably close to the period when the murders occurred is William Ritt's "1935–1938: The Head Hunter of Kingsbury Run" in *Cleveland Murders* published in 1947, itself part of a lurid collection titled *Regional Murder Series*. Ritt, not a Cleveland resident, apparently based his account on a cursory reading of the newspaper coverage; the piece is loaded with seemingly manufactured conversations and hobbled by simple factual errors. Howard Beaufait, who covered the crimes directly for the *Cleveland News*, contributed to *Cleveland Murders;* given his greater expertise, one wonders why he did not write, or was not asked to write, the section on the Kingsbury Run murders.

City papers dutifully, even enthusiastically, trumpeted any new investigative initiative from the police department, the coroner's office, or Eliot Ness. Unfortunately, unless those actions yielded both immediate and newsworthy results, editors saw little reason to keep covering them, hence a student of the crimes faces a series of tantalizing threads that simply

Cuyahoga County coroner Samuel R. Gerber standing before an exhibit of photographs and other Kingsbury Run artifacts for a conference of the National Association of Coroners at the Carter Hotel in August 1937. *Cleveland Press* Archives, Cleveland State University.

go nowhere. For example, in late August 1937, between one hundred and two hundred coroners from all around the country gathered at Cleveland's Carter Hotel for a convention of the National Association of Coroners. According to the *Plain Dealer,* then coroner Dr. Samuel Gerber and County Pathologist Dr. Reuben Straus decided to make a full presentation about the Kingsbury Run murders to the entire group in the hope "that in some way this presentation may stimulate your imagination so that you, in turn, may help us by pointing out some valuable clews [*sic*] or theories that we may have overlooked." Though a previously unpublished photograph in the *Press* archives shows Dr. Gerber standing before a large, ghastly display of morgue photos, human bones, and other Kingsbury artifacts put together for the conference, the papers never reported whether the assembled experts offered any useful insights.

Names of the people involved were a major problem. In the frantic rush to meet publication deadlines, newspapers often failed to double-check such details as the proper spelling of names. In the first *Plain Dealer* story reporting his murder, Edward W. Andrassy appears as Edward A. Andrasy. Surprisingly, police reports and autopsy protocols sometimes commit equally serious blunders. Florence Polillo, the third recognized victim, is consistently referred to as Florence Polilla or Pollilia in official documents; and some names were so badly mangled by authorities—Rudy Rige for Rudy Richko, for example—that I could correct them only by cross-checking street addresses given in the reports with the city directories, sources sometimes crippled by their own errors. Some individuals moved so frequently that they were missed by directory compilers, and wandering transients do not appear in the directories at all. If obtaining the proper spelling of a name proved impossible, I have noted all the recorded variants.

On an emotional level this was not an easy book to research or write. If one digs into a subject such as this long enough, human lives with all their

A desolate stretch of Kingsbury Run—a dark, dreary place filled with trash and debris. *Cleveland Press* Archives, Cleveland State University.

joys and sorrows eventually begin to glimmer behind cold public documents and the dry, formal wording of old police reports. At times, the sheer horror of it all was simply too overwhelming, and I had to walk away for a while. British authorities kept the scanty files on Jack the Ripper sealed for one hundred years. When I began to look into the Kingsbury Run murders seriously and in detail, I understood why. The Ripper documents were kept under official lock and key for a century to ensure that anyone directly touched by the crimes or the investigation, as well as their immediate descendants, was dead—thus potentially sparing innocent people both pain and embarrassment. The torso killings occurred over seventy-five years ago, and that is not such a long time. There are a few people alive who vividly remember seeing something or finding something connected to the case when they were children. Some of those directly involved in the murders as victims, investigators, or suspects have grandchildren, nephews and nieces, sons and daughters, even brothers and sisters still living. For many of these people, their involvement, or the involvement of loved ones, with the Kingsbury Run murders on any level became part of family legend. Most people shared their memories with me generously, graciously, and willingly. Some spoke as if recalling events that happened yesterday; some spoke as if finally relieving themselves of an old, heavy burden. Others were considerably more cautious. Occasionally people made it clear I was asking them to revisit something they had no desire to discuss. Some spoke to me grudgingly, a few not at all. One individual alternated compulsive outbursts of information with determined silences. The pain that still lingers around these killings for some individuals and their families remains enormous. I walked with ghosts; I wandered across minefields. "Just tell what really happened," responded one older woman to my cautious inquiry as to whether I might repeat the private information she had shared. I have tried, therefore, to be accurate and fair; I have tried to present the facts while respecting people's feelings and rights to privacy. To anyone who feels hurt or abused by my failure to always maintain that delicate balance, I offer my deepest apologies.

Compared to more recent serial murderers, the Kingsbury Run Butcher's known toll seems rather meager. The Green River Killer was responsible for far more deaths, and the details of Jeffrey Dahmer's bizarre behavior are considerably more gruesome. Why, then, the continued interest in the Butcher and his crimes after seventy-five years? No doubt because of the peculiarly brutal nature of the killings and the fact that the case is still officially unsolved. Would Lizzie Borden be anything more than an obscure footnote in the annals of American crime if her guilt were certain? Would Jack the Ripper continue to compel and fascinate 125 years after his crimes if they had been less ferocious and there were a face to place over his shadow?

NOTES

Some of the material in the opening sections of this chapter comes from interviews with Anne T. Kmieck, former curator at the Cleveland Police Historical Society Museum; Brian Albrecht of the *Plain Dealer;* and Tomi Johnson, granddaughter of Edward Andrassy.

The statistics on Cleveland's economic plight during the Great Depression are from *The Encyclopedia of Cleveland History* (Bloomington: Indiana University Press, 1987). David D. Van Tassel and John J. Grabowski, eds.

There are some terminology problems with the Scientific Investigation Bureau. The term "Scientific Investigation Bureau" seems to be the officially recognized designation for that specialized part of the police department, but newspaper stories and police reports generally refer to "Ballistics" or the "Ballistics Bureau"—occasionally the "Scientific Bureau." It is never clear whether "Ballistics" is a casually used synonym for the Scientific Investigation Bureau or a specialized unit within it. The problem is compounded by police reports that consistently refer to those individuals who photograph crime scenes as having come from the "Bertillon Department." The Swiss criminologist Alphonse Bertillon devised a system of criminal identification based on careful and minute body measurements. Though fingerprinting eventually superseded the system, it was widely used in Europe and America in the late nineteenth and early twentieth centuries—hence the term "Bertillon Department." Why Cleveland police officers continued to employ the outmoded term in official reports well into the 1930s is unclear. At least their usage of Bertillon Department appears to be relatively consistent; it seems to refer only to police photographers.

The tip letter sent to Eliot Ness is part of Detective Peter Merylo's files currently in the possession of his daughter Marjorie Merylo Dentz.

The bogus descriptions of Edward Andrassy's corpse come from John Bartlow Martin's "Butcher's Dozen: The Cleveland Torso Murders," *Harper's Magazine,* November 1949, 55–56, Howard Beaufait's "Kingsbury Run Murders," *Homespun,* November 1955, 32, and Stephen Nickel's *Torso: The Story of Eliot Ness and the Search for a Psychopathic Killer* (Winston-Salem, N.C.: John R Blair, 1989), 16.

September 5, 1934
THE LADY OF THE LAKE

Thirty-four-year-old Frank LaGassie of 21 Brookfield in Beulah Park was searching the beaches of Lake Erie for driftwood to burn. It was a regular part of his morning ritual, something he did every day before leaving for his job as a photostat operator at the Dodd Company. But this day would be different—one that would give Francis Xavier LaGassie a story to tell for the rest of his life.

The morning of September 5 was overcast and still; billowing dark cloud formations rolled low over the broad expanse of the lake. The cries of gulls punctuated the continuous, soft murmur of lapping waves. LaGassie was walking the shore just east of Bratenahl near Euclid Beach Park. Shortly before 8:00 A.M., he stood quietly, scanning the beaches, when something in the distance caught his eye. At first he thought the waves had washed up a major piece of good fortune. He saw what he initially identified as a piece of tree trunk, partly buried in the sand and stripped of its bark, in a pile of debris at the foot of East 156th. When he came nearer to claim his prize, he realized with horror that he was looking at the rotting lower half of a woman's torso, legs amputated at the knees. LaGassie knew he had to summon the police, but not wanting to alarm his pregnant wife, he ran to neighbor Charles Armitage's house and frantically asked him to place the call. LaGassie's apprehension grew as he nervously waited for the authorities. Finally, he could wait no longer; he had to get to work. He told his wife as gently as possible why the police would be arriving soon and implored her not to become upset. Twenty-one-year-old Virginia LaGassie, however, succumbed to the grim excitement around her and prematurely delivered her son Richard at home two days later.

Two weeks earlier and thirty miles east in North Perry, Joseph Hejduk, a handyman on a lakeshore estate, found what looked like the vertebrae and ribs of a human torso with some moldering flesh still clinging to the back. A dead gull lay beside the gruesome remains like some voodoo charm or evil talisman. Special Lake County deputy sheriff Melvin Keener judged Hejduk's discovery animal bones and ordered him to bury them in the sand along the shore. Close by a young boy hauled a box with a lid—three feet long, a foot wide, and a foot deep—out of the lake and idly sat on it as he lazily tossed his fishing line into the lapping waves.

Later on the morning of September 5, authorities finally collected Frank LaGassie's grim discovery and handed it over to Cuyahoga County coroner Arthur J. Pearce at the morgue. He immediately determined that this was not a medical specimen discarded by students as a prank; cataloging and numbering procedures at both the Western Reserve Medical School and the Ohio School of Embalming were too strict to allow for such a thing. Though he had precious little with which to work, a staff pathologist methodically began examining the grisly object. The woman had been dead for perhaps six months, and her body, at least this piece of it, had been in the water for about three or four. But the flesh was not waterlogged, suggesting that the piece had been packed in some sort of container when it was tossed into the lake. Pearce estimated her to have been about five feet six, 115 pounds, and in her mid- to late thirties. The only distinguishing mark on the torso was an abdominal scar, indicating that her uterus had been removed about a year before, but Pearce realized that this feature would be of little help in identifying the woman because the operation was so common.

A preservative of some kind had been poured or spread over the torso and had turned the skin reddish, tough, and leathery, thus explaining why it was not more decomposed. Pearce called in city chemists on September 6 to examine the skin in an effort to identify the mystery substance, which E. B. Buchanan initially speculated was probably one of approximately fifteen different forms of calcium salts. By the next day, W. H. Hay, director of City Chemical Laboratories, determined it was either calcium hypochloride or chloride of lime.

The next day, September 6, Joseph Hejduk read the newspaper accounts of Frank LaGassie's lakeshore discovery and contacted former Lake County sheriff James Moloney about the bones he had buried two weeks before at Special Deputy Melvin Keener's direction. Moloney passed the information on to Cleveland police, and Detectives Joseph Jacobs and Harry Hugo drove to the North Perry shore, where they joined Hejduk, Moloney, and Keener. Hampered by a hard rain and growing darkness, the group followed Hejduk along the shore for two hours searching unsuccessfully for the makeshift grave. Wave action and storms had shifted the sands during the two-week interval, and Hejduk simply could not locate the burial spot. Drenched and tired, they postponed their hunt until early the following day, September 7, when Lake County sheriff T. J. Kilcawley joined the group.

Sometime during the morning or early afternoon, Hejduk finally led the search party to a spot about three-quarters of a mile west of North Perry Township Park. The men carefully opened the shallow grave, gently removed and wrapped its contents, then transported them to Painesville, where acting coroner Dr. George Barnett declared them human remains. Pearce arrived in Lake County later in the day and, after a brief examination, determined that the upper torso exactly matched the lower half Frank LaGassie had discovered two days before. The dead gull Hejduk found with the remains could be explained if they had been covered with the same chemical preservative as the piece already in Pearce's possession.

Suddenly potential pieces of the bizarre puzzle turned up everywhere along the Erie shore. During the week before Labor Day, a fourteen-year-old girl had run frantically out of the lake near East 238th insisting that she had seen a human hand waving at her from the bottom. (The *Plain Dealer* reported the incident on September 8 but incorrectly identified the body part as a pair of legs.) In late August, a couple of fishermen on the breakwall at the foot of West 58th had snagged a line on something that broke loose as they tried to haul it in; as the freed line rose from the water, they noticed blond hair tangled on the hook. After ferryboat operator Harry Olasky later reported seeing an object that looked suspiciously like a human head bobbing near the same breakwall, police and members of the Coast Guard dredged the entire area for two hours but found nothing. Two boys reported they had buried some bones and flesh in late August or early September to keep neighborhood dogs away from them. On the night of September 5, two boys had found a grayish mass at the foot of East 256th. (Though initially identified by Euclid police as human brain tissue, Pearce determined it was just animal fat.) William Lentz of Euclid recalled that on the very day Frank LaGassie had made his grisly discovery, he and a friend had seen two fleshy objects rolling in the waves. After

The search for parts of the Lady of the Lake along the Erie shore in September 1934. The date on the back of this *Plain Dealer* photograph is September 14, nine days after Frank LaGassie's discovery. The cloth on the beach covers something small, perhaps an upper arm. *Plain Dealer* Collection, Cleveland Public Library.

managing to snag one of them, Lentz poked it with a stick. "It was flesh of some kind," he confidently told the *Press*. "It wasn't a fish."

On September 8, after first checking local cemeteries to make sure no grave robbers had been at work, police launched a full-scale search for other body parts along Lake Erie from downtown Cleveland all the way out to North Perry. Officers in rubber boots waded out in the waters off East 238th searching for the "waving" hand; others dug in the sand farther east, hunting for the material two neighborhood boys insisted they had buried the week before. Detective Sergeant Bernard Wolf of the Homicide Squad even contemplated calling in Boy Scouts to help authorities in their search. Police retrieved a trunk from the foot of Bonnieview Drive that some local children had found. After receiving a telephone call from a young boy, Detectives Joseph Jacobs and Emil Musil collected the large box—which turned out to be a discarded seaman's trunk—on which he had sat while fishing several weeks before. (The Scientific Investigation Bureau eliminated both as unrelated.) Except for the upper part of an arm found near Euclid Beach Park, no other pieces of the body were ever recovered.

At first, it was not even clear that this was, indeed, a murder. Some detectives initially speculated that the woman had been a suicide, her body sliced by the propeller of a passing boat—a theory that Pearce quickly deemed improbable. Microscopic examination of the vertebrae clearly showed knife marks, indicating that the torso had been cut in half with a large, sharp instrument—something akin to what a butcher would use. Obviously, whoever had performed these operations was familiar with the landmarks of the human skeleton, for the dismemberment was notably skillful. Only in the attempt to sever the right arm from the body had the Butcher's precision deserted him. Somehow he missed the joint, forcing him to hack through the shoulder blade with a saw to separate the missing appendage from the torso. "No surgeon ever would have used a saw," Pearce declared to the *Press*. "He would have known how to manipulate a knife around the joint."

Everything about this gruesome murder baffled the authorities. Why had the body been dismembered? Pearce theorized that the woman may have been killed some place where disposal would have been difficult, hence the killer cut the body into pieces, placed them in several boxes containing the preservatives, and dumped them in the lake, where wave action ultimately

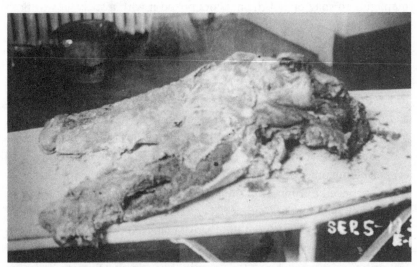

The Lady of the Lake at the morgue. Frank LaGassie said it looked like a piece of tree trunk stripped of its bark. Cleveland Police Historical Society.

forced them open, spilling the contents into the water. Why had the killer attempted to preserve the torso chemically? Police thought at first that the discoloration of the skin may have resulted from a botched attempt to burn the body, and Pearce wondered if the killer had meant to use quick lime to speed up the process of decomposition and had mistakenly used a substance that preserved it. "There are many persons," the coroner told the *Plain Dealer,* "who mistake slacked lime for quick lime and try to do away with bodies in that way." Where had the body come from? Pieces could have been thrown into the waters almost anywhere, even Canada, and been carried by the currents to the area close to Euclid Beach and beyond; they could have been tossed out of a boat or even dropped from an airplane. In the face of such seemingly insoluble perplexities, worrying about a motive seemed almost beside the point.

Standard police procedure was based on the assumption that murder victims knew their attackers; thus the first step in tracking the killer was to identify the victim. One attempt to identify the mysterious lakeshore torso produced a tale of love and intrigue so glamorously bizarre it could have graced the pages of a Hollywood script or a lurid romance novel. On September 8, Detroit police inquired about the torso, thinking it might be Agnes Tufverson, a New York lawyer who had mysteriously disappeared the previous December after marrying Captain Ivan Poderjay, a "Romanian adventurer" then in the custody of Viennese police and waiting extradition to the United States on an unspecified technical charge. At forty-three years of age, 130 pounds, five feet six inches, and marked by an abdominal scar, Tufverson at first seemed a reasonable match with Pearce's general description of the unidentified victim. Within days, however, police abandoned the attractive theory because of differences between the two women's respective scars.

Inspector C. W. Cody turned to the pile of yellow missing person reports stacked on his desk. They covered thirty-one women—of all ages and races, of various heights and weights—who had disappeared in the last six months, in other words, since March 1934, when Pearce speculated the woman had been killed. None of the missing women, however, bore the telltale abdominal scar. Since there were so many forms of calcium salts in common usage, all of them readily available, Pearce insisted that any attempt to trace the substance on the body would be futile.

With hindsight it seems clear that the story of the torso killings began along the shores of Lake Erie on that September morning of 1934. No one at the time, however, knew it was the beginning of anything; it was simply an isolated murder—fascinating, horrible, and strange. For six days the mystery woman was front-page news; on the seventh day, September 11, her remains were placed in a rough box bearing the number 102-3 and quietly buried in potter's field at Highland Park Cemetery. In case further examination proved necessary, the coffin was placed on top of two others so the remains could be quickly and easily retrieved. No arrests were ever made. The investigation into what seemed the perfect crime simply ended. Despite all their attempts, authorities were never able to identify the dead woman. Police called her the Lady of the Lake. When it ultimately became clear that she was a part of a series of murder-dismemberments, she would be stripped of her romantic title and given the coldly official designation victim no. 0. It would be another year before the case began officially, and then it would be in another part of the city—the infamous Kingsbury Run.

NOTES

Frank LaGassie's son Richard provided all the details relating to his father's experience on the morning of September 5, 1934.

The subsequent account of the police investigation comes from articles in Cleveland's three daily newspapers, September 5–18, 1934.

DOUBLE MURDER

Kingsbury Run is a broad, deep gorge, once a prehistoric riverbed, swinging in a long, lazy southeast arc from Cleveland's sprawling industrial area in the Flats out to about East 90th. Bordered on the north by Woodland Avenue and on the southeast by Broadway, the desolate area took its name from James Kingsbury, the first settler in the Western Reserve. In the late eighteenth and early nineteenth centuries, the Run served as a beautiful pastoral retreat, a picnic area filled with babbling brooks, trees, and flowers. By the 1930s, however, the picnickers and strolling lovers had long since disappeared, and Kingsbury Run had become a grim wasteland of weeds, bushes, trash, debris, and hobo jungles—an industrial channel, sixty feet deep at some points, scarred with more than thirty pairs of railroad tracks that linked the city's factories with the outside world. At night, darkness combined with industrial smoke to create an impenetrable blackness worthy of Milton's *Paradise Lost*—the silence interrupted by the shriek of locomotive whistles, the darkness pierced by fires from still operating factories.

The transients who haunted the shantytowns and prowled the Run escaped the brutality of Cleveland winters by catching freight trains to warmer climes in the South; children fleeing poverty at home often rode the rails in an aimless, unending search for a better life. Thus railroad police regularly patrolled the area, looking for hoboes, runaways, or adventuresome neighborhood boys who hopped aboard the freights for sport.

In the 1930s, Kingsbury Run served as a line of racial demarcation. The black communities gathered on the northern edge in the Woodland Avenue area; the neighborhoods to the southeast near East 55th and Broadway were home primarily to working-class central Europeans with names such as Krakowski, Pietrovski, Czech, and Blenka.

Monday, September 23, was a pleasant fall day in Cleveland with a high of 71 degrees. After school at about 5:00 in the afternoon, two young boys—sixteen-year-old James Wagner of 4511 Gallup Avenue and twelve-year-old Peter Kostura of 4465 Douse Avenue—tossed a softball back and forth along the upper edge of Jackass Hill, a sixty-foot slope on the south side of Kingsbury Run where short stretches of both East 49th and East 50th meet the gully. Neighborhood youngsters used the steep hill for sled riding during the winter. (The terrain has been altered since then. Part of Jackass Hill has been cut away, and only one lone house remains on the small stretch of East 49th just off Praha Avenue. It remains a remarkably isolated region, and it is difficult to believe that such an empty and desolate place could exist in the midst of a large city.) When the ball sailed over the rim of the hill and tumbled down into the gully, Wagner challenged Kostura to a time-honored test of teenage manhood—a race to the bottom to retrieve it. As the rapid transit passed by carrying commuters home to Shaker Heights, Wagner scampered down the slope into the Run leaving Kostura trailing behind. When he reached the bottom of the hill, he looked around for the missing softball. Suddenly he paused and then momentarily froze before tearing back up the hill. His eyes blank with horror and his voice a trembling, harsh whisper, he stopped Kostura with a startling revelation: he had seen a dead man with no head in the brush.

Twelve-year-old Steve Jeziorski and his older brother Leonard were watching as the two boys played, and as they followed Wagner's progress down the incline, they caught sight of a body, decapitated and discolored, lying in the bushes. "He certainly didn't try to hide it," the younger Jeziorski remembers. The startled brothers ran quickly to their nearby home on Praha Avenue as Wagner and Kostura headed off in a different direction. It would not become clear until later that afternoon that the body that had shocked the Jeziorski brothers was not the same one that had sent Jimmy Wagner rushing back up the hill in such terror.

Wagner and Kostura ran until they found an adult, an unidentified man who phoned the Erie Railroad police. Sergeant Arthur Marsh and Patrolman Arthur Stitt, who responded to the call, were the first authorities to see what had sent the two boys scrambling away from the base of Jackass Hill. The body of a white male, naked except for a pair of black cotton socks, emasculated and decapitated, lay on its side in the brush. The total absence of blood either on the body or on the ground convinced the two men that, whoever this was, he had been killed elsewhere, his body drained of blood, cleaned, and then merely dumped where Wagner had found it.

At 5:15, Marsh called in Cleveland police from the Sixth Precinct station. By the time Lieutenant Eugene M. Gorman and members of the no. 6 Police Emergency arrived, Stitt had found the body of the second man which the Jeziorski brothers had seen earlier from the top of the hill—older, shorter, and stockier than the first—lying about thirty feet away. The state of decomposition indicated that he had been dead for some time (initial newspaper estimates ranged from ten to thirty days), and the body bore evidence that some substance had been poured over it which had turned the skin reddish, tough, and leathery. Stitt and Marsh had also found the head belonging to the first corpse, buried in the ground about twenty feet from the body; just enough hair showed above the surface of the loose earth to ensure the police would find it.

At 5:20, Orley May and Emil Musil of the Detective Bureau responded to a radio call reporting the gruesome discovery and headed toward Jackass Hill. At about 5:30, a large contingent of uniformed officers and detectives under the direction of Assistant Chief Emmet J. Potts gathered at the ghastly crime scene and began systematically combing the area, moving in discernible patterns around the two bloodless and headless corpses. City police located the head of the second victim buried about seventy feet from the body; the severed genitals of both men lay in a mass close to one of the corpses. Nearby, they also found some clothing—a blue coat (with a label from B. R. Baker Company), a white shirt, some white trousers, and a light checkered cap. (One newspaper account added underwear and, oddly, a baby's undershirt to the tally, but Orley May's police report does not mention these additional articles.) Some of the clothing, which seemed to fit the second man, was blood-soaked, leaving authorities to surmise that he had been killed while dressed, then stripped and his body cleaned. Inexplicably, they found several pieces of rope, a railroad torch, and a two-gallon water bucket containing an oily substance that turned out to be car engine oil laced with partially decayed blood and a fairly large quantity of long, black hair which tests later concluded was probably human. Initially, authorities thought the killer might have tried to burn the body with the mystery liquid, perhaps accounting for the odd reddish discoloration of the skin. Coroner A. J. Pearce arrived at about 6:00; and in an absurd bit of officialdom, considering the condition of the bodies, solemnly declared both men legally dead, while Bertillon assistant Robert J. Blaha photographed the horrible scene.

Word of the terrible discovery spread quickly through the working-class neighborhood, and curious onlookers streamed to the base or the rim of Jackass Hill from all directions. Peter Kostura's cousin Anne Krupa eagerly joined a wave of children running toward the top of the hill to watch the bizarre spectacle below. "I saw the head," she remarks, the shudder still apparent in her voice. "That was a terrible thing for a child to see." Kostura's older sister Mary Lucak remembers the police taking both frightened boys to the Sixth Precinct station for their statements and her brother's utter terror when he returned home early that evening. She also clearly recalls the young Eliot Ness coming to the family home during later stages of the investigation. Michael Zemba, a boyhood friend and schoolmate of the two boys, stood among the spectators at the foot of the hill where he saw the partially decomposed head of the second victim before it was removed by county undertakers. He describes Wagner and Kostura as "good kids" and

The scene at the foot of Jackass Hill, September 23, 1935: Edward Andrassy's headless, emasculated corpse. Courtesy of Marjorie Merylo Dentz.

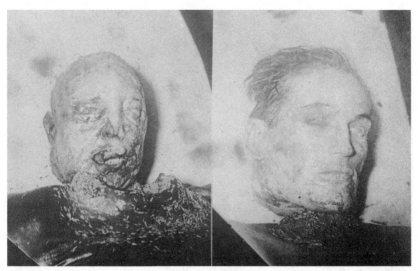

The recovered heads of the Butcher's first officially recognized victims. Victim no. 2 (*left*) and Edward Andrassy. Courtesy of Marjorie Merylo Dentz.

recalls that tragedy overtook both boys within a few years. On December 4, 1937, Peter Kostura was struck by a drunk driver on Broadway close to his home and, according to his sister Mary, died six hours later in St. Alexis Hospital; James Wagner was killed during World War II.

By 7:30 that evening, both bodies had arrived at the morgue and, according to the coroner's view slips, pronounced legally dead, apparently for the second time, by Deputy Coroner Wilson Chamberlain. By the time he began to perform the autopsies at 9:00 A.M., the first victim had already been identified through his fingerprints as twenty-nine-year-old Edward W. Andrassy of 1744 Fulton Road on the near west side.

Though hardly a major criminal, Andrassy was well known to the police as something of a gadfly, a perpetual source of trouble, a constant thorn in the side of law enforcement. He frequently haunted the sleazy establishments of Rowdy Row along West 25th and the Third District—a rough, rundown, crime-infested landscape of bars and tenements known as the Roaring Third, bordered by East 55th, Kingsbury Run, and Prospect Avenue. He shot craps with his friends and supposedly even slept off some of his drunks in a graveyard. He had been in trouble with the police any number of times, primarily for drinking and brawling, and had spent a month in the Warrensville Heights workhouse in 1931 for carrying a concealed weapon. John Bartlow Martin quoted a railroad detective who remembered Andrassy well.

Edward W. Andrassy, victim no. 1. This is a Cleveland Police mug shot and may date from Andrassy's 1931 arrest for carrying a concealed weapon. Cleveland Police Historical Society.

"Andrassy was the type fellow gives a cop a lot of lip when he's questioned. Once I had to knock him down." As nearly as anyone could determine, Andrassy had held only one steady job in his life; during the late 1920s and early 1930s he had worked in the old Cleveland City Hospital as an orderly in the psychiatric ward. At five feet eleven and 150 pounds, Edward Andrassy was a dashingly handsome man with brown hair and blue eyes. On the one hand, he enjoyed a reputation as a ladies' man; on the other hand, there were dark rumors of homosexuality and sexual perversion.

In the evening, police drove to the Andrassy home on Fulton Road to inform his family of his death. Detective Peter Merylo tagged along though he was not among the officers on the crime scene and would not be assigned to the case full-time until the summer of 1936. "It's not fun to crowd into a man's home and confront him with the murder of his son," he remarked to *Cleveland News* reporter Frank Otwell, "and ask him a lot of questions about his son's sex life."

Before Chamberlain performed the autopsies, police brought Andrassy's father, Joseph, and older brother, John, to the morgue to identify the body.

The elder Andrassy must have made that melancholy journey weighed down with a sense of tragedy so deep as to be beyond comprehension: thirteen years before, in 1922, his second-born son, Joseph Jr., had suffered a broken neck and died in a brawl at a friend's house on the near west side. Now, wrestling with grief and shock, he and his sole surviving son would have to face a nightmare. The police morgue photograph of Edward's head shows it bore the ravages of having been buried in the ground, perhaps for a couple of days, and it is doubtful there was enough time for morgue personnel, even with the help of a professional undertaker, to make it presentable for viewing by his father and brother.

Deputy Coroner Chamberlain estimated that Andrassy had been dead for two or three days, meaning he had been murdered Friday night or early Saturday; he carefully examined the body and recorded his findings with scientific precision: a mysterious, small pockmark-like scar on the forehead, an appendectomy scar on the abdomen, no abnormalities in the thorax or the abdominal cavities, the remains of a vegetable meal in the stomach, the heart virtually bloodless. The killer had severed the head from the body in the midcervical region with resulting fracture of the vertebrae; the skin edges were clean-cut, indicating that the knife had been wielded with notable strength and assurance. Slowly, inexorably, Chamberlain arrived at and recorded his shocking conclusion: "This man's death resulted from decapitation with a sharp instrument." This is not to say that Andrassy had been conscious when this unthinkable outrage occurred, but judging from the rope burns on his wrists, he may have been. An unidentified homicide detective present during the autopsy remarked, "That's odd. Usually a murderer kills by other means—stabbing, shooting, strangulation, poison. Sometimes, not often, the heads are removed to prevent identification, but almost never to kill. It's a hell of a job to remove a human head anyway." Pearce's official verdict virtually repeats Chamberlain's findings, but his final judgment is even more starkly brutal: "Murder and mutilation. Death due to decapitation and shock—Homicide."

The body of the second victim—a stocky five feet six and 165 pounds—posed a serious problem for the police and a much greater challenge to Deputy Coroner Chamberlain. The state of decomposition rendered identification through fingerprinting impossible and determining the cause of death far more difficult. Still, after noting the leathery condition of the skin and the presence of two small scars on the body, Chamberlain confidently attributed death, as with Andrassy, to decapitation in the midcervical region. Again, the edges of the skin were clean cut. Curiously, the left testicle was missing. Chamberlain estimated that the man was between forty and forty-five years old, placed the time of death anywhere from seven to ten days before discovery, and tentatively attributed the tanned, leathery condition of the skin to acid. (The superficial similarities between the skins of this second man and the Lady of the Lake found a year before seem to have escaped everyone at the time.)

The next day, on the 24th, the coroner's office sent skin samples for analysis to the Division of Health at the city's Department of Public Health and Welfare. The only record of those test results is contained in a letter which W. H. Hay, chief of laboratories, wrote to Dr. Samuel R. Gerber more than two years later on May 10, 1938. By then Gerber had succeeded A. J. Pearce as coroner, and apparently he had made inquiries about those test results. Hay estimated that the man had been dead for three to four weeks, far longer than Chamberlain's initial estimate of seven to ten days. He also attributed the condition of the skin to causes other than acid. After referring to the bucket of oil found at the crime scene, he added, "Appearances, together with certain findings, seem to indicate that this body after death was saturated with oil and fire applied. The burning however was only sufficient to scorch, hence the peculiar condition of the skin."

On Tuesday, the 24th, all three Cleveland papers rushed to report the gruesome murders in as much detail as was available. Next to a copy of Andrassy's police mug shot, the *Plain Dealer* called the killings "the most bizarre double murder here in recent years." "Vengeance for a frustrated love affair," proclaimed the *Cleveland News*. The *Press* weighed in with photos of James Wagner, Peter Kostura, and Andrassy, as well as a series of supposed police assumptions about the killings: the two men knew each other and had been killed by the same man; these were crimes of passion involving a woman rather than racket killings; each victim had been decapitated after his hands were tied, then stripped of clothing and further mutilated; the unidentified man had been first, "his body immersed in some sort of fluid until the murderer could trap Andrassy"; the bodies had then simply been dumped at the base of Jackass Hill.

Conventional law enforcement wisdom states that leads dry up after forty-eight hours, so over the next two days, Tuesday the 24th and Wednesday the 25th, the police launched a major investigation into the mysterious double murder. Detective Dudley A. McDowell of the New York Central Railroad reported seeing a suspicious green coupe several times in the past three weeks at the top of Jackass Hill at East 49th; the occupant, a white male McDowell thought looked Italian, kept surveying the area where the bodies where ultimately found with a pair of binoculars. Through the license number, Detectives May and Musil traced the car to Phillip Russo of East 140th; when they were unable to locate him, they sent out an alert that he, and anyone else found in the car, was to be held for questioning. (It would be a couple of years before police finally located him.) Detective Peter Merylo tells a strikingly similar story in the Otwell manuscript, except in this case, what began as a promising lead immediately dissolved into soap opera. The man with the binoculars was having an affair with a married woman who lived on the other side of the Run. She would frantically wave a white tablecloth when her husband left the house while her lover watched for her signal on the crest of Jackass Hill.

Police searched unsuccessfully for a fifty-year-old man who had been seen on Saturday, the 21st, in the area where the bodies were later found. John Pekarek and Steve Spalet, both of Trumbull Avenue, had watched the unidentified man stoop over some clothing in Kingsbury Run. As the two men approached, the strange man walked away, leaving Pekarek and Spalek to discover that the clothing was bloody. They asked Mrs. Christine Cole, also a resident of Trumbull Avenue, to call the police; unfortunately, she ignored their request.

Detectives Orley May and Emil Musil interviewed Jerome Kacirek, a twenty-five-year-old resident of East 49th, who had found a soiled, type-written note on the scene the day after Wagner and Kostura had discovered the bodies. The note, which appeared to be bloody, contained instructions for cremating a body; it was passed on to the morgue. Other officers looked into vague rumors concerning a deranged individual who lived near the Andrassy home on Fulton and had since disappeared; they even reached back thirteen years and questioned Anthony Hobart, the man responsible for the death of Andrassy's older brother.

With the second victim unidentified, there remained little for the authorities to do about him except check missing person reports—attempts to identify him as either Edward Faulkenberg or Raymond Stedronsky yielded nothing—and hope that he was, indeed, somehow linked with Andrassy. Louis Feltes, an Andrassy associate, identified his body at the morgue but, unfortunately, did not recognize the mysterious other man.

Detectives May and Musil also questioned Andrassy's parents, as well as his brother John and sister Edna, and this preliminary inquiry into Edward's life in the weeks before his death unearthed several potentially fruitful leads. His immediate family saw him alive for the last time at about 8:00 in the evening of Thursday the 19th; he was looking for his brother John. After having first checked his brother's home at 3123 West 52nd, Edward had driven up to his parents' house at 1744 Fulton, or had been driven, in a large, dark car that his mother, Helen, described as resembling one a gangster would own. Other witnesses also placed him in such a vehicle with a second man. Andrassy had walked into the house and demanded, "Where's John?" Since no one could tell him where his brother could be found, he left without saying where he was going; no one in the family saw him again until Monday night at the morgue. Exactly why he was so eager to find his older brother remains a mystery.

According to his family, about two weeks before his murder a strange man had come to the house and threatened to kill Edward if he did not leave the man's wife alone. Andrassy had denied any knowledge of the affair, declaring that the man must be crazy. Unfortunately, they could give police only the vaguest description of the angry husband. His sister Edna remembered that Edward had appeared upset and depressed in the weeks before his death because he had gotten into a fight with an Italian at the corner of East 9th and Bolivar and had stabbed him. Because of this incident, he feared "the gang" was after him. (A police informer even reported that he had hidden the frightened Andrassy for three days.) Though Edna tried to get more information out of Edward, he steadfastly refused to give her the supposed victim's name. Police checked their records but could find no mention of such an encounter at that time or at that location. His mother recalled that a taxi had brought him home one evening with his head cut; Edward could not remember how he got hurt, only that the cab had picked him up on that same corner of East 9th and Bolivar. "Andrassy was afraid to leave his home for several days before last Thursday when he disappeared," Sergeant Bernard Wolf of the Homicide Squad remarked to the *Cleveland News* on September 24. "Edward lived in continual fear of his life," declared his father, Joseph, to the *Press* on the same day. "He always told us to mind our own business when we tried to straighten him out."

Over the next two days, police delved more deeply into Andrassy's personal life. His exploits with women were impressive. Rudy Richko, a musician at the Night of Budapest on Buckeye, said the Andrassy had come to the nightclub several times, always accompanied by a different woman. Police questioned a certain Mrs. Szabo of West 35th, whom he had taken swimming on a couple of occasions, and twenty-one-year-old Margaret Gogany, a maid, who had been out with him twice and said she had a date with him on Sunday, the 22nd (a day or two after Chamberlain estimated he had been killed), but he had failed to show up. But the authorities also uncovered rumors of deviant sexual behavior. Informants hinted darkly at homosexual liaisons, one of them interracial; and Peter Feltes, who had known Andrassy since they were boys, told police a lurid tale involving his wife and Andrassy's claim that he was a "female doctor." The aggrieved husband said there was no use in trying to do anything about the incident since Andrassy was a much larger man and known to carry an ice pick. A subsequent search of Andrassy's room turned up two medical books, one of them on treating female disorders, and a number of what the police termed "physical magazines"—probably physical culture or body-building periodicals. The authorities were unable to link either Mrs. Szabo's spouse or Andrassy's acquaintance Peter Feltes to the outraged husband who had turned up at the family home a couple of weeks before his murder.

Feltes, however, did give the police a tantalizing clue, one that possibly could lead to identifying the second victim found with Andrassy. Feltes recounted that he had seen Andrassy with a good-looking, nervous man who had been introduced as Eddie, a chauffeur for a woman in Lakewood whom Andrassy claimed to be treating for female difficulties. Eddie drove a large, dark touring car, possibly either a Lincoln or a Buick, probably accounting for the car Helen Andrassy had seen her son get out of the day he disappeared. When May and Musil showed Feltes and his wife a photograph of victim no. 2's head, they both thought it resembled Eddie; when the couple looked over the clothes found with the bodies at the morgue, they identified the cap as the one the chauffeur had been wearing the last time they had seen him—a month before. The police, however, could never make a connection between the two men; and it seems improbable that Eddie could have been the second victim. After all, without Eddie, Andrassy obviously would have had no access to the large touring car his mother and other family members saw him in the day he disappeared, and no. 2 had been killed anywhere from a week to a month before Andrassy's murder.

On Tuesday, the 24th, Detectives May, Shibley, and Blackwell canvassed the neighborhood at the top of Jackass Hill, going door to door armed with Andrassy's photograph, but no one recognized him or remembered seeing him in the area. Toward the end of the day, the detectives returned to the scene where the bodies had been discovered, hoping to find further evidence. They found nothing, but perhaps it was then, alone in that desolate region, that they began to face fully all the imponderables and unanswered questions connected to the brutal double murder. Where had the two men been killed? Where had the corpses been kept, especially that of the second victim, until they were dumped? How had the killer managed to get the bodies to the foot of Jackass Hill, a spot virtually inaccessible by car? Had the bodies been rolled down the steep, sixty-foot slope or had they been dragged? The absence of any marks in the weeds on the hillside would suggest they had not. Had the murderer driven the bodies to the top of the hill? Did he actually carry each corpse, one at a time, down the slope? It would take a large, powerful man to accomplish such a grueling job. Why had he taken the time to bury the heads? Why had he simply tossed the severed genitals aside? Why was only one body burned? Did he actually try to burn it where it was found? If so, why hadn't anyone in the neighborhood at the top of the hill seen anything? Or if someone did notice flames, were they mistaken for a hobo's campfire? Why had he left the clothes, rope, and bucket of oil for the police to find? Had the pieces of rope been used to bind Andrassy's wrists? Had the murderer actually done all this in total darkness? Why had no one seen anything?

On Wednesday, the 25th, the body of the still unidentified second victim was taken to a potter's field and buried because, according to Coroner Pearce, the antiquated refrigeration facilities at the morgue did not allow keeping it any longer. Authorities had also turned Andrassy's body over to his family and undertaker Louis Bodnar, probably the day before, on the 24th. For one niece, this would be her first wake, a fearful experience for a little girl just six. Bodnar had apparently pulled the shirt collar up high to conceal the full horror of Edward's terrible injuries. "It affected me for years," she remarked, the emotion apparent in her voice. "My grandmother suffered so deeply." On Thursday, the 26th of September at 9:00 in the morning, a mass was performed for Andrassy at St. Mary's on Carroll Avenue. Following the service, a solemn procession including three limousines made the short trip from the church to the corner of West 41st and Clark for burial. One week to the day from the time his family had last seen him alive, Edward W. Andrasasy joined his murdered older brother in St. Mary's Cemetery.

Edward Andrassy would remain one of only two victims to be positively identified and the only one with deep roots in Cleveland; consequently, whenever the murder investigation hit a snag or stalled, authorities returned to him—feeling that somehow the key to the mystery rested with someone he knew—and dug into his life and background with greater determination.

Cleveland once boasted the largest Hungarian population in the world, second only to Budapest. The first great wave of Hungarian immigration occurred toward the end of the nineteenth century and extended well into the first years of the twentieth. The vast majority settled on the east side in the Buckeye-Woodland area close to the factories where most found employment. A much smaller Hungarian colony began to form on the west side of the city. The two groups differed largely in class: blue collar to the east, blue blood to the west.

Twenty-six-year-old Joseph Andrassy of Silesia brought his twenty-year-old wife, Helen (or Lena), two-year-old son, John, and infant son, Joseph Jr., to Cleveland in 1902. There was at least one other Andrassy in the city at the time; so he may have been following relatives already established, a process called chain migration. Ultimately, there would be five children in the family; Edward, who would become the most notorious, was born on September 3, 1906. By 1910 Joseph Andrassy had settled his family on the near west side in the area around West 50th, and although there would be several moves over the years, they would all take place within a narrowly defined geographical area. His decision to join the Hungarian colony on the west side may have been prompted by his name. In the old country, the Andrassys were of the nobility, and a certain Count Andrassy was reputed to have been Maria Teresa's lover. However aristocratic Joseph's ancestry and pretensions, his job history remained distinctly working class—painter, shoemaker, polisher, metal worker.

Edward took a job as an orderly in the psychiatric ward of City Hospital, apparently about 1925, when he was nineteen years old. By then, the family was living at 5702 Storr Avenue in a large row house building with several family units, a relatively short walk away from Edward's job at the hospital. According to Detective Peter Merylo, hospital records showed Andrassy had been hired and fired eleven times over an eight-year period. As other victims accumulated over the next three years, the presence of rope burns on Andrassy's wrists, suggesting he may have been conscious when he was decapitated, would remain a unique feature. It is tempting to speculate that his murder bears the unmistakable signs of a payback, and, indeed, the police based their investigation on the assumption that Andrassy had been killed out of revenge, perhaps by one of the unsavory characters with whom he associated. The surviving police records indicate that authorities dug deeply into his work history at the hospital, focusing most of their attention on other orderlies he had known and with whom he had worked. Could he, however, have met someone else at the hospital, a patient perhaps, someone who would carry a grudge for a personal offense, real or imagined?

Except for his on-again, off-again job at the hospital, Andrassy's work history remains sketchy. He sold magazines door to door for a time and was rumored to be involved in pushing marijuana. He worked as a laborer and put in a brief stint on a government relief project. The city directory for 1931 lists him as a bellhop but does not indicate which hotel employed him. Cynics might assert that he used his position as a cover for solicitation or pimping. Whatever the case may be, the question remains: did he offend or cheat someone while on the job, someone who bore him a grudge so fierce and deadly that four years would pass before the killer acted on it?

On November 12, 1928, he apparently offended his parents' sense of class by marrying a middle-class girl of German background named Lillian Kardotska, a nurse he had met at the hospital, who, according to the marriage license, lived in the same building as the Andrassys on Storr Avenue. Lillian had come to Cleveland from Vickery, Ohio, near Sandusky, where she worked at Good Samaritan Hospital, to study psychiatric nursing, ultimately finding work at City Hospital in 1927. According to family legend, her meeting with Edward was the stuff of Hollywood. Among the patients under Lillian's care was a woman who spent her days sitting on the floor in a catatonic state. Doctors considered her extremely dangerous, and the young nurse had been warned to keep her distance. One day, however, when Lillian saw her sitting by an open window with rain pouring in on her, she entered the room either to move the woman or at least close the window. The deranged patient viciously attacked her, and a handsome young orderly named Edward Andrassy rushed to her rescue.

Lillian married Edward on the rebound; she had been seeing someone else directly before they met. She quickly succumbed, however, to his charm and undeniable good looks. He was a very dapper dresser, a quality she admired until she learned that he, like many others during the Depression, bought his clothes from a fence. In an odd move for two west siders, the couple traveled to Shaker Heights to be married by Justice of the Peace William J. Zoul—perhaps a show of defiance toward Edward's disapproving parents. The marriage was apparently stormy; it was certainly short-lived. Within three weeks, Lillian, now pregnant, grew weary of her husband's behavior—he was rarely home—and left him after a furious quarrel during which she cracked him across the forehead with her high-heeled shoe, hence the pockmark-like scar Wilson Chamberlain noted in the autopsy protocol six years later. In a rage, Lillian stormed back to her parents in Vickery, Ohio, where she ultimately bore Edward's daughter and finally sued him for divorce.

Edward's daughter saw her infamous father only once, in 1933 or 1934, when she was about four years old. While sleeping on a lounge chair at her grandparents' farm, waiting for the lunch which was for her the high point of their weekly card games, she heard someone at the door ask, "Where's Lillian?" Her grandfather's angry response prompted the voice to reply, "I've got to talk with her." Timidly she looked toward the shadowy figure at the door; he turned in her direction and asked, "Is that the kid?" She remembers there was another man with him, perhaps the mysterious chauffeur Eddie. How else could Andrassy have made the long trip from Cleveland?

She vividly remembers the day her grandmother sat her down on her knee and told her that her father was dead. "It didn't mean anything because I didn't know him at all," she remarked. She did not learn that he had been murdered in an infamous series of killings until several years later—possibly in 1949 with the publication of John Bartlow Martin's article about the killings in *Harper's*—when someone told her she had read about her father in a magazine article.

When she became the district manager for Raydelle hair care products, she traveled to Cleveland every month for business lunches. At one such gathering in the 1950s, a stranger came over to her table, struck up a conversation, and then began asking very pointed questions. When she bristled at the extremely personal nature of the man's inquiries, her inquisitor apologized and introduced himself as a Cleveland police detective. Even in the 1950s, the official investigation was still going on.

In January 1938, the authorities suddenly shifted their attention back to Edward Andrassy. By then, the Butcher's tally stood officially at nine, and no new bodies had turned up for six months. Andrassy had been dead for almost two and a half years, and the police had already questioned family members many times and scoured his room for clues. That they would refocus their efforts on him and his associates shows just how frustrating an impasse the investigation had reached. Police returned to the infirmary at the Warrensville Workhouse where Andrassy had worked as an orderly during his incarceration for carrying a concealed weapon, trying to get a lead on a black man named John Laster whom Andrassy had befriended. They tied him to the criminal element in the Scovill-East 30th area and checked out a dive at East 22nd and Central where Andrassy had frequently visited another black man suspected of being a "pervert." They linked him to a "voodoo cult" known as the Black Rite. They also searched, unsuccessfully, for a WPA worker who allegedly accompanied Andrassy to the bootleg joints around East 14th and East 16th. They even tracked down his former wife in Vickery, Ohio, and asked her to comment on a list of thirty orderlies who had worked with him at City Hospital in 1927. They subsequently questioned John Galvin of Sackett Avenue, a former hospital orderly who had lived with Andrassy for between one and six months sometime in 1929 or 1930. Galvin reported having last seen him on the High Level Bridge in 1933, at which time Andrassy confided that he was involved in "a very risky business" mailing out unspecified "samples," apparently in violation of federal law.

Realizing what the Andrassy family had been put through by police and press in the two years since Edward's murder, Detectives Peter Merylo and Martin Zalewski reluctantly called at the Andrassy home and asked permission to go through his belongings yet again. Sorting carefully through notebooks and other personal articles in Andrassy's trunk, they turned up four photographic negatives that had somehow eluded the police during previous searches. When they held them up to the light, they saw four different poses of what appeared to be the same man—standing, sitting, reclining on a bed. When the pictures were developed, there was Edward W. Andrassy in all four, dapper and handsome, surrounded by the decadent splendor of rococo decorations, prints of nude or seminude women, and a garish Japanese lantern.

At the time, detectives regarded the four photos as their best clue, not only in Andrassy's murder but also in the entire series of mutilation killings. Who had taken them? Where had they been taken? The answers to those questions could lead to the murderer's lair and even to the perpetrator himself. "Do You Know This Room, Where Torso Victim Is Shown?" asked a headline in the *Press* on April 12. Underneath all four pictures of Andrassy, the paper exhorted its readers, "If you recognize the settings, the furniture, the pictures on the wall or the decorations, call or write the Cleveland Police Department or *The Press* city editor."

The next day, John Moessner—a fifty-six-year-old bachelor who lived with his two sisters on Fulton Road near Lorain, close to the Andrassy home—came forward and announced that he had taken the pictures several years before when he was living at 1734 West 28th in what is now Ohio City. The restaurant food checker and former head usher at Public Hall said he had met Andrassy in Brookside Park in 1930. "Have you got a match, fellow?" he remembered Andrassy asking. "I've got a bad toothache and need a smoke." Moessner described the murdered man as a "nice boy" and admitted that Andrassy had visited him at his West 28th address five or six times. On one of those occasions, Andrassy had shown up with a camera and had asked him to take the four pictures. Moessner insisted that he had nothing to do with Andrassy's murder and maintained he could not even remember when he had seen him for the last time.

When police checked the room on West 28th where the photos had been taken, it had been completely redecorated; Merylo recognized it only by a distinctive light fixture visible in the photographs. A similar check at the amateur photographer's present residence revealed that he had decorated his room in the same bizarre style as the room in the pictures. (His sisters had once entertained the hope that he would become an interior decorator!)

Suddenly the cooperative photographer became a potential suspect. A young west side man told police that he recognized the room in the published photographs as one he had visited several times and that Moessner had wooed him with an offensive combination of liquor and sexual advances. Moessner also had a police record—a conviction for petty larceny in 1929—and when police searched his room, they uncovered sixty-seven pieces of silverware belonging to different Cleveland hotels.

Far more damning were the suspicious dark stains on the floor of the attic, two pairs of similarly stained trousers, and a small box of personal items containing love notes from young male acquaintances and a wicked-looking hunting knife with a six-inch, discolored blade. When Lloyd Trunk of the Scientific Investigation Bureau announced that preliminary tests of the attic stains showed them to be blood, the police placed the middle-aged man under arrest. His sisters immediately jumped to his defense. Not only was he subject to nose bleeds, they maintained, he had come home one day covered with blood after falling from a streetcar. They insisted he led a quiet life, never went out late and never had visitors. They could not recollect Andrassy's visits to their previous home on West 28th, nor could they remember their brother ever talking about him or his death. When David L. Cowles of the Scientific Investigation Bureau later announced that neither the stains in the attic nor those on the man's pants were blood and that the discoloration of the knife was rust, the police realized they had a very weird character on their hands—a man who would be later tried and convicted on "sodomy" charges unrelated to the murders—but not a viable suspect. Though a photograph in Moessner's possession of a sailor that closely resembled a later victim killed in the summer of 1936 momentarily linked him with that victim, police could not connect him to the murders.

Over the years, members of the immediate Andrassy family would be constantly and painfully reminded of Edward's terrible death. His parents, Joseph and Helen, patiently endured unwanted attention for years from journalists and, no doubt, the police. Every new article about the case opened family wounds all over again; with each retelling of the story, the portrait of Edward became blacker—an unredeemable low life who enthusiastically embraced every vice he encountered. While commentators stopped short of suggesting he deserved what he got, they did indicate that, given the nature of his activities, it was hardly a surprise that he would cross paths with someone who would kill him so horribly. As time went on, the term "pervert" became attached to his name. Both police and press probably share responsibility for this association. At the time, "pervert" was an unofficial catchall term for any activity deemed sexually deviant.

More than seventy years after his murder, it is impossible to arrive at an accurate and balanced assessment of Edward W. Andrassy. Certainly, he was no altar boy proudly sporting a chest full of Boy Scout merit badges, and at the time of his death, his lifestyle clearly distressed his parents. He was, however, as much a victim of press coverage and the circumstances of his life as he was of his killer. At sixteen he had to cope with the senseless murder of his older brother, Joseph; for him life during the Depression

One of the four photographs John Moessner took of Edward Andrassy. This one most clearly shows the garish surroundings. Courtesy of Marjorie Merylo Dentz.

was unpredictable, hard, and cheap. Much of his totally negative image is based solely on the often sensational, contemporary accounts of his brutal murder and the subsequent police investigations, and the authorities were looking for someone who had reasons to kill him, not those who cared about him. His former wife, Lillian, for example, contemptuously dismissed the allegations of homosexuality, confidently telling their daughter, "He was anything but."

Through other members of the Andrassy family, Edward's daughter ultimately learned about the gentle, human side of her father, coming to know him as more than a Depression-era con man surviving through his wits with little to show for his life other than a string of run-ins with police. Her cousins remembered their fun-loving uncle who would hoist them on his shoulders at Edgewater Park and wade out into the lake, laughing with them as they alternately squealed in terror and giggled with delight. "To me he was a sweetheart," one family member recalls fondly.

Joseph Andrassy died in 1948, thirteen years after the murder of his third-born son. His older daughter Irene followed four years later in 1952. Perhaps fearing yet another round of unwanted intrusion into family privacy, neither obituary mentioned Edward. Not until his mother, Helen, died in 1960 did the Andrassys again publicly acknowledge and embrace their wayward, unfortunate son.

NOTES

The information surrounding the discovery of Edward W. Andrassy's and victim no. 2's bodies comes from a variety of sources. The police reports from Detective Orley May in the coroner's files—case no. 44996 (Edward Andrassy)—contain the most detailed and reliable descriptions of the scene and the subsequent investigation. All three Cleveland dailies ran extensive coverage of the double murder on September 24, 1935. Other specific details come from the Frank Otwell/Peter Merylo manuscript and my interviews with John Kostura, Steve Jeziorski, Anne Krupa, Mary Lucak, and Michael Zemba.

The railroad detective's colorful assessment of Andrassy appears in John Bartlow Martin's "Butcher's Dozen: The Cleveland Torso Murders," 57.

All anatomical findings are reported in the autopsy protocols—case nos. 44996 (Andrassy) and 44997 (victim no. 2). The quotation from the unidentified detective present during the Andrassy autopsy comes from Howard Beaufait's "Kingsbury Run Murders," 33.

The history of the Andrassy family in Cleveland was supplied by Edward's granddaughter Tomi Johnson and other family members, who requested anonymity. His daughter—who also requested anonymity—provided the description of her father's movements the day he disappeared, the personal details of her parents' relationship and marriage, the account of her brief encounter with her father in Vickery, Ohio, when she was a child, and her meeting with an unidentified Cleveland policeman in the early 1950s. Some additional information on the Andrassy-Kardotska marriage can be found in the divorce papers, case no. 315896.

The only detailed account of the subsequent phase of the police investigation into Andrassy's murder that began in January 1938 is contained in Detective Peter Merylo's daily reports from January to July 1938 and his personal memoirs. The three Cleveland dailies give the fullest description of John Moessner, his background, and police efforts to link him to the murders, as well as the history of the four Andrassy photographs, April 12–19, 1938.

A FROZEN CORPSE

It was a brutally cold winter night. The city lay locked into the sort of unrelenting cold snap with which Clevelanders are all too familiar, and freezing weather had hung on for weeks. It was the kind of bitter cold that drove people inside and kept them there. The area around East 20th and Central Avenue near Charity Hospital was a decaying neighborhood: a ramshackle collection of small manufacturing concerns, a few shops, run-down houses, old apartment buildings, and brothels. In the early Sunday morning hours between 2:00 and 2:30, James and Josephine Marco of 2108 Central Avenue were awakened by the mournful barking of their dog, confined on the back porch. They huddled against the cold and let the chow continue to fret, but as Josephine listened to the rustle of the wind and the howling dog, she detected the faint sounds of someone moving around in the yard outside.

As the night wore on, the temperature inched down into single digits. Irving Gartland of 2091 East 19th passed through the snow-covered area behind the houses and shops repeatedly on his regular beat as night watchman for several neighborhood establishments, but he saw no one and noticed nothing unusual; nor did Emmett Gogan, night watchman for the Waite Cab Company, which parked some of its vehicles in a vacant lot beside the Hart Manufacturing plant at 2315 East 20th.

At 6:00 A.M., Frank and Angela Felice, residents of an apartment building at 2340 East 22nd, heard furious knocking next door and the excited voice of a man demanding entry. At about the same time, Angela's mother, Frances Capo, who lived with the couple, overheard two women talking, apparently in a different apartment. Though she spoke little English, she picked up enough of their conversation to realize they were discussing a black man they had seen who had chased a dog away from the yard area behind the Hart plant, put something in his pocket, and then run away.

As the cold, gray day began to dawn, sleepy residents heard yet another dog begin to bark—this one, named Lady, belonged to sixteen-year-old Nick Albondante of 2100 Charity Avenue, directly across Cedar, north of Hart Manufacturing. At 9:00 A.M., Charles Frater, a toolmaker at Hart, drove in the rear driveway of the plant but saw nothing out of the ordinary. At the same time, the intoxicated Tawa (or Iowa) Yosaf (perhaps Yosal or Jowef) of East 74th stumbled through the yard area behind the Hart building. He was apparently the first person to see the two half-bushel baskets sitting in the snow against the back wall of the building. He gave the baskets and their contents a cursory examination, noticing what he thought were pieces of pork wrapped in newspapers and placed in burlap bags. As he wandered away, it occurred to him that he should alert the police, but he did not.

At 11:00 A.M., an unidentified black woman had had her fill of the barking dog, so she bundled herself up against the cold and went outside to investigate. She too found the two half-bushel baskets resting in the snow; she too looked inside and examined the newspaper-wrapped packages. She then walked down the alley beside Hart and entered the White Front

Pieces of Flo Polillo's body behind Hart Manufacturing on January 26, 1936. Courtesy of Marjorie Merylo Dentz.

Meat Market at 2002 Central and announced to owner Charles Page that she had seen some hams in a couple of baskets behind the manufacturing plant. Apparently thinking his shop had been burglarized, Page rushed up the alley to the back of the Hart building and made the sickening discovery that the baskets contained frozen pieces of a human body.

At 11:25, Lieutenant Harvey Weitzel of the Detective Bureau responded to Page's call, arriving with a full contingent of police, including Lieutenants Kreuger and Peter Vargo; Sergeants James T. Hogan, head of homicide, and Walter Kirby; Detectives Gordon Shibley and Herbert Wachsman; Captain Thomas G. Duffy; and members of cruisers D-2 and no. 3. Behind Hart Manufacturing they encountered one of the most bizarre crime scenes any of them had ever seen. Neatly packed in the two half-bushel baskets, they found the lower half of a female torso, two thighs, and a right arm and hand. Cinders and coal dust were embedded in the skin, and the lower piece of the torso bore the indentations of lump coal. Everything had been wrapped in pieces of newspaper: the August 11, 1935, issue of the *Cleveland Plain Dealer* and the January 25, 1936, issue of the *Cleveland News.* The baskets had been covered with two burlap sacks. Close by they located a two-piece set of cheap, white cotton underwear wrapped in the November 19, 1935, issue of the *Cleveland News* and a small tag bearing the name of William Danches's poultry store on East 105th. An immediate search of the surrounding area failed to turn up the rest of the body—though later in the day a third burlap bag, blood-stained and with chicken feathers adhering to it, turned up close by on East 18th. After police had taken a set of fingerprints from the hand and the scene had been photographed by the Bertillon Department, the body parts were taken to the morgue around 1:00 P.M. All through the frigid morning, curious neighborhood onlookers gathered behind Hart Manufacturing. They stood and watched silently, shivering against the bitter cold, as police explored the ghastly crime scene. When the authorities dispatched the body parts to the morgue, they gradually wandered away, obscuring the footprints the killer had left behind in the snow.

The police swung into action immediately. While the severed remains were en route to the morgue, Detectives Emil Musil, a veteran of the Andrassy investigation, and George Zicarelli had begun to comb through the missing person reports and had already eliminated a couple of likely prospects. Detectives Leo C. Duffin and Roland C. Sizler checked out whorehouses on East 16th and East 20th but found all the "white girls" accounted for. By the time the body parts had been officially viewed at the morgue at 1:30, George Koestle, head of the Bertillon Department, had identified the woman through the fingerprints of the right hand as Florence Polillo—well known to the police as a part-time waitress, part-time barmaid, part-time prostitute. She was a hard-drinking (probably an alcoholic), hard-living woman in her early forties with dyed red-brown hair and bad teeth. A chunky 160 pounds, she stood at five feet four. She had been arrested in Cleveland as a suspected prostitute in 1931, in Washington D.C., for soliciting in 1934, and again in Cleveland in October 1935 for selling liquor at 1504 St. Clair Avenue. Her police mug shot, widely printed at the time and published on several occasions thereafter, remains the only known photograph of Florence Polillo. The deeply lined, almost ravaged face, suggests an age far beyond her forty-some years.

Two different people filled out the coroner's view slip at the morgue, one of them Wilson Chamberlain, who had performed the autopsies on Andrassy and his still unidentified companion. But in this case, County Pathologist Dr. Reuben Straus performed the formal autopsy. He noted that the torso had been bisected at the second lumbar vertebra and that a longitudinal incision ran the length of the lower half; the thighs—which he described as obese—had been severed at the hip, close to the torso; the right arm, which showed signs of rigor mortis, had been removed at the shoulder joint. Sometime before her death, her entire reproductive system had been removed along with half her appendix. Although Straus indicated in his report that all the cut surfaces had clean edges, Arthur J. Pearce's official verdict, somewhat surprisingly, described the cutting as "crude." Death, which had occurred two to four days before the pieces of her body were found, was attributed to murder and "criminal violence."

Later that day, Detectives Musil and Zicarelli checked out William Danches, the name that appeared on the poultry store tag found at the scene, at his shop on East 105th and got a lead to the Cleveland Feather Company at 1838 Central Avenue, very close to where the pieces of Flo Polillo's body had been found. They interviewed co-owner Adolof Osteryoung, but he was unable to identify the burlap bags as having come from his plant. The police searched the premises carefully, especially areas like the boiler room, but came up empty. Maintaining that no women had worked for him in the past year, Osteryoung provided the detectives with the names of his three male employees, none of whom they were able to locate that day.

Ultimately, they picked up John Willis, a driver for the company who had collected the feathers from Danches's poultry shop, but after searching his home and questioning him, they let him go.

Since the frozen pieces of Flo Polillo's body had been discovered early Sunday morning, all three Cleveland papers had time to gather the facts and prepare their stories for the Monday editions. This was sensational stuff, and the press responded with lurid, detailed stories that milked the terrible crime for all it was worth. "Find Pieces of Woman's Body in Bags," screamed the front page of the *Plain Dealer,* and the *Press* shouted back with its own page one account: "Woman Slain, Head Sought in Coal Bins." The *Plain Dealer* treated its readers to a photo of David L. Cowles of the Scientific Investigation Bureau examining one of the baskets. The *Press* responded with Flo Polillo's mug shot and a photograph of the dog, Lady, whose barking had led to the discovery of her partial remains. The *Cleveland News* linked Polillo's murder to the Lady of the Lake, parts of whose body had washed up on the Erie shore fifteen months before: a remarkable, even surprising connection

This Cleveland Police mug shot is the only known photograph of Flo Polillo, victim no. 3. Cleveland Police Historical Society.

since standard Kingsbury legends have always maintained that no one—not the police, not the public, nor the press—saw any connection among these various killings until the summer of 1936. Yet, the paper noted on January 27, "The speedy solution of the identity of Mrs. Polilla [*sic*] recalled the still unsolved torso murder of a woman, the dismembered pieces of whose body was [*sic*] washed ashore at the foot of E. 156th st. early in September 1934. Police never were able to identify her."

A native of Ashtabula, Ohio, Florence Polillo had come to Cleveland by way of Buffalo, New York, and Erie, Pennsylvania. Her past was littered with curious personal and "business" liaisons—two of them legitimate marriages, another only rumored to be. She brought with her a bewildering number of names: Florence Genevieve Sawdey (perhaps Sawdy or Saudey, her maiden name), Florence Ghent (her first husband's name), Clara Dunn, Florence Martin, Clara Martin, Florence Gallagher, Florence Davis, and, of course, Flo Polillo. During her years in Cleveland, she had moved frequently, piling up as many different address as names; since May 1935, however, she had lived in a rooming house at 3205 Carnegie Avenue.

Her landlady, Mrs. Ford, told police she had last seen Pollilo leaving the house on Friday, the 24th, at 8:30 A.M. wearing a black cloth coat with a gray fur collar, brown stockings and shoes, and a small black hat. In the light of Straus's estimate of the time of death, she must have been murdered and dismembered later that night. "She usually ironed on Saturday, and when I found she wasn't here, I was worried," Mrs. Ford remarked to the *Press* on January 27. "She never gave us any trouble, and the only bad habit I noticed was that she would go out occasionally and get a quart of liquor—bad liquor, too—and drink it all by her lonesome in her room. When she was drinking she was pecky—quarrelsome, you know." Mrs. Ford, however, apparently liked her tenant; she was quiet and pleasant—except when drunk—paid her rent on time with relief checks, and if she was soliciting, Mrs. Ford knew nothing about it. Three months before her death, Mrs. Ford had taken pity on Polillo when her mother died and had driven her to Pierpont, Ohio, for the funeral.

The cooperative landlady also supplied the press with those touchingly personal details about Flo Polillo usually described as human interest. The dead woman owned a collection of over a dozen dolls, each with its own name, neatly arranged on chairs, the davenport, and her bed. She played frequently with Mrs. Ford's three small girls, readily sharing her dolls with them.

Among her personal effects, police found a notebook and some letters containing the names and addresses of people from Buffalo, Girard, Pennsylvania, and Conneaut, Ohio. In one letter, a man named Elmer Bollanberg claimed he had been arrested on a vice charge in Blawnox, Pennsylvania, and asked Polillo to raise the ten dollars he needed to pay his fine. In a second letter, bearing a Pittsburgh postmark, Bollanberg wrote that he had pawned her radio but would retrieve it if she would send him the necessary two dollars. A Spokane Avenue address in Polillo's notebook led investigators to Mrs. Herbert Coates, who insisted that she had not seen the dead woman for ten years but recounted that she had undergone treatment at the old Lakeside Hospital. Subsequently, police looked for a Dr. Manzella, to whom Polillo had listed a number of payments, but no doctor by that name could be found in Cleveland.

The next day, investigators began a sordid odyssey through cheap cafes and hotels, brothels, gambling joints, and bootleg operations, tracking down Florence Polillo's acquaintances and tracing her movements in the days before her death. Through informants, Detective Ralph Kennedy received a tip that an unsavory character named "Chink" Adler, who hung around the gambling spots on East 105th and Superior, had been Polillo's pimp for several years. He also hunted for two known prostitutes, reputed to be good friends of Polillo's, who lived in an apartment at the corner of East 86th and Carnegie. Neither of these potentially fruitful leads produced anything valuable. Detectives Musil and May located and eliminated from suspicion a black man named Ben Cotton who had asked for and received three burlap bags at Wayand's Grocery on Euclid three weeks before the remains were found. They also searched for a bootlegger named Albert N. Carlotta for whom Polillo was supposedly working when she was arrested for selling liquor in October 1935. (He was not found and cleared until July 1937.)

According to the police reports, the gallery of unsavory, even grotesque lowlifes in Polillo's life seemed endless: an "ugly" Italian on relief with bushy hair and dark complexion with whom she had once lived; "a very dirty looking" Italian whom she met frequently at East 22nd and Scovill the summer before her death; an addict named Al, who supposedly furnished her with drugs; a peddler who reportedly said he would cut her up if he ever found her; a black man called One-Armed Willie who had lived with her and fought with her the day before her death; a bootlegger to whom she had tried to sell a gun two days before she was murdered. Police could not implicate any of them in Polillo's death and dismemberment.

Anna Hughes, the manager of the dingy Lexington Hotel on Walnut Avenue, handed the police their first solid suspect—a tall, blond, "nice looking" truck driver for the Cleveland Transfer Company named Harry Martin. He was supposedly an army man who at one time had sold army buttons on the street. Apparently he had come to Cleveland with Polillo from Washington, D.C., sometime in 1934 after her arrest there on prostitution charges. Polillo insisted he was her husband. Hughes described Martin as a violent man who had beaten Polillo and blackened both her eyes repeatedly. Polillo had also been arrested several times during the couple's residency at the hotel and had even been sent to the workhouse. They had moved out two years before, taking all their possessions with them. Hughes remembered that Polillo had returned to the hotel six weeks before her death in the company of a young, unknown Italian man asking for some jigsaw puzzles that the hotel used to keep around for the guests. When Hughes told her the puzzles had all been given away, Polillo and the Italian left. Harry Martin had shown up on his own at the hotel for a short stay six months after his departure with Polillo, but Hughes had not seen him since. The police were never able to find him.

On January 28 Sergeant James Hogan took a statement from Andrew Polillo, a mail clerk from Buffalo, New York, who had come to Cleveland by bus after being notified of Flo's murder. He had married Flo in either 1922 or 1923; he was unsure of the exact date. She had been a hard drinker even then; so when, six years into their marriage, she told him she wanted to visit her mother in Ashtabula for about two weeks in an attempt to "get straightened out," Polillo readily agreed. Fifteen days later, he saw her outside the Charles Restaurant in Buffalo in the company of another man, and the next night she gathered up her clothes and left their apartment. She agreed to a divorce and ultimately moved to Erie, Pennsylvania, where she was arrested, probably for solicitation, in August 1928. The scar from an old operation that Dr. Straus noted during the autopsy was, according to Polillo, for a tumor and had been performed after she left him but before her move to Erie.

Detectives Wachsman, Carlson, and Harris responded to a call on Friday, February 7 at 5:45 A.M. and drove to 1419 Orange Avenue. In the early evening darkness, the three men trudged through the melting snow to the rear of the vacant house. In grim silence, they gathered around a shallow depression in the ground and looked down at its grotesque contents: the upper half of a female torso, minus the arms and head. The frozen, dirty surface was dotted with masses of charcoal, chicken feathers, and hay. About six feet away next to a fence lay both lower legs and the left arm dumped in a heap. Official confirmation from the coroner's office would come later, but the detectives no doubt knew they had found the rest of Flo Polillo's body—everything except the head, which would never be recovered.

When sixteen-year-old Walter Piszczek, a paper boy who delivered both the *Press* and the *News,* coasted into the Standard Oil service station at the corner of Orange and Broadway on his bicycle shortly after 6:00 A.M., two stern-looking men approached him and asked if he had seen anyone strange over on Orange recently. Piszczek replied, "There's a cat house over there. Everyone is strange." The two strangers looked disgusted and turned away. The station attendant identified the pair as detectives and told the startled newsboy that if he wanted to see a dead body, he should go across the street where paddy wagon lights cast a garish, eerie glow and hand-held flashlights cut through the gathering darkness. With a mixture of horror and awe, Piszczek, now joined by his older brother, watched as a detective wearing gloves nudged the torso piece with his foot to loosen it from the frozen ground and then carried it to a waiting police vehicle. "Here's the arms and legs," called a policeman close by. "The legs are cut below the box."

The killer could have discarded these additional pieces as far back as the morning of January 26 at the same time he had left the baskets containing the first set of partial remains behind Hart Manufacturing at East 20th and Central; the intersection of Orange Avenue and Broadway lay only a few blocks south. Police further reasoned that the killer might also have wrapped this second set of body parts in newspapers or burlap bags, which had blown away in the two-week interval since he disposed of them. In any case, the pieces would have remained hidden until the cold snap abated and the snow began to melt. Mary Cimino, who lived nearby on Orange Avenue with her husband, Anthony, remembered hearing their dog bark on the evening of Monday, February 3 but paid no further attention. The torso had been discovered by John Gaembeline, an employee of the Bennett Trucking Company on Orange Avenue, as he crossed the yard behind the house shortly after 5:00 on an errand. He had alerted his boss, Harry Bennett, and after the two men had hurried back to the site, they found the pile of dismembered limbs and subsequently summoned the police.

The Ciminos did not recognize Flo Polillo from her photograph, nor did John Gaembeline. Curiously, Harry Bennett did recognize her as someone he had noticed on several occasions during the last few months walking along Woodland Avenue in an apparently inebriated condition. He had last seen her a couple of weeks before her death arguing drunkenly with an equally intoxicated, shabbily dressed black man of about fifty.

The next day on February 8, Sergeant James Hogan and a contingent of detectives that included Orley May and Emil Musil, fanned out through the vacant lots in the vicinity of East 14th and Orange Avenue in a fruitless effort to find the missing head. Hogan was also present at the morgue later in the day when Dr. Straus examined the second set of Flo Polillo's remains. According to the pathologist, she had been decapitated at the level of the fifth cervical vertebra; a longitudinal incision, which had been noted in the lower piece of the torso, ran the entire length of the upper half, the clean edges indicating a knife rather than a saw; the heart, as in Andrassy's case, was virtually bloodless. The killer had apparently been in a rage when he dismembered the body. In his police report, Hogan noted that the Butcher had cut the skin around the arms and legs and then "wrenched" them "from the socket." At the end of the day, police sent a letter to Andrew Polillo in Buffalo informing him that several more pieces of his former wife had been located.

Seven months later, in September, Detectives Orley May and Emil Musil uncovered an intriguing lead. A woman, who asked not to be identified, told the two detectives that while she had been in the workhouse, another inmate named Helen O'Leary had identified Jack Wilson, a former butcher who had worked at a meat market on St. Clair, as the murderer of Flo Polillo. Wilson, according to the nameless informant, was a known "Sodomist" who carried a large butcher knife. May and Musil spoke to Detective Cooney, who knew of the deviant former butcher and promised to haul him in for questioning. Whether Jack Wilson was ever questioned is not known, but police were apparently unable to implicate him in Flo Polillo's murder.

After months of hard, frustrating work, the police had virtually nothing to show for all their detailed checking and drudgery. Every lead, no matter how insignificant, had been doggedly pursued. As with the investigation into Edward Andrassy's murder, promising leads all led nowhere, and eventually they simply dried up, leaving the authorities with nowhere to turn. Police had examined every detail of Polillo's sordid life and had tracked her every movement until she left the rooming house at 3205 Carnegie at 8:30 on the evening of Friday, January 24. After that, she simply disappeared. Within hours, she met the man who would kill her, violently dismember her corpse, and dispose of the pieces; but no one noticed anything. No one saw him when he placed the two half-bushel baskets containing the neatly wrapped pieces of her body in the snow behind Hart Manufacturing; no one noticed when he dumped the additional parts in the vacant lot on Orange Avenue. The only apparent witnesses to her fate were a pair of barking dogs. Flo Polillo's murder remained an enigma.

Her name, however, would continue to crop up during the investigations into subsequent killings. On January 17, 1938, a woman's winter coat and hat were found, along with other articles of clothing, in a vacant lot on East 65th near Jackass Hill. By then, six additional decapitation murders had been added to the Butcher's tally, and a jittery populace, taking the discovery as a sign that yet another dismembered corpse would turn up somewhere nearby, waited in grim expectation. No new bodies were discovered. When pieces of victim no. 10, a relatively petite female, began to appear in April, the police made an unsuccessful attempt to match the clothing with her. Though probably too small, they bore a resemblance to the clothes Flo Polillo had been wearing when she left her rooming house for the last time, almost exactly two years before.

In March 1939, more than three years after Flo Polillo's murder, the severed remains of a young woman were found in Havana, Cuba, and Gerber dispatched information on the Cleveland killings to the Havana police. In mid-July, Dr. Israel Castellonas, director of the Cabinete Nacional de Identifacion in Havana, specifically asked for and received a copy of the survey of anatomical findings in Flo Polillo's case. Nor was the curious odyssey of her remains over. At about the same time as Dr. Castellonas was making his request, parts of her body, which had been kept at the Western Reserve University Medical School since her death, were returned to the morgue, perhaps for further study. An official permit for removal and transfer in the coroner's files documents the mysterious move but fails to provide any reason for it.

The investigation into Flo Polillo's murder may have ground to a frustrating halt, but at least the police had a name, several in fact, to work with. Flo Polillo was a victim with an identity. This would be the last time investigators enjoyed such a luxury.

NOTES

The fullest account of the January 26 discovery behind Hart Manufacturing, the events leading up to it, and the subsequent investigation are in the police reports of Detectives Orley May, Emil Musil, Leo Duffin, and Ralph Kennedy, as well as Lieutenant Harvey Weitzel and Sergeant Walter Kirby. The events of February 7 and 8 are covered by reports from Detective Herbert Wachsman and Sergeant James Hogan, head of homicide. All of these reports, as well as a transcript of Hogan's interview with Andrew Polillo, are contained in the coroner's files on Flo Polillo, case no. 45371. The three Cleveland dailies, January 26–27, 1936, offer additional information on the first phases of the police investigation.

All anatomical findings for both sets of remains are recorded in the autopsy protocols, case no. 45371.

Walter Piszczek recounted his experiences on the evening of February 7 during a personal interview.

The background information on Harry Martin and the descriptions of some of the individuals sought by police were culled from now missing reports by John Bartlow Martin and are contained in his article "Butcher's Dozen: The Cleveland Torso Murders," 59.

The paperwork relevant to Dr. Castellonas's request for the anatomical findings in the Polillo case and the transfer of her remains from the Western Reserve University Medical School to the morgue are part of the coroner's files, case no. 45371.

June 5, 1936

THE DECAPITATED TATTOOED MAN

As the summer of 1936 approached, city leaders had reason to be optimistic about Cleveland's economic and financial future. First, the city had landed one of the season's two prize political plums—the Republican national convention. After the city had spent $150,000 to spruce up Public Hall's yawning interior, the Republicans gathered there between June 9 and 12, nominating Alf Landon to challenge Franklin D. Roosevelt for the presidency. Fifteen days later, on June 27, the Great Lakes Exposition opened for a one-hundred-day run. The project, intended to celebrate the centennial of Cleveland's incorporation as a city, was the brainchild of Frank J. Ryan and Lincoln J. Dickey. Cleveland philanthropist Dudley S. Blossom chaired a civic committee that raised $1.5 million to convert a 135-acre stretch of lakeshore real estate—embracing the Mall Area, Public Hall, and the Stadium—into a massive exposition site which drew four million visitors to the Erie shore the first year and three million more in 1937. The Townsend Club—a relatively minor organization born out of the Depression and devoted to the concept of a government subsidy for senior citizens—planned to hold its convention in Cleveland in mid-July, and the American Legion would follow suit in September. If the city's movers and shakers had their way, the summer of 1936 would be a golden one, lifting both the city's spirits and its financial prospects. The last thing anyone wanted was negative publicity about Cleveland.

On the morning of Friday, June 5, workmen put the finishing touches on Public Hall, readying it for the Republican delegates who would be arriving four days later. Several miles away at about 8:20, two young African American boys—eleven-year-old Louis Cheeley of 2635 East 65th and thirteen-year-old Gomez Ivey of 5800 Haltnorth Court—were walking south through Kingsbury Run along a path by the New York Central Railroad tracks. Though Kingsbury oral tradition holds that they were on their way to Outhwaite School, the youngsters were actually playing hooky to go fishing. In the early morning stillness, the two boys strolled through the desolate landscape close to where the East 55th Street bridge spanned the gorge. About a thousand feet southwest of Kinsman Road, between the train tracks and the rapid transit line, the boys spotted a pair of brown tweed trousers, wrapped in a bundle under a willow tree. "We see the pants all rolled up," Gomez Ivey later told the *Plain Dealer* on June 6, "and we think maybe there's money in the pockets." The boys tentatively poked at the bundle with a fishing pole, causing it to unroll slowly. Beneath one of the pant legs, a grimy human head appeared. "We're so scared we run straight

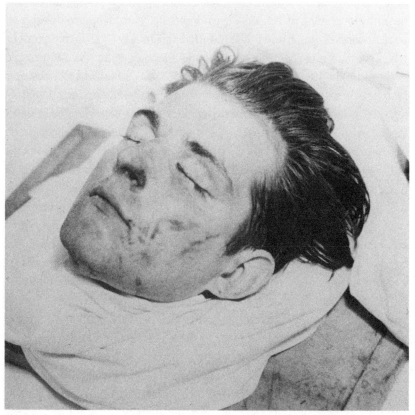

The head of victim no. 4 found in Kingsbury Run on June 5, 1936. Morgue personnel cleaned it before putting it on public display. Cleveland Police Historical Society.

home," Ivey related. "I wanted to ask my mother what to do but she wasn't home. When she came in at about 5 o'clock she tells us to see a policeman."

The boys then told Patrolman Hendricks of the Fifth Precinct station at East 55th and Woodland about their grim discovery. He seems to have tried to locate the head before radioing for help, but because the two boys had fled in terror and could not be sure of its exact location, Hendricks could not find it. The by now familiar cast of law enforcement personnel began to gather on the scene. At 5:40, Detectives Orley May and Emil Musil, both of whom had been deeply involved in the Andrassy and Polillo murders, responded to the radio call, joining Sergeant James Hogan, head of homicide, David L. Cowles of the Scientific Investigation Bureau, officers from the Sixth Precinct and others in the desolate setting of Kingsbury Run.

Before police examined the pants, Bertillon Assistant James Benacek took a picture of the boys' grisly find. The badly faded photograph shows the filthy head lying on its side—eyes closed, lips parted—partially exposed beneath one of the trouser legs. Stuffed inside the legs of the trousers, which were torn in the back, police found a bloody white polo shirt ripped at the shoulder and bearing the label "Park Royal Broadcloth," a similarly bloodied dress shirt with brown stripes and the label "Desmonds," a pair of blue striped men's shorts, and a size 32 black leather belt trimmed in white leather with a nickel buckle. The right rear pocket yielded a soiled white, man's handkerchief. The blood on the shirts made it impossible to make out the laundry marks at the crime scene, so the clothing was turned over to Cowles for further analysis. About twenty feet from the head lay a pair of size 7½, badly worn oxfords (the police reports differ on whether they were tan or oxblood in color), their laces tied together and stuffed with a pair of dark striped socks with orange tops; thirty feet away to the northeast in an open area covered with cinders, police found a dirty, oily brown cap.

None of this had been there the day before. New York Central Railroad detective Dudley A. McDowell of Charles Avenue, who had provided police with a lead in the Andrassy murder, patrolled the area regularly, looking in the bushes and under the trees for stolen goods. He had last checked the area at 3:00 A.M. on June 4, about eighteen hours before Ivey and Cheeley made their nasty discovery. In the late evening or early morning darkness, the killer had moved silently through the isolated region, picking his way carefully across the railroad tracks with his grisly package under his arm.

But there was no body. The police carefully combed the entire area. They walked through the gullies and depressions, looked in the empty boxcars which stood idle close to the scene and checked the nearby hobo shanties. There was nothing, not even a trace of blood.

If the assembled lawmen had turned to the southwest that late afternoon, they would have seen Jackass Hill about a mile away. Nine months before, two other equally traumatized boys had found the naked, headless bodies of Edward Andrassy and his still unidentified companion. The bucket of oil, the pieces of rope, and the severed genitals of both men had been casually abandoned or simply dumped—just as the shoes and hat of this victim had been dumped or tossed aside, just as Flo Polillo's legs and left arm had been dropped in a heap behind a house on Orange Avenue.

Yet the Butcher also proudly, defiantly, perhaps tauntingly displayed his handiwork. The head of this fourth victim had been carefully rolled up in his pants and deliberately deposited under a willow tree, just as pieces of Flo Polillo's body had been neatly wrapped in newspapers, packed in baskets, and deposited behind Hart Manufacturing six months before. When he disposed of his victims, the Butcher seemed to manifest an odd combination of obsessive neatness and casual sloppiness. Or, despite appearances, was everything carefully arranged? Was there some dark, obscure personal meaning behind every detail of the scenes he left behind?

Even though police had worked on a large number of cases in the intervening months, the striking similarities between the gruesome murders were immediately apparent to law enforcement officials; and they were clearly not lost on the reporters for the city's three daily newspapers who began to use terms such as "fiend," "maniac," "maniac killer," "crazed killer," and "human butcher" to describe the perpetrator. "In each case a very sharp knife was used," mused Coroner Pearce to the *Press* on June 6. Sergeant James Hogan also conceded the similarities in the crimes, and if, according to the *Plain Dealer* (the *Plain Dealer* and the *Press* disagreed about his position on this issue), he was inclined to keep Flo Polillo off the official tally of the Butcher's activities, the newspapers were not: the *Press* ran a huge photo spread on Saturday, June 6, including a morgue shot of the head found the day before, a photo of Kingsbury Run with an arrow marking the spot where it had been discovered, as well as Andrassy's and Polillo's mug shots.

The head arrived at the morgue about 7:30 A.M.; and, judging from the handwriting on the coroner's view slip, Wilson Chamberlain, who had performed the Andrassy autopsy, was the first pathologist to examine it. The head belonged to a young man, somewhere between twenty and twenty-five, with fine features, brown eyes, thick reddish-brown hair, and, though five were missing, a reasonably good set of teeth. (Police thought he was Central European, possibly a Pole or Slav.) The victim had been killed approximately forty-eight hours before discovery; the head had been severed from the body, with multiple hesitation cuts, under the chin at the axis. Either David Cowles or A. J. Pearce made a plaster casting of it in case circumstances forced burial before the victim could be identified.

Police feared that without an identification of the victim, finding the killer would be virtually impossible. And with no body to fingerprint, identification would have to come from the head itself. The coroner's office, therefore, dutifully cleaned it and put it on display in the morgue. From the evening of June 5 to the morning of June 6, an estimated two thousand people filed through the morgue, but no one recognized the handsome young man.

As they had done in the cases of victim no. 2 and Flo Polillo, police immediately checked through missing person reports. Early on June 6, Detectives Theodore Carlson and Herbert Wachsman took a photo of the head to the homes of three different individuals reported missing since June 1. At the last address they checked, an aunt and a neighbor thought the picture strongly resembled missing Tony Luksic, but they changed their minds after viewing the head at the morgue. Sergeant Ernest Molnar thought that the unidentified man may have been an associate of Edward Andrassy's—the two men resembled each other somewhat and were close in age—and suggested bringing residents near Andrassy's home at 1744 Fulton Avenue into the morgue to view the head.

A major break in the case came swiftly at 1:00 on the afternoon of June 6. New York Central crane operators Peter J. Fagan and Louis G. Mackey found a naked, headless corpse lying on its side covered with twigs just east of the East 55th Street bridge, between the New York Central and Nickel Plate railroad track—about a thousand feet from the spot where the boys had found the head the day before and eight hundred feet away from where Andrassy and the other victim had been discovered the previous September. By 2:00 A.M., Sergeant James Hogan, Detective Theodore Carlson, Acting Detective Inspector Charles O. Nevel, and others had responded to the call. Lieutenant Frank C. Rezac noted the pools of blood in the area and confidently reported to Captain Daniel J. O'Brien that they had found the murder site.

Determining the identity of the young victim now seemed a certainty. Not only was the corpse fresh enough to yield a good set of fingerprints, it bore six different tattoos on various parts of the body: a butterfly on the left shoulder, the comic strip character Jiggs on the outer surface of the left calf, crossed flags and the letters W. C. G. on the left forearm, a heart and anchor also on the left forearm, a cupid and anchor on the outer surface of the right calf, and the names Helen and Paul on the right forearm. Even though only the anchors were particularly nautical in nature, investigators believed the dead man may have been a sailor.

At the morgue, pathologists quickly filled in the victim's vital statistics. He was five feet eleven and weighed about 165 pounds. Unlike Andrassy and victim no. 2, he had not been emasculated. For some reason, Reuben Straus did not perform the autopsy until June 8, two days later. Considering the speed with which the coroner's office had moved on the previous cases, the delay is inexplicable. By the time Straus went to work, the body had undergone what he blandly described as "considerable postmortem change": areas of the skin had turned green, the cut surfaces swarmed with maggots, and the body itself was swollen with foul-smelling gas. He detected a blood alcohol level of .03 percent and found a small amount of undigested food, including baked beans, in the stomach. Death was attributed to decapitation and the resulting shock.

The discovery of the body kept the killing on the front pages, where it vied for attention with the Republican national convention. Acting Detective Inspector Charles O. Nevel seemed glad, even anxious, to share his theories about the murder with the press. He described the killer for a *Plain Dealer* reporter on June 7 as a "maniac with a lust to kill," conjuring up an image of a phantom butcher who silently prowled Kingsbury Run in search of potential victims. The young man, Nevel theorized, was a stranger to the city who had arrived by rail and simply fallen asleep in Kingsbury Run, where the killer just happened upon him. "While he was sleeping this maniac attacked him. First he cut his throat. Then he hacked away at the neck. Then he undressed the victim." When asked why the killer would bother to strip the clothing from the body, Nevel rather darkly declared, "That's a maniac's trick."

The fingerprints turned out to be a dead end; the victim's prints were not on file with any official agency, including the FBI and the State Identification Bureau in Columbus. By Wednesday, June 10, detectives had begun to canvass every laundry in the city, hoping for an identification through the laundry mark "J. D. X" on the victim's clothing. The X, they believed, would be the key since it was used to differentiate among other customers of the same laundry who shared the initials J. D. Police also had the tattooed initials W. C. G. on the victim to work with. They scoured every public and private record, every list of names from every agency looking for a J. D. or a W. C. G., even a W. G. A few matches led to persons still very much alive. (Authorities received an anonymous postcard in March 1937 suggesting that the victim might be William or Walter "Chuck" Griffith of Phoenix, Arizona—a man the writer thought might once have worked at Cleveland's Wayfarer's Lodge, but no one by that name had ever been associated with the Lakeside Avenue home for transients.) Police managed to trace a shirt label to a California manufacturer, but there the trail ended.

At least three different photographs were taken of the head at the morgue, one before it had been cleaned for public viewing. Police passed the two least shocking over to the newspapers for publication and had them showed to countless tramps, informants, and tattoo artists all over the country. A detailed description of the victim even went out over the radio. Again, they came up empty.

Authorities decided to turn the popular Great Lakes Exposition to their advantage, so they put the victim's plaster death mask—presumably the same one either Pearce or Cowles had cast earlier—on display. Over the summers of 1936 and 1937, thousands of exposition visitors filed by the lifelike mask and gazed at its placid, handsome features. But no one recognized him.

† † †

In January 1938, a year and a half later, Everett Hanson of Minneapolis saw an outline drawing of victim no. 4 showing the tattoos (how or under what circumstances is unknown) and wrote Cleveland police about a young man he remembered seeing at the Brace Memorial Newsboys Home in New York City in June 1932. "I distinctly remember the comic character 'Jiggs' on one of his legs," Hanson insisted. He suggested that if the initials W. C. G. on the victim's arm were actually his, the police could probably identify him through registration records at the Newsboys Home. Police immediately checked the establishment, but yet another promising lead yielded nothing.

In the spring of 1938, the tattooed man suddenly became the focus of the entire investigation again, this time through a mysterious photograph in the possession of John Moessner, who admitted to having taken the four published pictures of Edward Andrassy in the bizarrely furnished room on West 28th. While detectives were searching Moessner's Fulton Road

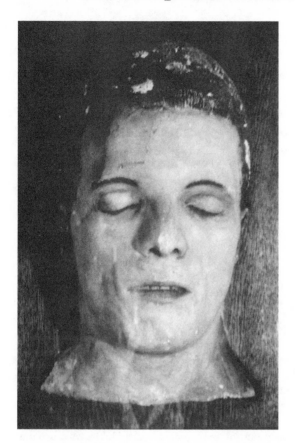

This casting of victim no. 4's head was displayed at the Great Lakes Exposition in the hopes that someone would recognize him. Today it hangs in the Cleveland Police Historical Society Museum. Cleveland Police Historical Society/ Richard Karberg.

home for potentially incriminating evidence linking him with Andrassy, they turned up a photo of a handsome, young naval officer, who they felt bore a striking resemblance to the still unidentified fourth victim. Moessner insisted that the picture was at least twenty years old, that it had been taken while he tended bar somewhere in downtown Cleveland, and that he had no idea what the officer's name was. According to the *Press* of April 14, he told police, "I don't think you will ever find him." "I don't think I will ever find him either," retorted Detective Peter Merylo in the same article. "But if he is alive, I have got to find him. If he is dead I have got to know how he died. There is too much resemblance between this man and the one whose severed head was found in Kingsbury Run in June of 1936. The bulging forehead, the bridge of the nose, the ear—all are the same." But the circumstantial evidence surrounding John Moessner collapsed, leaving the police with yet another tantalizing clue that led nowhere.

† † †

The authorities made a thorough and determined effort to identify this mysterious fourth victim. Never again over the next two years would they pursue an identification with such persistence; never again, however, would they have as much to work with. The death mask still hangs, with other relics from the Kingsbury Run murders, at the Cleveland Police Historical Society and Museum, where he is known to this day only as victim no. 4.

NOTES

Facts relating to the Great Lakes Exposition are from Van Tassel and Grabowski, eds., *The Encyclopedia of Cleveland History.*

The police reports from Detective Orley May and Sergeants Ernest L. Molnar and James McDonald cover the discovery of no. 4's head on June 5; reports from Detective Theodore Carlson and Lieutenant Frank C. Rezac deal with the subsequent discovery of the body. All are contained in the coroner's files, case no. 45781. Additional information comes from the three Cleveland dailies, June 6–7, 1936. John Bartlow Martin's "Butcher's Dozen: The Cleveland Torso Murders" and Howard Beaufait's "Kingsbury Run Murders" provide information about subsequent phases of the investigation.

All anatomical findings are recorded in the coroner's files, case no. 45781.

Detective Peter Merylo mentions the anonymous postcard in the Otwell manuscript.

Everett Hanson's tip letter is part of Peter Merylo's personal collection of documents.

The three daily papers provide the details covering the discovery of the naval officer's photograph in John Moessner's room, April 12–19, 1938.

July 22, 1936
MURDER WITHOUT A CLUE

Marie Barkley was an attractive seventeen-year-old who had no idea she would earn a small niche in the history of Cleveland's most notorious murders. She had simply decided to take advantage of the pleasant summer weather by hiking through a wooded area close to where she lived. In the late morning of July 22, 1936, she left her home at 7808 Hope Avenue and walked south, probably down West 73rd; she crossed Denison and the Baltimore & Ohio railroad tracks—a trek that took her outside Cleveland proper to Brooklyn. The north end of the southwestern suburb was a sparsely populated area dotted with a few homes, small farms, and industrial plants. She headed toward a patch of woods south of Clinton Road near Big Creek, perhaps passing the remnants of the hobo campfires that the police would later investigate. Whether she first noticed the terrible stench or actually caught sight of the sickening corpse is not known; but at about 11:30, she came upon the naked, headless body of a white male in an advanced state of decomposition lying on its chest in a gully near West 98th and the Rayon Plant.

Sergeant James Finnerty, the first Cleveland policeman on the scene, did not arrive until 1:20, nearly two hours after Barkley's discovery. (Brooklyn police may have been summoned first, but there is no existing record of whether they ever responded to such a call or, indeed, even received it. There is also no record of how Cleveland police became involved. Brooklyn authorities may have alerted them when they recognized the similarity between Marie Barkley's discovery and the previous killings in the city proper.) Initially, Finnerty did not see the head but ultimately found it between ten and eighteen feet away, lying on top of and partly hidden by the victim's clothing, some articles stained with blood: a single-breasted, dark gray suit

Victim no. 5, the only one found on Cleveland's west side, had been dead for two months when his body was found on July 22, 1936. Courtesy of Marjorie Merylo Dentz.

(the arms of the jacket turned inside out, a slash in the right sleeve), a dark brown leather belt with a plain nickel buckle, well-worn size 8 black oxfords, a light blue polo shirt, light blue socks, a black cap with gray stripes, and white underwear. The man had apparently been killed where his body lay.

At 1:30, Sergeant James Hogan and Detectives Orley May and Thomas F. McNeil joined Finnerty and members of no. 10 Cruiser in the isolated spot. Hogan and May were savvy, experienced veterans of the force. Orley May had been one of the first Cleveland detectives at the base of Jackass Hill the previous September when Jimmy Wagner and Peter Kostura discovered Edward Andrassy's body, and he had worked on every torso case since. He had seen solid leads in the Andrassy and Polillo murders evaporate. After exploring the area, both men realized that there were few clues and no leads at all: only an isolated crime scene—later determined to be about two months old—and a rotting corpse. Because the body lay in a spot surrounded by railroad tracks and dotted with the remains of hobo camps, police assumed the victim had been a vagrant. A more thorough investigation of the area turned up nothing. Without a bit of luck in this case, authorities realized their efforts would be futile. Since the skin of the face was so badly decomposed, fingerprinting and missing person reports were the only possible ways to identify the victim. Given the condition of the remains, the former method would have been next to impossible; but the police tried to take a set anyway. After Bertillon Assistant James Benacek photographed the body, county undertaker Frank G. Nunn took it to the morgue, where Coroner Pearce declared the man legally dead at 5:20 P.M.

The victim weighed about 145 pounds, was five feet five, and possessed longish brown hair. Pathologist Reuben Straus judged him to be approximately forty years old. Straus's autopsy report reads like a catalog of horrors: the skin on the back and legs remained intact but was hardened and brownish, an observation borne out by Benacek's photograph. The viscera of the chest had been largely destroyed by decomposition, rats, and insects; after opening the abdomen, Straus noted "innumerable worms and other forms of bugs in great numbers throughout the skin and viscera." The head had been separated from the body between the third and fourth cervical vertebrae. He estimated the man had been dead for about two months—meaning he had been killed before the tattooed man whose body was discovered in early June.

An odd and potentially significant disagreement over the exact cause of death arose in the coroner's office. Because Straus's detailed examination showed the bones in the neck to be smooth, with no knife marks at the points of separation, he hedged in his autopsy report, calling the death a "probable murder (method unknown)." Pearce was far more emphatic; in his official verdict he called the case a homicide and attributed death to decapitation. Yet in statements to the press, he backed off, stating that the cause of death was uncertain. "There is nothing to indicate that there was any violence on skull or body," Pearce told the *Plain Dealer* on July 23. "The whole thing was so decomposed that it is possible for the head to have dropped off and to have been carried a few yards by a dog or other animal." To the *Press,* Pearce suggested that, assuming the man had been murdered, the killer would have to possess the skill and anatomical knowledge of a surgeon to sever the head from the body so cleanly. Why the equivocation? Had Pearce spoken to the press before Straus's autopsy, or did he simply change his mind?

With no usable fingerprints, no identifying marks on the clothing, and no papers or other forms of identification in the pockets, police immediately turned to the missing person reports that had been filed in the last six months, but none of those individuals matched the admittedly vague description of the dead man. A two-month-old report of a missing forty-year-old WPA worker whose general physique matched the victim's caused a brief flurry of interest, but the sketchy document did not even indicate who had reported the man missing. According to the *Press* on July 23, some detectives even began to wonder if all the deaths could be attributed not to a lone individual but to "a group of thrill-killers."

All three city newspapers linked this latest decapitation murder to the other four. In the rush to get their stories on the street, many errors crept into their recapitulations of the previous killings; the accuracy of the historical record became blurred. The intensity of the coverage also rose by several degrees, led by the *Cleveland News* on July 23. Under a headline trumpeting "Madman or Cool Killer? Police Probers Groping for Leads in County's Five Headless Murders," the paper asked:

> Is there somewhere in Cuyahoga county a madman whose god is the guillotine?
> What fantastic chemistry of the civilized mind converted him into a human butcher?
> Does he imagine himself a legal executioner of the French Revolution? Or a religious zealot determined to save the human race from perdition with an ax? Or a modern Jack-the-Ripper who terrorized London many years ago?
> Or is he merely a cool and calculating killer who decapitates his victims with the skill of a physician?
> Does he dissect his victims in some grisly workshop, carrying them to the isolated sections of the county where they are found?
> Or does he lure them to the outdoor scene of the execution, acting upon some fairly reasonable motive in each case?

In what seemed an ominous move, the killer had ventured to the west side for the first time in search of a victim; but, though no one could have known it then, this was the only such foray he would make across the river. In their zeal to lump together all five of the victims killed since September 1935, the papers missed the startling similarities between the tattooed victim no. 4 and the just discovered victim no. 5. The fourth victim had been dispatched a few days before his head and body were found on June 5 and 6. If the coroner's office was correct in its determination that victim no. 5

Cuyahoga County coroner Arthur J. Pearce. *Cleveland Press* Archives, Cleveland State University.

had been dead for about two months, then he was murdered in late May or very early June, perhaps within days of the tattooed man's death. Both men had been killed outside, presumably at the sites where their bodies were eventually found (unlike Edward Andrassy, no. 2, and Flo Polillo); both had been decapitated and stripped, but neither had been emasculated as had Andrassy and the second victim. In both cases the killer left the victim's clothing and head on the scene or close by.

The investigation into this particular murder died shortly after it started; only the slow, methodical working of prescribed police procedures gave it any illusion of life. At this point, the authorities may have begun to realize that one perpetrator was responsible for the entire chain of killings, but that had not yet significantly altered their approach to the case. Basically, they were still trying to solve individual crimes, one at a time. Since both the murders of no. 4 and no. 5 had apparently been committed in isolated spots, the police could pursue their investigations of those scenes in relative privacy. Within two months, however, a crime scene would be transformed into a ghoulish public circus.

NOTES

Because victim no. 5 had been killed outside Cleveland, little official documentation relevant to the investigation remains. (Ripperologists will note the similarity between victim no. 5 and Catherine Eddows—the only Ripper victim to be killed outside Whitechapel in London proper.) Only two police reports—one from Sergeant James Finnerty, the first officer on the scene, and the other from Detective Orley May—are in the coroner's files, case no. 45960. All three Cleveland newspapers covered Marie Barkley's discovery thoroughly on July 23, 1936; and Peter Merylo adds a few more details in the Otwell manuscript.

All anatomical findings are from the autopsy protocols, case no. 45960.

September 10, 1936
CIRCUS AT A STAGNANT POOL

Sergeant James T. Hogan was deeply apprehensive. Although the chief of homicide had not been among those at the foot of Jackass Hill when the bodies of Edward Andrassy and his unnamed companion were discovered a year before, he had been one of the first behind Hart Manufacturing the following January to investigate the death of Flo Polillo. He also had led the futile search for her missing head along Orange Avenue thirteen days later when more pieces of her body turned up, and he had been present during the pathologist's examination of that second set of remains. He had responded to the call when Louis Cheeley and Gomez Ivey found the head of the tattooed man in Kingsbury Run on June 5, 1936, and had been among the first on the scene when the body was discovered the next day. Up until early June 1936, he had regarded the killings as separate crimes, but the murder of the still unidentified tattooed man forced him to reassess his position and see them as linked.

Initially he had been reluctant to add Flo Polillo's murder to the official count, but the discovery of victim no. 5 on the west side in Brooklyn probably caused him to reexamine that assumption as well. The police were now confronted with what the *Press* termed on September 10, "a modern Bluebeard mystery" and "a blank-wall of clueless mystery." Hogan was a veteran of the police force, a solid professional with the tough, handsome features often associated with marine sergeants. He had joined the force in 1905 and had been promoted to chief of homicide in November 1935. Though neither the term nor the concept "serial killer" held the same relevance for him as it does for society now, he possessed the sure instincts that can come only from thirty-one long years of experience, and those instincts, according to the *Press* on September 10, 1936, told him there would be another killing soon. Cleveland was facing a serial killer.

Jerry Harris was a vagrant. On the morning of September 10, 1936, at 11:15, the twenty-five-year-old black man, a native of St. Louis, sat on an abutment along the side of a foul, virtually stagnant waterway optimistically referred to as a creek in Kingsbury Run near East 37th, waiting to hop a freight train that would carry him east. Suddenly he caught sight of the two halves of a white male torso—headless, armless, and legless—bobbing and swirling slowly in the murky waters close by. He fled to the Socony Vacuum Oil Company tank station at 2846 East 37th and alerted storage clerk Leo Fields, who, in turn, summoned the police.

Within fifteen minutes Sergeant Hogan, as well as Detectives Orley May, Emil Musil, and Gordon Shibley had responded to the call. For reasons left unexplained, Bertillon Assitant Ohlrich could not get a photograph of the two pieces in the creek, so police hauled them out of the dirty water and immediately sent them to the morgue. At a point where the water emerged from a large tunnel into a twenty-foot-deep pool, the police found some small bits of human flesh adhering to a ledge, apparently where the killer had thrown the pieces over the edge into the creek. After a cursory examination of the torso pieces by the pool, Hogan speculated that the man had been dead for no more than three or four days and confidently told the press that this latest victim had been murdered by the same man responsible for the five previous victims in the series.

The fire rescue squad, under the leadership of Lieutenant Charles G. Eisenhart, arrived and began dragging the foul waters with grappling hooks in a fruitless attempt to locate the rest of the body. When they switched to ceiling hooks, however, they managed to snare the lower half of both legs, which were promptly dispatched to the morgue. May and the others continued the largely futile dragging operation from a small boat borrowed from the Coast Guard.

All this activity attracted the attention of the already restless residents in the neighborhoods on the rim of Kingsbury Run. There had been five extraordinarily gruesome murders in the space of a single year, three of the bodies left in the Run itself, and the police still had no real clues or viable suspects. Now the killer had dumped his sixth victim right on their doorstep. "Hacked Body Found in Kingsbury Run," proclaimed the *Press* on the front page of the September 10 edition. On September 11, the *News* estimated that "hundreds" of curious onlookers gathered to watch the grim search, and the *Plain Dealer* printed a photo of the impressive spectacle the same day. The investigation had become a public circus.

As in each of the previous murders, the police found some clothes on the scene. This time the tally included a blue denim work shirt, a gray felt hat with a small black band, and a twelve-by-sixteen-inch piece of faded green underwear bearing the laundry mark "J. W." on the waistband. The shirt had been found, wrapped in the September 4, 1936, issue of the *Plain Dealer*, along the bank of the waterway at the point where authorities assumed the pieces of the body had been dumped. Orley May spotted the dirty hat the next day in the weeds, 125 feet northwest of the creek. The shirt bore blood stains and knife cuts at the neck, as well as a crude patch above the right front pocket and a label stamped with no. 5 above the left; the underwear was spotted with blood. The hat had a label that read "Loudy's Smart Shop, Bellevue, Ohio." All of these articles of clothing were turned over to David L. Cowles for further analysis by the Scientific Investigation Bureau.

Other bits and pieces of tantalizing evidence also began to accumulate, but they refused to cohere into a discernible pattern. On Wednesday, the 9th, the day before Jerry Harris discovered the first floating pieces of the body, railroad detectives had been scouting the area looking for some stolen wire; and they assured police the torso pieces had not been in the pool then. In the evening of the same day, Roland Strasser and Emil Hayden, two Nickel Plate Railroad switchmen, saw a truck parked with its lights out above the abutment near where police theorized the pieces had been tossed into the pool. Police located a bloody stone that they surmised could have served as the killer's chopping block. On Friday, the 11th, Coroner Pearce joined the hunt and found a charred object he at first thought might be a human bone while raking through the remnants of a hobo campfire under the East 34th Street bridge; it turned out to be nothing. Authorities even drafted onlookers to canvass the area surrounding the pool in a fruitless search for additional clues.

At 1:00 A.M. on the 10th, the day Harris discovered them, pathologist Straus examined the body pieces at the morgue. He estimated the victim weighed about 145 pounds and stood approximately five feet ten; he placed his age between twenty-five and thirty years. The rest of Straus's report had a frighteningly familiar ring. The head had been severed from the body with two powerful cuts—one from the front, the other from the back—between the third and fourth cervical vertebrae. (The longish hair at the base of the neck indicated the victim had medium brown hair.) The killer had similarly bisected the torso about two inches above the navel between the third and fourth lumbar vertebrae, slicing the stomach and both kidneys in the process. As with both Andrassy and victim no. 2, but unlike the tattooed victim no. 4, this man had been emasculated; about one inch of his penis remained in the groin area. All the dismemberment had been accomplished with few or no hesitation marks. Coroner Pearce's final verdict attributed

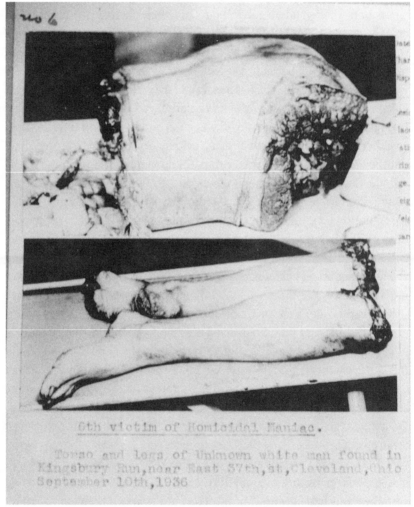

Two photographs of the recovered parts of victim no. 6. The special mounting suggests that they may have been part of Coroner Samuel R. Gerber's display for a conference of the National Association of Coroners in late August 1937. Cleveland Police Historical Society.

death to "probable murder by decapitation and section of body." Deputy Cononer Wilson Chamberlain told the *Cleveland News* on September 10 that the examination of the victim's heart showed he had still been alive when the killer began to dismember his body.

Like brush daubs in an impressionist painting, some of Straus's observations began to coalesce into an image of the killer: a powerful man with considerable anatomical knowledge. The pathologist noted that the cuts at the shoulders had been made "without hesitation and in the proper site for clean amputation." "Judging from the character of the cut through the bone," he remarked in reference to the torso itself, "it would require either considerable force with a heavy knife or some heavier instrument as a hatchet or cleaver to do this." Pearce gave these conclusions, as well as some of his own, to the press, and the *Cleveland News* dutifully passed them on to an already jittery and apprehensive public on September 11: "The killer is apparently a sex maniac of the sadistic type. This is indicated by the condition of his victims. He is probably a muscular man. The slayer definitely has expert knowledge of human anatomy. The incisions of his knife are clean and were made in each case without guesswork. He may have gathered his knowledge of anatomy as a medical student. Or it is possible that he is a butcher."

Without arms and head, identification would be impossible, so the largely futile search for the rest of the corpse went on for almost a month. On Friday, September 11, Hogan ordered the fire department to bring a large-nozzled pump in hopes of stirring up whatever pieces of the body might remain at the bottom of the pool. When that proved unsuccessful, police reverted to dragging the water with grappling hooks in a boat supplied by the Coast Guard. When this too failed, they returned to using ceiling hooks and managed to snag the right thigh. On Saturday, September 12, police arranged for planks to be placed across the creek so the dragging operation could continue from these makeshift bridges, but their only reward for the day's work was the left thigh.

In the evening of the 12th, County Prosecutor Frank T. Cullitan and Detective Inspector Joseph M. Sweeney made arrangements with veteran marine diver John D. Stanton to coordinate a diving operation in the dark waters of the pool. "We never see anything," Stanton told the *Plain Dealer.* "We have worked in the Cuyahoga River so long we operate by sense of touch. If there are any more pieces of the body in the water we'll find them." So in spite of all the dangers posed by rocks and rubbish, on Sunday, the

13th, diver Richard Boyce searched unsuccessfully for five hours along the bottom of the pool and in a tunnel that led into it.

All through the day people from the surrounding neighborhoods—the morbidly curious, the deeply concerned, the frightened—came to the search area even though there was little for them to see. Some just passed by; others stayed to watch. The *Cleveland News* estimated that an astounding one hundred thousand onlookers gathered at the pool at some time during the day. Extra police were even called to manage the increased traffic flow—probably on East 37th, the only road, save for the East 34th and East 55th Street bridges, linking the north and south sides of Kingsbury Run. Cars backed up for a half mile in both directions, and one onlooker counted an astonishing fourteen hundred automobiles cruising by. Detective Peter Merylo relates in the Otwell manuscript that hundreds of curious bystanders wandered over to the morgue in hopes of seeing the grisly body parts, forcing an angry Coroner Pearce "to close the place to these 'tourists.'"

Curious onlookers from the nearby neighborhoods watch the police search for pieces of victim no. 6 in the stagnant pool near East 37th in Kingsbury Run. Couresty of Marjorie Merylo Dentz.

The city was reeling from the discovery of what at first seemed to be another decapitated victim. On Monday, September 14, in a bizarre scene reminiscent of an old horror movie, ten-year-old Andrew Larned and his six-year-old brother David stumbled upon human bones sticking above the ground in an East Cleveland field as they walked home from school. The terrified boys alerted their father and older brother, who returned to the weed-infested lot to verify the grim discovery and then notified Detective Horace B. Weaver at the East Cleveland station. Police uncovered a woman's skeleton, minus the skull, buried in a small open box about a foot beneath the surface. The brief but intense flurry of interest and speculation about a seventh victim dissipated quickly the next day when L. D. Mennell, a Cleveland schoolteacher, stepped forward and explained to the *Press* that he had inherited the skeleton from his father-in-law in 1934—some of the bones were, indeed, wired together—and had paid a couple of neighborhood boys to bury it. He was moving to Lakewood and did not want to be bothered taking it with him. The only embarrassment in the whole affair was Coroner Pearce's initial hasty guess to the *Plain Dealer* on the 15th that the woman had been dead for about a month when, according to Mennell, the skeleton was over fifteen years old.

On October 2, Sergeant Hogan tried to have the creek pumped dry. (Earlier plans to drain it through dynamiting had been deemed impractical.) At this point, he must have been motivated solely by a strong sense of professional dedication and personal pride. Even if the missing body parts could be dredged up through such heroic measures, the advanced decomposition would make identification impossible—though Hogan did hold out hope that any dental bridgework found with the head could be the key to determining who the victim was. When the pump supplied by the utilities department proved too small for the job, police brought in one borrowed from the East Ohio Gas Company and yet another from the city fire department. The operation continued for the entire morning and into early afternoon—draining off an estimated three million gallons of water—until only two feet of dirty water remained and the pumps began to clog with thick muck. Then, aided by men from the utilities department, Detectives Gordon Shibley, Herbert Wachsman, and Peter Merylo raked the foul bottom of the creek. "And nothing to show for it," Merylo growled in the Otwell manuscript, "nothing but junk." At the end of the day, a frustrated Sergeant Hogan wrote his superior Lieutenant Harvey Weitzel, "It is my opinion that the missing parts were not thrown into the creek when the Torso [sic] was thrown in." He vowed to keep looking (almost a week later, on the 8th, he was still commanding the pumps and a contingent of twenty men), but the missing arms and head would never be found.

Police did not confine their attempts to identify this sixth victim to the murky pool in Kingsbury Run. A week after Jerry Harris had discovered the first pieces of the body, police thought the victim might be Patrick Casey, a twenty-eight-year-old section hand for the New York Central Railroad, originally from Youngstown, who had disappeared from his room at the Congress Hotel on Woodland Avenue on August 31, leaving behind a twenty- five-dollar paycheck. A preliminary check with his acquaintances also revealed that, for whatever reason, the missing Casey frequented Kingsbury Run. But, as had happened so often before, this tantalizing lead simply evaporated.

Police drained the pool in a vain effort to find victim no. 6's head. Courtesy of Marjorie Merylo Dentz.

For a while all official attention focused on the gray felt hat Orley May found near the pool, even though stains on it turned out not to be blood. Based on newspapers descriptions, Mrs. Charles Hoffman of Bellevue and her twenty-one-year-old son Melvin recognized the hat as one she had given to a hobo who had come to their house and begged for clothing two weeks before. Their recollections about the transient bore a resemblance to Straus's description of the latest victim, but the beggar turned out to be very much alive. Again, authorities ran up against a blank wall.

Frustrated by the lack of identification, police felt stymied and grabbed at any remotely suspicious person and any potential lead, no matter how slim. "Don't ever veer from the path of strictly normal behavior in this town," wrote a *Cleveland News* reporter as late as September 9, 1938. "One slip, and an inquisitive detective may come visiting." Sergeant Hogan arrested a powerfully built, mentally disturbed man wearing a mission band cap and carrying a collection cup simply because he showed up at the pool with the rest of the crowd whenever the police were there and showed keen interest in what they were doing. Hogan was convinced that the killer lived somewhere in the vicinity of Kingsbury Run, so police concentrated their efforts in the surrounding neighborhoods, especially those to the south, close to Broadway. Shortly after the body had been discovered, Detectives Ralph Kennedy and Leo Duffin picked up a Mexican named Frank Gomez—a poor pushcart operator who lived at East 33rd near Central and had served several terms in the workhouse for intoxication—because they saw him wandering near Kingsbury Run at East 14th and Broadway. He was sick, Gomez explained, and had gone to the area where he was arrested to pick grass for a home remedy. Detective Emil Musil held a thirty-five-year-old resident of the Wayfarer's Lodge for questioning simply because he was known to have lived in a shack in Kingsbury Run. Hogan interrogated a young scrap collector who insisted he had watched two men carry a box from a large sedan parked near the pool on Wednesday, the 9th, but then released him without taking a formal statement because of the discrepancies in his story. Police hauled in an "oriental" with a long-bladed knife whom, according to John Bartlow Martin, reports described as "Stocky, full round face, black shaggy hair, stooped over, feet turned out." There was an escapee from the Athens State Hospital—violent, paranoid, and plagued by hallucinations; there was an insane former butcher who chased people with a large knife. Six detectives searched Kingsbury Run unsuccessfully for a heavyset bearded man who had reportedly accosted a young man from Chicago as he waited for a west-bound freight train at East 37th. Handpicked members of the police department hid in the bushes in the Run and held a succession of grim, unsuccessful night vigils.

Railroad workers in Kingsbury Run grew increasingly apprehensive, and some car inspectors began to work in pairs for protection. Railroad police concentrated their efforts on the incoming train traffic, regarding each hobo as a potential killer or potential victim. Some inhabitants of the Run's jungles spoke fearfully of a man who lived under the Lorain-Carnegie Bridge and surrounded his den with between four and five hundred pairs of women's shoes. Nickel Plate detectives Anthony Kotowski and Paul Troutman tried to find him, but the shoe collector evaded detection, leaving nothing behind but chicken feathers and size twelve footprints.

The investigation soon spread far beyond the borders of Kingsbury Run. Police searched through old files, looking for similar killings, and even revisited a grotesque case from 1928. A black "voodoo man" living on East 40th had been charged with murder when authorities, initially alerted by reports that the man's dog was playing with a severed human head in the yard, discovered a headless corpse in his basement. The man had been tried and acquitted because, according to the *Press* on September 14, 1936, identification of the victim had not been possible. In an eerily similar case, a mutilated, decapitated corpse had been found in a field near East 40th and Woodland in 1929, and the police now searched for a forty-two-year-old man who had been detained at the time. (Contemporary newspaper accounts confuse the two killings, and it is not clear whether these are two separate cases or merely one.)

Investigators also checked into the recent releases of "known perverts and sadists" from all the public institutions in Ohio and surrounding states. They launched a determined search for a man who possessed a history of "sadistic aberrations" and had escaped from the State Hospital for the Insane at Newberg, Ohio, five years before, as well as a fifty-year-old Clevelander who had escaped from the "violent ward" of the Athens State Hospital the previous September, a few days before the murder of Edward Andrassy and victim no. 2. Acting on a tip, Detectives Musil and Shibley arrested, and ultimately released, a west side doctor who had been acting strangely.

Since becoming Cleveland's safety director in December 1935, Ness had racked up an enviable record of success by concentrating on illegal gambling, labor racketeering, and corruption in the police department. He had remained aloof from the grisly killings that had begun in September

1935, perhaps because the onetime G-man who had battled such traditional and recognizable enemies as Al Capone knew the case was quicksand for the unwary. By the end of the summer of 1936, the police realized that all six brutal killings of the past year were not isolated acts of violence but part of an inexplicable series. The press realized it as well, and each new killing prompted a detailed review of the previous cases. In the face of growing public concern, Mayor Burton summoned his safety director to a meeting at city hall and asked him to become more directly involved. "He had to do something," recalled Peter Merylo in the Otwell manuscript. "The mayor was on his neck; so were the Chamber of Commerce and the Come to Cleveland Committee and some of the people who rode home to Shaker Heights through the Run on the Rapid Transit. But so was the whole town, for that matter. It was getting to be something of a national disgrace, Cleveland's uncaught torso murderer." But Burton's request created a potential problem. In a situation virtually unique to Cleveland, the lines of authority between safety director and chief of police had never been precisely drawn; it was not exactly clear with whom responsibility ultimately rested. Most of the time, this gray area didn't cause any serious difficulties, but the torso killings put enormous pressure on the entire law enforcement establishment. It is a tribute to the professionalism of both Ness and Matowitz that no major conflicts erupted between them in spite of growing public pressure and intense newspaper scrutiny.

On September 12, Ness officially took charge of the torso investigation and ordered a major contingent of police into Kingsbury Run. Starting at East 24th, the small army swept east through the dilapidated jungles of shanties, boxes, and old piano crates, rounding up the desperate inhabitants for questioning. The word had already gone out over the invisible hobo communication network that Cleveland was to be avoided because a mad butcher haunted the city. Railroad police reported a steady stream of indigents abandoning Kingsbury Run and a virtual halt to incoming hobo traffic. Ness also personally combed through all the records associated with the murders and interviewed the main investigators. Whether he wanted it or not, the Kingsbury Run murders now became Eliot Ness's case.

NOTES

Police reports from Detective Orley May and Sergeant James Hogan—contained in the coroner's files, case no. 46118—provide the official documentation for this killing. Because of a variety of circumstances, the newspapers devoted more coverage to this murder than any in the series up to this point, September 11–October 10, 1936. No. 6 was the third victim within slightly more than three months; and by the end of the summer, it had begun to sink in that a lone butcher was prowling the city. The saga of what the papers liked to call "the headless dead" also made for sensational reading against the backdrop of the city's civic activity; and the ongoing search for body pieces at the stagnant pool gave the press something tangible on which to focus.

All anatomical findings are from the coroner's files, case no. 46118.

Some of the suspects rounded up by police are mentioned in John Bartlow Martin's "Butcher's Dozen: The Cleveland Torso Murders," 62.

As indicated in the text, some material is taken from the unpublished Otwell/Merylo manuscript.

CLEVELAND'S SHAME

Murders of the Rue Morgue: Cleveland's Shame
—*Cleveland News* editorial, September 12, 1936

The summer of 1936 faded into autumn, leaving Cleveland a markedly changed city. When the head and body of the tattooed man were discovered in early June, authorities began to realize that the brutal murders they had initially regarded as isolated crimes were, in fact, connected. Over the summer, as the mutilated remains of two more victims appeared and the police seemed unable to find a viable suspect, that realization began to cut deeper into the social fabric and weigh more heavily on the public consciousness. Every segment of society was affected.

Detectives Orley May, Emil Musil, and George Zicarelli, veteran members of the Detective Bureau, had been dedicated foot soldiers on the case since the Andrassy murder in September 1935 and, along with Sergeant James T. Hogan, head of homicide, would continue to work on the murders until the investigation stopped. During the summer of 1936, the police department put twenty-five detectives on the case full-time. This was a temporary move prompted by growing public concerns and increased publicity, and most of the detectives gradually returned to other duties.

In the summer of 1936, however, Chief of Police George Matowitz assigned Detective Peter Merylo to the case full-time; and along with Eliot Ness, he would become the lawman most frequently associated with the murders. Born in the Lvov region of the Ukraine in 1895, Merylo immigrated to the United States as a teenager. He joined the army during World War I though he never saw any combat. Finding the discipline of military life to his liking, he entered police work in 1919. His first assignment was as a crossing guard for children.

In the summer of 1936, he had been assigned to the Roaring Third on a 12:30 to 8:00 A.M. shift. On the morning of September 10, his professional and private life changed irrevocably. In his unpublished memoirs, he writes that he had to attend juvenile court proceedings after going off duty and did not arrive home until 11:00 A.M. The exhausted detective left instructions with his wife that he was not to be disturbed for anything and then flopped into bed. Two hours later, she gently roused him saying that someone from the office wanted to speak with him on the phone about a vitally important matter and would not leave a message. Merylo grumbled and went to the phone. "This is Lieutenant Zeman, Pete; I hate to get you up, but I just want to inform you that you are assigned to special detail by the Chief, George J. Matowitz." Since winning a promotion to the Detective Bureau in 1931, Merylo had worked a daunting series of special details, some of them extremely dangerous. "Again, another special detail?" he muttered sleepily into the receiver. Zeman asked Merylo to report for duty at 4:00 that afternoon.

Chief of Police George J. Matowitz. He personally selected Detective Peter Merylo to investigate the Kingsbury Run murders full-time. Courtesy of Marjorie Merylo Dentz.

Detective Peter Merylo, the policeman most closely associated with the investigation in the Kingsbury Run murders, worked on the case from 1936 until his retirement in 1943. Courtesy of Marjorie Merylo Dentz.

When he arrived at the Detective Bureau, John Zeman informed a startled Merylo that Chief Matowitz had sent down an order placing him on the torso murders full-time. He was to work any hours he thought necessary and pick anyone he wanted for a partner. Zeman recommended Detective Martin Zalewski, a twenty-three-year veteran who had put in several years as a beat cop in the Jackass Hill area. Like Merylo, who spoke seven eastern European languages, Zalewski was multilingual, which meant both men could converse easily with the diverse immigrant populations living in the Kingsbury Run area. Merylo replied he would accept anyone Zeman suggested as his partner—so long as he was willing to work.

Inspector Joseph Sweeney made the official announcement to members of the press. "This job will take endless patience and determination because there are literally no clues," he remarked. "But I know these men will work day and night without becoming discouraged." And, indeed, both men would live up to Sweeney's prediction by working with incredible tenacity, often on their own time. The new partners sat down with the accumulated files, which already numbered several hundred pages, and started to familiarize themselves with all aspects of the case.

The next day Merylo went to see Chief George Matowitz. He respected Matowitz because he had proven himself on the job and had earned his position through solid work and experience. Merylo was contemptuous of those who climbed departmental ranks by passing a written test but possessed little investigative savvy. Why, Merylo wanted to know, had the chief picked him out of the fourteen hundred men available in the department for the torso detail. "I have faith in you,'" replied Matowitz; "'if you don't find the killer, no one else will.'"

On September 13, three days after Chief Matowitz had handed Merylo his new assignment, the safety director summoned him to his office. The day before, Mayor Burton had ordered Ness to become more directly involved in the torso investigation. Eliot Ness may not have been much of a political animal, but he recognized political heat when he felt it. With his personal assistant, John R. Flynn, looking on, Ness demanded to know what progress Merylo had made on the case so far. That he would press Merylo for results so soon after Chief Matowitz had assigned the veteran detective to the case demonstrates how much pressure Ness was getting from above. Surely, he knew that it had only been three days since Merylo had received his marching orders, and that was hardly enough time for him to absorb all the official documents related to the case. Merylo describes the confrontation with Ness in his unpublished memoirs, and his irritation is evident despite the relatively dry formality of his language. He replied that he was still digesting all the material relevant to the investigation and could say little at this point except he felt the murders were sex crimes.

The Kingsbury Run murders would make Peter Merylo famous to some, infamous to others. On the one hand, he was a cop's cop, a total professional—dedicated, tough, thorough, and absolutely incorruptible. He was a skilled, shrewd investigator as well as the force's pistol champion. On the other hand, he was a sensitive, gentle man who harbored a lifelong love for the violin. His daughter Marjorie Merylo Dentz remembers the rapt expression that would steal over her father's face whenever he heard a particularly beautiful violin solo on the radio.

If Ness's political instincts were minimal, Merylo's were nonexistent. At the time the Cleveland Police Department was still somewhat compromised by political patronage and corruption, and in taking on such a major case, Merylo was entering a public arena that, with the passage of time, became highly politicized. On the job, he was a bulldog who always gave 200 percent and could sometimes be intolerant of those who gave a mere 100. For him politics and the police department did not mix, and his distaste for political appointees extended all the way up the ladder of authority to the safety director, himself. "You can't bring up Eliot Ness to Peter," his wife, Sophie, told her sister. "He starts to get nasty. He did not like the man." According to his daughter, his blunt manner, independence,

Eliot Ness, Cleveland's safety director from 1935 to 1942. *Cleveland Press* Archives, Cleveland State University.

and tendency to speak his own mind—consequences be damned—did not sit well with those in local government and law enforcement who had little direct involvement with the murders but used them to court personal publicity in the press. "Was you there, Charlie?" he growled sarcastically at anyone who made pompous public declarations about the case. "Those were the days when every man was his own expert," Merylo declares in the Otwell manuscript, "and the papers, with an eye to dramatic reading matter, quoted a lot of would-be experts."

Merylo established a reputation for unorthodox methods and following his own instincts, no matter where they led him, that persisted in the police department long after his retirement in 1943. According to one colleague, Peter Merylo was a vice cop who had worked vice for too long and had begun to see the world in terms of the people he dealt with daily; over time, he became obsessed with what he judged to be sexual perversion. His daughter Marjorie remembers one common pleas court judge remarking that whenever he saw that Peter Merylo had been the investigating officer, he knew the case would be rock solid; yet, according to one of Merylo's colleagues, prosecutors were sometimes reluctant to put him on the stand because they feared his rough language might shock jurors.

Peter Merylo was a complex, private man, and the public saw him only through the eyes of Cleveland's dailies as a tenacious bulldog who always wore a straw hat during the summer and a felt one in winter. A famous *Plain Dealer* photograph shows him with his cold weather headgear pulled down low on his forehead, wryly examining two monstrous butcher knives. But behind the tough professional facade lived a deeply religious and compassionate man, a side of his nature his daughter Marjorie remembers well but feels he hid from the rest of the world. (He had considered the priesthood in his youth and had actually spent some time in a monastery.) No doubt because of the degradation and sheer horror he saw daily, he became extraordinarily protective of his family. "I was in elementary school at the time of the murders," reflects Marjorie, "and I can remember him sitting at the table going over stacks of reports and photographs; but he kept it all away from me until I was older." Crimes against children invariably roused him to fierce professional efforts—superhuman even for him. "It could have been you," he would say simply to his daughter.

When Peter Merylo was promoted to detective in August 1931, a friend, George L. Brock, wrote him a congratulatory letter. "I note with pleasure that the powers that be have seen fit to promote you to the detective bureau service. This surely is a case where merit is rewarded." Ironically, Brock closed his letter on a note more prophetic than anyone could have imagined. "I am confident that you will make a wonderful Sherlock Holmes and that it will not be long until we will see your name in big type on the front page."

† † †

By the end of the summer of 1936, the police began to think about the crimes and the investigation in what were for them nontraditional terms. The old rules of engagement between law enforcement and criminal held that murderers killed people they knew for such readily understandable reasons as anger, greed, revenge, or jealousy; the path leading to the killer's arrest, therefore, began with identification of the victim. But both Edward Andrassy and Flo Polillo had been positively identified, and the extensive investigations into their deaths had ultimately ended in failure. Could they have been murdered by a total stranger for reasons no one understood? At the end of summer, police found themselves with three more bodies—there was actually a fourth, but a year would pass before anyone knew it—that, in spite of their most diligent efforts, they could not identify. But did that matter if the victims had been killed by someone none of them knew? Suddenly, the old rules of criminal investigation did not seem to work, and no one knew what the new rules were.

Taken individually, the details of the bizarre crimes were frightening enough; taken together, the series of murders was horrifying. All three major Cleveland dailies responded to the situation by devoting more space and larger headlines to the killings. On the one hand, this was the sort of sensational stuff that built circulation numbers (one man remembers how quickly newspapers disappeared in the family-owned drugstore whenever the murders were the top story); on the other hand, the authorities did not want public panic, nor did they need so much negative publicity while the city played host to the Republicans, the American Legion, and the crowds attending the Great Lakes Exposition. Not only were the murders becoming embarrassing front-page news nationally, they were fueling the anti-American propaganda mills in both Nazi Germany and fascist Italy. Whether or not the editors and publishers of the city's papers ever wrestled with such political-ethical issues, the level of coverage and the sheer intensity of the rhetoric increased dramatically throughout the summer. The Kingsbury

Run murders invaded the editorial pages and became an ongoing story. "Of all horrible nightmares come to life, the most shuddering is the fiend who decapitates his victims in the dark, dank recesses of Kingsbury Run," proclaimed the *Cleveland News* in an editorial on September 12. "That this creature, sly, crafty, inhumanly skilled in butchery, is a menace to every man, woman and child who walks the streets of Cleveland does not have to be emphasized." "Why these dead? Why this darkest of all Cleveland murder mysteries?" wailed the *Press* on the same day. "He kills for the thrill of killing," the paper stated emphatically. "He kills to satisfy a bestial, sadistic lust for blood. He kills to prove himself strong. He kills to feed his sex-perverted brain the sight of a beheaded human. He must kill. For decapitation is his drug, to be taken in closer-spaced doses. Yes, he will kill again. He is, of course, insane." None of this was calculated to calm an already nervous public, and the fear that gripped the neighborhoods close to Kingsbury Run began to spread out and infect the residents of the city's suburbs.

Although the rapid transit line from Shaker Heights ran through a part of Kingsbury Run on its way downtown, for most suburban dwellers, the desolate industrial landscape was just a name—a blur passing by outside the train window, barely noticed by commuters absorbed in their morning or evening papers. But all that changed on Friday, September 11, when *Press* staff reporter William Miller took Clevelanders on a guided tour of the area now made infamous by four out of the six linked butcheries. "Last midnight I went down in Kingsbury Run," he began. "Kingsbury Run, that lonely, mysterious gully where prowls a mad butcher." Miller and a companion headed down into the darkness with two neighborhood youths, Joe Dylong of East 68th and Henry Tobias of East 66th, clinging to the running boards of his car to act as guides. They crossed over the railroad tracks and cruised through the vast empty blackness. As they passed by heaps of trash, derelict buildings, small clumps of hobo shanties, and dense patches of sumac bushes, the boys spoke of the fear in the surrounding neighborhoods and shared their own pet theories about the killer and his victims with Miller. "I can testify," Miller confided to his readers, "that if you enjoy feeling your flesh creep—feeling the small hairs rise on your neck and your heart pound with shameless fear—if that's what you like, just take a midnight tour through Kingsbury Run." By the end of the summer of 1936, those commuters from the Heights watched thoughtfully as the gloomy landscape passed by the windows, their newspapers unread in their laps.

In a move that probably stood somewhere between self-promotion and civic concern, the September 12 issue of the *News* promised a one-thousand-dollar reward—a huge sum for the time—for information leading to the arrest and conviction of the Kingsbury Run murderer. The same day, Councilman Joseph Artl announced that he would present a resolution to the city council offering the same monetary incentive. The murders now became a political football, and those who headed up the investigation, especially Safety Director Eliot Ness, became unwilling players in an exceedingly rough and nasty game of local politics. Martin L. Sweeney, the colorful, maverick Democratic congressman from Cleveland's Twentieth District, blasted the Republican administration repeatedly and proclaimed that if voters would turn Mayor Burton out of office, "we can send back to Washington the prohibition agent who now is safety director." In a fiery speech before the League of Independent Voter Clubs on March 6, 1937, which a *Plain Dealer* editorial the following day labeled "a new low in political morality even for the oft-elected gentleman from Cleveland's Twentieth District," Sweeney dubbed Ness Burton's "alter ego" and charged that both men were wasting time and manpower on such trivial matters as graft in the police department when they should turn the entire force loose on the torso murders.

The increased publicity about the killings, coupled with the announcement that Eliot Ness would now head up the investigation, brought out the nuts, the cranks, and the crackpots. A seemingly endless stream of people, many of them transients perhaps eager for the spotlight, descended on the Central Police Station with stories ranging from probable to wild to impossible, such as the tale offered by one man who assured police he had been washing a shirt in a gully in Garfield Heights when he narrowly escaped an attack by a muscular man dressed in black with close-cropped hair wielding a large, curved knife and wearing black leather gloves. A wave of letters, most of them unsigned, offering various solutions to the crimes also poured on to Ness's desk. One eight-pager named a hospital employee who had been a friend of Edward Andrassy's and had access to both drugs and scalpels. Michael R. Collegeman, head of the federal narcotic bureau in Cleveland, solemnly and pompously assured police and public in a *News* article on September 6, 1936, that the killer was most likely a marijuana addict because "both the desire for a thrill and a homicidal obsession are easily induced by the loco weed cigarettes."

Suddenly the scope of the investigation changed dramatically. Newspaper reporters in Cleveland picked up news stories from Pennsylvania that an unknown killer or killers had been committing similar acts of butchery for close to ten years in and around New Castle, a small industrial town in the western part of the state, close to Youngstown. Between 1925 and 1934, four murders, a couple of them virtually identical to the Cleveland killings, had occurred; all of the victims had been found in a remote, desolate, swampy area close to the city—rather similar to Kingsbury Run— that the locals referred to as the Murder Dump or the Murder Swamp. Since Youngstown mobsters had been disposing of victims in the swamp for years, local police initially attributed the killings to bootleg violence when headless corpses began turning up. The discoveries, however, of three mutilated bodies within the span of a single month, October 1925, had rocked New Castle and neighboring West Pittsburg to their very core. Nothing remotely similar to these atrocities had ever happened in the area. Despite the valiantly determined efforts of local law enforcement, all of these unfortunates remained unidentified; and police never came remotely close to identifying a perpetrator. Predictably, such sensational stuff produced an avalanche of lurid local press coverage that succeeded in ratcheting up public interest and panic to an incredibly high degree. In late October 1925, the concerned citizens of both New Castle and West Pittsburg assembled on the outskirts of the treacherous swamp and embarked on a carefully planned and executed march through the thick brush and marshy swamp on a determined hunt for clues or, just possibly, more victims. The coordinated search, which had been enthusiastically trumpeted and supported by the local press, yielded very little that was useful. It is rather curious to note that Cleveland police learned about these seemingly similar butcheries from local newspaper reports, not law enforcement authorities in Pennsylvania. Police in Ohio's neighbor to the east certainly knew about Cleveland's Kingsbury Run agonies; the murder-dismemberments had become an embarrassing national story. Their reluctance to alert Cleveland to their own set of grisly murders may have stemmed from the belief that these were gangland killings and, therefore, proceeded from very different causes than the gruesome events in Ohio.

During the last week in June 1936, however, the Murder Swamp's sole resident, Oscar Wukovich, noticed hawks circling over a string of twenty-three boxcars that had been abandoned on a siding since 1930. Pittsburgh & Lake Erie Railroad inspectors routinely checked the empty cars and had last done so on June 10, but Wukovich's sighting sent inspectors E. B. Benn and H. C. Goodhart back to the deserted string on July 1. In one of the cars, they found the naked, headless body of a white male lying chest down on parts of three different newspapers—one of them from Cleveland dated August 30, 1933. The eerie similarities between this victim and his Cleveland counterparts mounted quickly: bloodstained underwear found nearby, the decapitation clean and expert, the severed head never found, the man never identified. (The *Press* erroneously reported that all the Cleveland victims had also been found lying on their chests, a condition that applied only to no. 5.) Ness's executive assistant, John Flynn, traveled to New Castle to check out this latest murder site, convinced that Cleveland's

Exploring a possible connection in New Castle, Pennsylvania. *Left to right:* New Castle sheriff Edward Pritchard, Lieutenant George P. Kennedy of the New Castle Police Department, and Eliot Ness's assistant, John R. Flynn. Courtesy of Marjorie Merylo Dentz.

butcher had either expanded his range of activities or copied the modus operandi of the Pennsylvania killer. Armed with the scanty files on the Pennsylvania cases, New Castle lawmen Sheriff Edward Pritchard, Police Chief R. A. Criswell, and Lieutenant George S. Kennedy took Flynn on a guided tour of the desolate area. When Flynn arrived back in Cleveland, the antagonism between the safety director's office and Chief Matowitz's hand-chosen Butcher hunter deepened. "Flynn returned to Cleveland a little dubious about the New Castle torsos," Merylo reflects in the Otwell manuscript. "He wasn't sure those murders had been committed by the man responsible for those here. I was sure."

The situation demanded a grand public gesture, and Coroner A. J. Pearce supplied it. In a dramatic move, he called for an emergency "crime clinic" or "torso clinic" to be held in the Central Police Station at 8 A.M. on September 15. Over thirty police officials and medical experts would examine and discuss every bit of evidence collected in the case so far. Among the law enforcement luminaries Pearce invited were Eliot Ness, Police Chief George Matowitz, ballistics expert David L. Cowles, County Prosecutor Frank Cullitan, Sergeant James T. Hogan, and all the detectives who had worked on the case; to cover the scientific angles, the coroner brought in Dr. Royal H. Grossman (psychiatrist in the probation department), Dr. Guy H. Williams (superintendent of the Newberg state hospital for the insane), as well as Drs. T. Windgate Todd and Wilson M. Krogman from the Western Reserve Medical School. (There is no press or police record indicating whether Peter Merylo and Martin Zalewski were present, but, since they were assigned to the case five days before the meeting, it is logical to assume they were.) The unprecedented conference provided a forum that would allow authorities and medical personnel to pool their knowledge, and, since it was open to an eager press, it served to reassure an uneasy public that something was being done.

County Pathologist Reuben Straus, who had performed the autopsies on most of the victims, led off with a chart comparing all aspects of the killings such as manner of dismemberment and general condition of the bodies. Dr. Guy Williams advanced the theory that the murderer was probably insane, though he admitted he could not fit his activities into any known pattern of insanity. According to press reports, Ness sat quietly through most of the presentation, listening to the parade of speakers and asking occasional pertinent questions. When the conference ended at 10:30, the participants had not agreed on any particular course of action, though Ness's assistant,

David L. Cowles of the Scientific Investigation Bureau with the shirt of victim no. 6. He revolutionized the science of crime detection in Cleveland. Cowles was one of Eliot Ness's most trusted associates. *Cleveland Press* Archives, Cleveland State University.

John R. Flynn, suggested checking every house in the neighborhoods north and south of the Run. Sergeant Hogan—no doubt wearied and frustrated by his fruitless search for the head and arms of victim no. 6—shrugged his shoulders and remarked, "Gentlemen, tonight we're right where we were the day the first body was found."

In spite of Hogan's negative assessment, Pearce's conference did produce some assumptions about the killer. It would take a large, powerful man to wield a knife with such strength and to haul the bodies into areas of Kingsbury Run inaccessible by car. His ability to move through the Run without being noticed suggested that he probably lived, and maybe even performed some of the dismemberment, somewhere in the surrounding neighborhoods. Interestingly, the medical men—perhaps class conscious and unwilling to believe that someone as well educated or socially prominent as a physician could commit such brutalities—argued that the killer was not a surgeon but more likely a butcher or hunter. There was no evidence to indicate that the murderer knew any of his victims, so the assertion that he was acquainted with them, at least in the weeks or months before he killed them, remained problematic and may simply reflect the old, standard, official prejudice about the relationship between victim and killer. Ness even wondered if the decapitation and disposal of the head was simply a method of foiling any witnesses who may have seen the two together. Though the participants branded the killer a sex pervert and assumed he was most likely insane (some argued he may have been keeping the heads as trophies), they felt that he probably led a normal life to all outward appearances.

As the flurry of publicity surrounding Pearce's conference abated, the authorities doggedly pursued their investigation. From mid-September into October, Ness launched a public probe into bribery and other forms of corruption in the police department, an investigation which, at least temporarily, usurped the murderer's headlines and gave the safety director a task far more to his liking than the hunt for a phantom butcher. John R. Flynn became a casualty in his boss's war against official misconduct. He suddenly resigned. According to Paul W. Heimel, author and authority on Ness, Flynn had climbed the ladder of political patronage. Though he and Ness enjoyed a good working relationship, the safety director's crusade put Flynn in the uncomfortable position of defending some of Ness's prime targets. Merylo was probably not sorry to see him go. Not only did Flynn's assessment of the New Castle killings conflict with his own, but Ness's executive assistant had also wondered publicly—with no evidence to support his musings—whether the killer might be a woman. He "should have known better," grumbles Merylo in the Otwell manuscript. "If she were, and we never had the remotest indicaton it was a woman, she must have been a super-Amazon." Ness immediately replaced the departing Flynn with one of his own friends, Robert Chamberlin.

In the November elections, Democrat Frank Cullitan won reelection as county prosecutor with the active help and support of the Republican safety director. Ness liked and worked well with Cullitan and would not allow politics to stand in the way of law enforcement efficiency. In spite of all his diligent work, however, Republican A. J. Pearce was defeated in his bid for reelection as coroner by the young Democrat Samuel R. Gerber.

Sometime after Pearce's public conference—perhaps as much as a year or more later—Ness set up a private meeting at his Clifton Boulevard apartment with David Cowles and an unnamed editor from the *Cleveland Press,* conceivably Louis B. Seltzer. The paper was willing to finance any methods necessary to end the Butcher's citywide reign of terror and wanted to explore possible options with the safety director. Believing that the underworld could be instrumental in tracking the killer, the trio adopted a bold and somewhat unconventional strategy. Cowles would establish a group of eight undercover men—to be chosen by and known only to him, who would report back, rather like Sherlock Holmes's Baker Street Irregulars. He subsequently picked his men, set up meeting places and times, provided any needed police support, and took care of paying them—presumably with the *Press*'s money. Only three of the gang members were ever identified. Two of them, Tommy Whalen and James Limber, were brand-new cops who had been recruited right out of the police academy by David Cowles. They could move easily through the city's shady underworld without attracting attention because no one would know they were policemen. The third gang member to be identified was Joe Teran, a Mexican marijuana dealer that Cowles had first busted in 1930. The trio who had gathered in Ness's apartment to plot strategy kept their secret well; nothing more is known about this shadowy group or their activities.

Following a model that had served him well in his Chicago days, Ness set up a small independent team of investigators in Cleveland called the Unknowns. Funded privately by a group of anonymous businessmen and civic leaders concerned about growing labor racketeering, the carefully handpicked operatives could work quietly outside of official circles and the public spotlight on the fringes of the law. It is impossible to say when, but Ness seems to have turned the shadowy group loose on the torso case as well. Was the safety director deliberately keeping city police out of the loop? If so, did he doubt the effectiveness and reliability of his department? Or was he more concerned about the rising intensity of newspaper coverage? Ness gladly courted the press when it served his purposes, but did he decide in this instance that too much publicity could compromise a sensitive investigation employing unorthodox methods? Could he and his closest associates accomplish more by allowing the sensational press coverage of Merylo's and Zalewski's investigations to screen their activities? Whatever Ness's reasoning may have been, as work on the murders ground down in the late 1930s and early 1940s, there seem to have been two separate but parallel investigations going on: a very public one more or less under the control of James Hogan with Merylo and Zalewski serving as point men and a secret one headed by Ness and Cowles.

† † †

In the days immediately following their assignment to the murders, Merylo and Zalewski looked for a black man who had been seen exposing himself in Kingsbury Run and checked into the possibility that the crimes were related to racketeering at the Northern Ohio Food Terminal. Following up on a lead from some frightened prostitutes, they hunted a strange man who paid women to singe his chest hair with a burning piece of paper while pretending to stab him. Acting on a report from a terrified woman who insisted she saw a man hacking something in Kingsbury Run that looked like bloodied flesh, the pair swooped down on the remains of a butchered watermelon. Some months later, they arrested a thirty-six-year-old former slaughterhouse worker for chasing his neighbors with an ax. The clearly deranged man insisted that it was not people he was after; he was chasing evil spirits that he would kill once he determined if they were male or female.

But extraordinary crimes demanded extraordinary measures. The word went out from the highest level of the department that all police officers were to randomly stop and check any cars on the road in the late night to early morning hours in hopes of snaring the killer while he was en route to drop a body. Working on the assumption that the Butcher must be covered with blood after his killings, investigators canvassed every laundry in the city.

They uncovered a lot of bloody clothing, evidence of every kind of mishap imaginable, but in each case the stains could be logically accounted for.

According to the Otwell manuscript, Merylo and Zalewski canvassed all of Cleveland's slaughterhouses on the southwest side "at the behest of some prominent businessmen who wanted to play detective." Merylo emerged from this two-week odyssey convinced that the murderer could not be an ordinary butcher.

A far more ghoulish turn in the investigation took the pair to potter's field where, acting on the assumption that someone might be stealing and cutting up indigent bodies as a sick joke, they opened recently dug graves to make sure each plain box contained a corpse. After Merylo and Zalewski had disinterred dozens of bodies, unidentified "medical men" ended the grim work by alerting the pair to a fundamental anatomical fact. "That fundamental," Merylo declares in the Otwell manuscript, "which in our ignorance of anatomy we had overlooked, was this: if the bodies had been dug up from the grave, traces of blood would still have been evident in the arteries. In the torsos, there was no blood."

Police continued to haunt the Run and the surrounding neighborhoods, convinced that the killer and his "laboratory" were somewhere in the area. The September 15 conference had spawned the notion that the police could, perhaps, apprehend the murderer by disguising themselves as hoboes and acting as decoys; therefore, some dedicated and brave men, including railroad police, donned rags and descended into the nighttime blackness.

Merylo wanted to take the operation several steps further. He asked Chief Matowitz for permission to go underground. Dressed as a hobo, he could blend into the transient population of Kingsbury Run—a step, Merylo argued, that would dramatically increase police chances of catching the Butcher. Matowitz refused; it was just too dangerous. "There was something in the Chief's look as I left his office that September day," Merylo recalls in the Otwell manuscript, "that said as plainly as words: 'Pete, I don't want you to get killed, but you're no detective if you don't do just about what you suggested.'"

After letting his beard grow for a few days, Merylo strapped on a shoulder holster with his .38, dressed in the oldest clothes he owned, and quietly stole into Kingsbury Run alone one night in late September 1936. He moved carefully through a long, dark tunnel that led to the rapid transit repair shops in a side gully. In the yard in front of the shop's huge doors illuminated by a foundry at the rim of the Run, Merylo could see waist-high stacks of car wheels, scrap metal, and rails. To the left of the repair shop stood a small deserted building, a single, naked bulb feebly lighting its interior even though the doors were locked. Merylo could hear the muted, echoing crunch of his own footsteps as he entered the blackness inside the repair shop and felt along the wall with his hands. Just inside the door, he found a bench. As he sat quietly, allowing his eyes to adjust to the darkness, it suddenly occurred to him that Edward Andrassy and victim no. 2 could have been killed on that very bench. "A strong man could have carried those headless bodies to the place they were found only a few hundred yards away," he reasons in the Otwell manuscript. (When he investigated the site later during the day, however, he could not find any traces of blood, either on the bench or the surrounding ground.)

As Merylo trudged out of Kingsbury Run that dark night in late September 1936, he could not have known that his nocturnal foray was only a dress rehearsal for a deeper and far more dangerous plunge into the gritty hobo world. Nor could he have known that he was taking the first steps on a quest that would consume the rest of his professional life. The industrial gully had been branded with an infamy that would still mark it over seventy-five years later, but, though no one could have known as the fall of 1936 approached, the phantom Butcher had abandoned Kingsbury Run forever.

NOTES

Peter Merylo recounts the events leading up to and including his assignment to the torso murders in his unpublished memoirs. His daughter Marjorie Merylo Dentz—with whom I talked several times, both formally and informally, beginning in April 1999—provided the details of her father's background and the descriptions of his character. Andrew R. Schug (former member of the Board of Trustees of the Cleveland Police Historical Society), Anne Kmieck (former curator of the CPHS Museum), and researcher Don Stragisher participated in one of those formal interviews. Merylo's nephew Allen P. Pinell recounted his uncle's negative assessment of Eliot Ness during a conversation with Andrew Schug, Don Stragisher, and me. The less flattering descriptions of Merylo come from a former colleague who requested anonymity. Inspector Joseph Sweeney's glowing assessments of the Merylo-Zalewski partnership for the press are from a *Plain Dealer* retrospective on the case of May 30, 1937. The congratulatory letter from George L. Brock is contained in Peter Merylo's papers.

The events of September 1936, including Coroner Pearce's clinic, are chronicled in Cleveland's daily papers. The coverage of the New Castle killings also appears in local newspapers, September 17, 1936. Peter Merylo discusses the New Castle killings in both his memoirs and the Otwell/Merylo manuscript; he also covers Coroner Pearce's "clinic" in the Otwell manuscript. For an in-depth look at the history of the Pennsylvania murders and their possible link to the torso killings in Cleveland, see James Jessen Badal's *Hell's Wasteland: The Pennsylvania Torso Murders* (Kent, Ohio: The Kent State University Press, 2013).

The account of the meeting among Cowles, Ness, and an unnamed editor from the *Press* is contained in the transcript of a taped interview with David Cowles conducted by Florence Schwein of the Cleveland Police Historical Society and Lieutenant Tom Brown.

As indicated in the text, author Paul W. Heimel provided the reasons for John Flynn's sudden departure.

Peter Merylo describes some of the outlandish figures with whom he and Zalewski had to deal in his police reports, his memoirs, and the Otwell/Merylo manuscript. His assessment of John Flynn and his account of his nighttime exploration of Kingsbury Run in late September 1936 are in the Otwell/Merylo manuscript.

February 23, 1937

A SECOND LADY OF THE LAKE

History was about to repeat itself. On a cold winter afternoon of biting wind and lead-gray sky and water, fifty-five-year-old Robert Smith of 40 Brown Street, Beulah Park—a community close to ten miles northeast of Kingsbury Run—went down to the Lake Erie shore to check on a sailboat he had stored there for the winter. Afterward, he wandered along the beach looking for driftwood to burn. Two and a half years before, Smith's neighbor and acquaintance Frank LaGassie had been walking along the same path on a similar mission when he came upon the lower half of a human torso—the unidentified woman police called the Lady of the Lake. At 1:40 in the afternoon, near the foot of East 156th, Smith noticed a white object just offshore. "At first I thought it was the body of a dog or a sheep," Smith told the *Plain Dealer* on February 24, "but then I saw it [was] part of a body, so I notified the police."

The first officer on the beach was Lieutenant William Sargent. Bracing himself against the chilly winds, he saw the upper half of a woman's torso, headless and armless, grounded a few feet offshore. Soon after, he was joined by Sergeant James T. Hogan, Detective Inspector Joseph M. Sweeney, Detective Orley May, and three other detectives. As Hogan waded out into the bitter cold waters to retrieve the grisly object, he noted that the only footprints visible in the sand belonged to Robert Smith and Lieutenant Sargent. The torso had washed up on the beach; no one had carried it there. "The piece probably appeared in the last two days," Hogan mused to the *Plain Dealer* on the 24th. (Some boys had been on the beach the day before, and it had not been there then.) "If it had floated up when the waves were high it would have been thrown far up on the beach." Noting the quantity of sand and gravel embedded in the flesh and adhering to the cut surfaces, Hogan surmised, "With the lake rolling the way it has it is possible the body was placed in the lake anywhere between Beulah Park and Lakewood. And it is possible there are other pieces lodged in the breakwall which runs to E. 79th Street." A couple of storm sewers emptied into the lake nearby, but blockage from snow and ice prevented any immediate search. (When the sewers became passable several days later, Merylo and Zalewski, accompanied by three workers from the city sewer department and a newspaper reporter, explored a ten-mile stretch but found nothing.) After Hogan had dispatched the torso to the morgue, where County Pathologist Reuben Straus awaited its arrival, he and the other detectives fanned out a mile southwest and northeast along the beach in a fruitless search for other parts of the body.

Straus began to work on the torso at 3:30 that same afternoon. The woman had fair skin and light brown hair. From the condition of her lungs, Straus determined that she was a city dweller. He guessed she was between twenty-five and thirty-five years old, weighed about 120 pounds, and stood anywhere from five feet five inches to five feet eight. The dismemberment had been accomplished with a large, heavy knife; all the cut surfaces bore evidence of multiple hesitation marks. The exact cause of death, which had occurred during the last two to four days, eluded Straus. It had not been caused by decapitation; her heart had already stopped beating when the killer removed her head.

An interesting set of disagreements arose within both the police department and the morgue. Coroner Gerber believed the development of the breasts indicated the woman had given birth at least once, perhaps twice; Straus thought otherwise and argued that she had never borne a child. Much more to the point, was this yet another victim of Cleveland's phantom Butcher? Detective Inspector Sweeney said "no" to the *Plain Dealer* on the 24th because "dissection was not marked with the same skill displayed in the others," and Hogan was inclined to agree with him. After all, the torso half had also been found far away from Kingsbury Run and the other discovery sites, and death in this case could not be attributed to decapitation. After the chaos surrounding the discoveries of three victims the previous summer, all culminating in then Coroner Pearce's well-publicized conference, the investigation had made little if any headway. Sweeney's and Hogan's initial unwillingness to add the dead woman to the Butcher's tally may have been motivated by both official caution and an understandable reluctance to endure another major burst of publicity about the case—the discovery of the torso half became immediate front-page, headline news—when police still had so little to show for their efforts. Pathologist Straus maintained, a bit cryptically, that whatever had motivated the previous murders had motivated this latest as well. Detective Orley May was simply resigned. "He gives us one regularly every five months," he shrugged. Ultimately, the weight of authoritative opinion determined that the unidentified woman was, indeed, victim no. 7.

Police immediately uncovered leads that ran a gamut from solid to mysterious and tantalizing to simply lurid. Missing persons reports of two women who matched Straus's understandably vague description surfaced immediately: Anna Zibert of Sylvia Avenue, separated from her husband, had simply vanished in late January; Flavia Pillot of Canton, who had come to Cleveland to stay with her brother on East 97th, disappeared after a row on Saturday, the 20th. Hogan regarded Pillot as an unlikely prospect, and Zibert removed herself from the list of possibilities by popping up at the Central Police Station on the 25th.

On Feburary 25 Charles F. Fisher, pastor of the Collinwood Congregational Church on Cleveland's northeast side, wrote Merylo a letter reporting dark rumors about an "Abortion Farm" on Lake Shore Boulevard, somewhere between East 105th and Euclid Beach. The existence of what the *Press* termed "a baby farm or abortion clinic" on February 24 raised the possibility that the woman had died of a botched illegal operation. Suddenly the Gerber-Straus dispute over the victim's childbearing history assumed far greater importance. Hogan ordered his men to search for the establishment, even though Straus continued to insist that the torso showed no signs of post-operative infection caused by an illegal abortion.

On February 24, Frank Frederick, an assistant manager at Euclid Beach Park, reported seeing two men in a small boat about a thousand yards offshore—odd in itself, considering the time of year—the Saturday before Robert Smith found the torso. These shadowy figures took on momentary significance when Detectives Merylo and Zalewski discovered two zigzagging trails of blood beginning on Lake Shore Boulevard and terminating close to the Erie shore. Two men in an automobile, Merylo theorized, pulled up to the curb and headed toward the beach by two different, intentionally devious routes to avoid attracting attention (the *Press* even printed a map showing the paths on the 25th), each carrying a blood-dripping parcel containing dismembered body parts. Even though the two-man theory did not quite square with previous notions of a lone killer, and in spite of Ho-

Detectives Peter Merylo (*left*) and Martin Zalewski sifting for clues in Kingsbury Run. *Cleveland Press* Archives, Cleveland State University.

gan's insistence that the torso half had washed up on the beach, Merylo's surmises apparently made enough sense to bring out David Cowles from the Scientific Investigation Bureau to gather samples of the blood for analysis from the snow-covered ground. Merylo's theoretical scaffolding fell with a resounding thud, however, when a newsboy came forward and told Detective Herbert Wachsman that he had seen a dog hit by a car and had watched as the poor animal limped aimlessly back and forth leaving blood behind. Police confirmed his tale when they located the dog at its owner's gas station. In an unfortunate display of his legendary stubbornness, Detective Merylo continued to insist to the papers that the blood he had found was human; it was not his finest hour. Hogan accepted the dog story with quiet resignation.

Predictably, the city newspapers immediately increased the pressure on law enforcement officials. "Magazines which exist by appealing to morbid tastes cannot devise fiction more gruesome than the hard facts of Cleveland's series of torso murders," proclaimed a *Press* editorial the day after Robert Smith's discovery. "Bewildered and outraged as the chilling discoveries mount, Cleveland faces a dilemma which holds the nation disagreeably fascinated. It is useless to say simply that something must be done. Certainly the horror of the mounting torso murders is sufficient to call for the most exhaustive efforts of police to run the murderer down." What the *Cleveland News* had termed "Cleveland's shame" the previous September now become embarrassing national, even international, news, and unexpected aid came from a national source: federal postal authorities announced that they would provide local police with a list of Cleveland residents whom they suspected of "unbalanced sexual tendencies."

† † †

Police realization that they were searching for one killer responsible for a series of deaths—a single investigation rather than several unrelated smaller ones—meant that the hunt could go on in spite of the regrettable lack of much physical evidence and the paucity of solid leads associated with a single murder. The sheer intensity of the investigation also produced some perhaps unexpected dividends: the police solved twenty other outstanding cases, ranging from violation of immigration laws to contempt of court, and managed to get about a dozen visibly disturbed individuals off the streets and into mental institutions. "Even though the torso killer has been able to evade capture with uncanny success to date," Police Chief George Matowitz told the *Plain Dealer* on May 30, "there does seem to be some consolation in the fact that almost two dozen other serious law violators have landed in jail as a result of the Kingsbury case."

Some of the astonishing figures Merylo, Zalewski, and other detectives searched for or snared during their investigation defied credulity: a man who pulled into a gas station at East 55th and Sweeney Avenue, waved what looked like a bloody butcher knife, and declared he had cut a black man on the arm; a hobo bundled up in two suits, two coats, and four hats preparing a drink from the juice of canned cherries; a strange creature dripping with beads and amulets who said he possessed the secret of transplanting human heads; a former medical student and army man who offered to demonstrate his technique for grafting human limbs; a man who swung Tarzan-like on a cable, dug tunnels, and strangled rabbits. Most intriguing of all was a strange duo, living in a dilapidated house on the rim of Kingsbury Run, who claimed they earned a living as ragmen. One of the pair could easily have walked off the pages of the most lurid pulp fiction novel: a hunchbacked former wrestler in possession of a bloodstained butcher's apron, five incredibly sharp butcher knives, a suspiciously stained ax and hatchet, a framed painting of a medieval beheading, and a selection of contemporary erotica. The stains on the ax and hatchet—that police chemists could not identify as human blood—were caused by "chopping mahogany," while the cutlery collection was used solely for "cutting up macaroni." After intense questioning, the police could not crack their alibis and were forced to set the odd couple at liberty. Such a parade of lunatics and grotesques gave the newspapers colorful copy but did not provide the authorities with viable suspects. Such antic behavior was at odds with one of the conclusions reached during the September 1936 conference that, though insane, the killer probably appeared normal, and no one as seriously disturbed as some of these poor individuals could act with the cold cunning of the Kingsbury Run Butcher.

In mid-April, Floyd Purnell of Battle Creek, Michigan, wrote a letter alerting Cleveland police to the discovery of a woman's arm in the nearby town of Marshall. Later in the month, Merylo and Zalewski began pursuing some vague leads about a religious cult that had been operating for about two years somewhere near East 49th. At the same time, Chief Matowitz drafted a letter to the editors of the city newspapers asking them to implore their readers to report anything suspicious, especially pools of blood, either to Chief of Detectives Joseph Sweeney or directly to him.

† † †

On Monday, May 5, almost three months after Robert Smith discovered the upper half of victim no. 7, Howard Yochem, a concessionaire at the Great Lakes Exposition, was testing a swan boat when he found the lower half of a woman's torso in the lake just off of East 30th. Sometimes forensic science is a simple business. At the morgue, Gerber matched the newly discovered piece with the upper half found in February, now hardened and somewhat discolored from refrigeration, by placing them together on a table. A morgue photo documents the perfect fit. The cold waters of Lake Erie had kept the lower half in a remarkably good state of preservation.

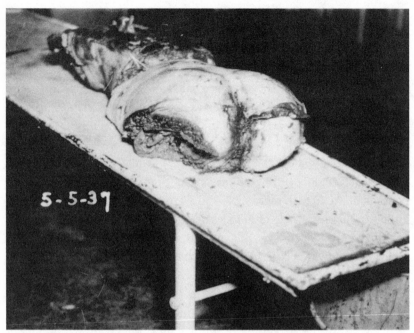

A morgue photograph showing the two halves of victim no. 7's torso. Cleveland Police Historical Society.

Hogan believed that, because of the easterly lake currents, the two halves had been tossed into the waters at different points but at the same time. He guessed the missing and less buoyant legs, arms, and head were probably lying somewhere on the bottom of the lake. Unfortunately, the lower torso half yielded no additional information, so Gerber announced that for the first time in the cycle of slayings, he would test for poisons in the system in hopes of learning something about the killer's methods.

None of the other body parts would ever be found; the woman would remain unidentified. The *Press* pointed out to its readers that Robert Smith had discovered the upper half of this seventh victim's torso near East 156th—almost exactly where Frank LaGassie had found a piece of the Lady of the Lake in September 1934. Just as Hogan had been reluctant to include Flo Polillo among the Butcher's victims, he now refused to concede that the two female lakeshore victims were the work of the same maniacal killer.

While the *Plain Dealer* stuck with the already established numbering, the *Press* and the *News* began to speak of eight victims rather than seven; the Kingsbury Run murderer apparently had been active longer than anyone had realized.

NOTES

The details of Robert Smith's discovery on the morning of February 23, the disagreements within the coroner's office, police speculations over whether the dead woman belonged with the recognized torso victims, and the account of the injured dog are carried in Cleveland's daily papers, February 23–25, 1937. Additional information comes from Peter Merylo's daily reports, February–May 1937.

The brief account of Merylo's and Zalewski's search of the nearby sewers comes from Peter Merylo's unpublished memoirs.

All anatomical findings are from the coroner's files, case no. 46672.

The letters from Charles F. Fisher, pastor of the Collinwood Congregational Church, and Floyd Purnell of Battle Creek are in Peter Merylo's files. Chief Matowitz's letter to the press is also among Merylo's papers.

The descriptions of the suspects corralled by police have been culled from the daily papers and Merylo's memoirs. The account of the hunchback and his companion is from George Condon's "The Mad Butcher of Kingsbury Run: A Strange Unsolved Case," *Cleveland Magazine,* March 1984, 79–80.

The discovery of the lower half of victim no. 7's torso is covered in the Cleveland dailies, May 6, 1937.

June 6, 1937
BONES IN A BURLAP BAG

Fourteen-year-old Russell Lauer was riding the bus on his way home from the movies. He was about to become part of an emerging and deeply disturbing pattern: children making terrible discoveries. As the bus headed toward Cleveland's near west side shortly after 5:00 P.M., the boy idly looked out the window and noticed a group of people crowded together on the bank of the Cuyahoga River. Lauer left the bus at the next stop to investigate. Two days before, on June 4, Charles Gallagher, a member of a tugboat crew, had been lost in the river, and the Coast Guard was still dragging the waters for his body. Lauer watched the search until about 5:20 and then took a shortcut through the Flats to his Scranton Road home. He walked through Stone's Levee, a barren field west of the river sometimes used as a trash dump. The arch of the Lorain-Carnegie Bridge towered high above, and the muted roar of rush hour traffic mingled with the sounds of the river. As Lauer passed by the second abutment of the bridge at 5:40, he caught sight of a strange object partly buried in a relatively fresh pile of dirt and refuse. As he approached to get a better look, something suddenly caught the glow of the late afternoon sun; from the glittering gold teeth, Lauer realized he was looking at a human skull.

The call came into the Detective Bureau at 6:00 P.M. James Hogan and Detective Orley May, along with Lieutenants Harvey Weitzel and Walter Keary, Detective Diskowski, and Sergeant James McDonald, headed to Stone's Levee. While Patrolman Robert Blaha of the Bertillon Department photographed the skull, the assembled officers combed the area, locating a heavy, white wool cap—now gray—with a tassel, the sleeve of a woman's dress, and a "toupee" of kinky black hair. As they dug the dirt away from the skull, they unearthed a dirty, greasy burlap bag, saturated with a grayish-white powder and held closed with a piece of rotted twine; inside they found a human skeleton minus the arms and legs, a fairly large piece of blackish-gray tissuelike material, and an undated advertisement and partial review from the *Plain Dealer,* "N. T. G. [Nils T. Grantlund] and his Girls Review, at the Palace Theatre." Weitzel, noting that the sack was not covered with much refuse, surmised that it had been dumped rather than deliberately buried.

Stone's Levee under the Lorain-Carnegie Bridge. Fourteen-year-old Russell Lauer points to the spot where he found the skull of victim no. 8. *Plain Dealer* Collection, Cleveland Public Library.

Save for the fact that the extremities were missing, there was virtually no physical evidence linking these skeletal remains with the Kingsbury Run butcheries; nor, for that matter, was there any indication that the individual had even been murdered. There was no bullet hole or any other sign of trauma on the skull. The skeleton found in East Cleveland the previous September had been a false alarm, and Hogan and the others no doubt hoped that this one would prove unrelated to the case as well. The signs, however, were ominous: the head had been separated from the body in some fashion, and the torso had been placed in a burlap bag—recalling the manner in which the killer had disposed of some of Flo Polillo's remains. The next morning, June 7—before the autopsy even took place, before anyone knew whether the skeletal remains were male or female—*Plain Dealer* headlines raised the possibility of a "Torso Case Link."

And later that same morning, shortly after 11:30 A.M., the coroner's office formally confirmed that link. It would probably be more accurate to describe the procedure as an examination of the bones rather than an autopsy, and Coroner Gerber brought in anatomy professor Dr. T. Windgate Todd of the Western Reserve Medical School to aid pathologist Reuben Straus. Todd had been a major player in A. J. Pearce's conference the previous summer, and the invitation for him to participate may have been as much a matter of public relations as forensic science. Though the two men could not determine the exact cause of death, the autopsy protocols noted "definite knife marks" and "evidence of hacking and cutting" on the vertebrae, all pointing to decapitation. Suddenly, Orley May's words from the previous February took on a prophetic, haunting echo: "He gives us one regularly every five months."

From the anatomical details of the skull and pelvis, Straus decided that the victim was a petite African American woman about five feet tall and weighing approximately one hundred pounds. He almost immediately revised his initial estimate of the victim's age of from between twenty-five and thirty-five years upward to between thirty and forty. From the rusty hairpins and a piece of dried tissue, Straus determined that the black "toupee" the police found was actually part of the victim's scalp; the gray, soggy mass discovered in the sack was badly decomposed tissue. Although none of the surviving autopsy protocols estimate the time of death, the police dated the ad found with the skeleton through theater booking records as from June 1936, and both the *Plain Dealer* and the *Cleveland Press* carried Gerber's assurance that the woman had, indeed, been dead for about a year on June 7. (The *Plain Dealer* reported his statements in its morning edition before the formal autopsy had been performed.) Chemical tests conducted a month later confirmed that the powdery material saturating the burlap bag was lime.

Except for Edward Andrassy and Flo Polillo, all previous efforts to identify the murderer's victims—all of the bodies fresher and most of them more complete than this latest—had been fruitless. Now, dogged by weariness and frustration, the authorities faced the daunting job of identifying an incomplete skeleton. Their best chance rested with the three gold crowns and the bridgework in the upper left side of the skull. Shortly after Russell Lauer's discovery and before the official autopsy, Detective Robinson was checking missing person reports filed since January 1, 1934, in the General Records Room, looking for someone possessing such distinctive dental work. Elverta Nash, missing since the summer of 1935, was the only one who fit; but by the evening of the 6th, Detectives Carl Obert and Rudolph Charvat had eliminated her as a possibility. Detectives May and Diskowski questioned the manager of the Palace Theater and learned that none of the girls in Grantlund's company had been missing during their local appearance in June 1936.

By mid-June, Merylo had tentatively identified the dead woman as forty-year-old Rose Wallace of 2027 Scovill Avenue. Her age and general appearance were close to Straus's estimates about the skeletal remains, and records of her dental work that Coroner Gerber received from Cinncinati matched the distinctive bridgework found in the skull. Rose Wallace, however, had reportedly disappeared on August 21, 1936—a time at odds with the *Plain Dealer* review found with the bones and almost three months after Gerber's estimates about the time of death. Dr. Hall, the Cinncinati dentist responsible for the bridgework, had been dead for fifteen years, rendering any positive identification of the crowns and bridgework virtually impossible. But a name gave the victim an identity and a past. Her movements could be traced and her acquaintances tracked down and questioned. Perhaps for these reasons alone, Merylo enthusiastically accepted an identification about which some of his colleagues remained more skeptical and Gerber flatly rejected. In his official reports, however, Merylo hedged; he used the name "Rose Wallace" but invariably qualified the identification with phrases such as "suspected to be."

Ten months later in April 1938, a young African American man walked into the Detective Bureau and said he might be able to provide a positive identification of victim no. 8. After looking over all the police notes, including

Rose Wallace, tentatively identified as victim no. 8. Drawing by Michael Nevin, based on a lost newspaper photograph.

a description of the distinctive dental work found in the skull, he declared, "That's my mother. That was Rose Wallace." Her son's declaration only confirmed what Merylo already suspected. Now, in his own mind, he was sure of victim no. 8's identity.

On the afternoon of her disappearance, Merylo learned, Wallace had been doing her laundry when a friend arrived and informed her that an unidentified man wanted to see her at an East 19th and Scovill bar close to her home. She left her laundry in the tub and headed for the sleazy establishment. According to witnesses, she later left with a dark-skinned white man named Bob for a party on the west side. Later still, a woman identified only as Mrs. Carter of Hazen Court reported seeing her in a car with three white men, but after that, Rose Wallace simply vanished.

Merylo dug into the Wallace disappearance with his usual tenacity and diligence. Suddenly for the first time since the series of killings began, he uncovered threads that seemed to tie some of the victims together. Wallace was reportedly going to a party on the west side—where Andrassy had lived. An informant said that a black male named One-Armed Willie—the same One-Armed Willie with whom Flo Polillo had argued the day before her murder in January 1936—was the only man with whom Wallace had maintained any steady relationship. Like Polillo, Wallace was at least a part-time prostitute and may have vanished from the same bar. Merylo insisted to the *Plain Dealer* on April 11, 1938, that Wallace had "disappeared in the same circumstances as Florence Polilla [*sic*]." Unfortunately, Merylo could never make these tantalizing and tenuous connections add up to anything meaningful. Nor, for that matter, was he ever able to establish the dead woman's identity conclusively; victim no. 8 would remain an unknown hidden behind Rose Wallace's shadow.

NOTES

All three Cleveland papers related the details of Russell Lauer's discovery on June 7, 1937, and the subsequent identification of the victim on April 11, 1938. Police reports from Detectives Orley May and Carl Obert, Sergeant James McDonald, and Lieutenant Walter Keary cover the same ground and document the first phases of the investigation. These reports are contained in the coroner's files, case no. 47022.

All anatomical findings are from the autopsy protocols, case no. 47022.

Peter Merylo details the steps of the investigation in his daily reports, June–July 1937, and relates the incident confirming the Rose Wallace identification in the Otwell/Merylo manuscript.

July 6, 1937

SAVAGERY ALONG THE CUYAHOGA

There were labor troubles in the Flats that summer. In May 1937, the Steel Workers Organizing Committee struck Republic Steel, Youngstown Sheet & Tube, and Inland Steel over the companies' refusal to recognize and deal with the union. Ohio governor Martin Davey managed to get negotiations between the two warring parties started, but by mid-June talks had broken off, precipitating violent confrontations which included a strikebreaker attack on the union's headquarters and soup kitchen in Cleveland. Federal appointment of a mediation board failed to break the deadlock, and Republic Steel declared it would reopen on July 6 with workers wishing to return to their jobs or with replacement labor, if necessary. Fearing the worst, Mayor Burton and Cuyahoga County sheriff Martin O'Donnell asked the governor to send in the National Guard to maintain order.

On July 6, the 147th Infantry took up positions in the Flats at the Upson Nut Division of Republic Steel. The exact sequence of events on that morning remains somewhat sketchy, and it is not always perfectly clear who saw what and when. The search for Amelia Earhart captured local headlines and kept press coverage of the torso slayings to a minimum, and though the newspaper stories and the police reports do not exactly contradict each other, comparing the two sets of accounts raises some interesting questions. To further complicate the picture, some of the details in Sergeant James Hogan's July 6 report differ sharply from those in a second report submitted the same day—though by whom it is impossible to tell since the signature is unreadable.

At 5:30 A.M. Private John Smith saw something white bobbing in the Cuyahoga River but wasn't sure what the object was. Apparently at about the same time, or perhaps shortly thereafter, Private Edgar M. Steinbrecher of Middletown, Ohio, walked out on to the West 3rd Street bridge to watch a tug cruise by underneath and recognized the lower half of a male torso, presumably the object Smith had seen, floating in the dirty water. But no one called the police until 10:00 A.M. Sergeant James Hogan maintains in his report that Smith didn't think anything about his sighting (but what about Steinbrecher?) until hours later when he and Private Charles Demesne caught sight of a floating burlap bag—which, it turned out, contained the upper half of the torso. (The bag was apparently retrieved and opened before the police arrived.) Hogan also says that Captain Marion Ratterman summoned the police when he saw the torso's lower half in the river—presumably at about 9:55. The second report submitted on July 6 relates that Private Demesne saw a leg floating in the river at 5:30 A.M. (suggesting that Demesne was confused with John Smith) but did not notify Captain Ratterman until later in the morning. The two reports do agree that Ratterman placed the call that sent Hogan, Orley May, and Emil Musil to the scene under the West 3rd Street bridge. Someone put in a call to Captain Crapo of the Coast Guard, who then dispatched a motorboat to retrieve the lower half of the torso and search the Cuyahoga for other pieces of the body. At about 11:00, Patrolman Clayton Chute came across the right thigh lodged in a bridge piling; other parts of the body—the left thigh, left lower leg, and left upper arm—turned up at various points on the river at about the same time.

The torso's upper half had been wrapped in three-week-old newspapers and packed in a burlap bag whose red-letter inscription proclaimed it contained one hundred pounds of Purina chicken feed. The bag also yielded one of the most perplexing clues the police would deal with in the entire series: a cheap woman's silk stocking, in good condition save for a single runner, which contained a lone black and white dog hair and several short, blond human hairs.

Inspector Joseph Sweeney was convinced, he told the *Cleveland Press* on July 7, that the murderer had dumped the pieces in the river in hopes they would ultimately drift out into the lake. (Perhaps the Lady of the Lake and victim no. 7 had been disposed of in a similar fashion.) Detectives May and Musil slowly cruised the waters throughout the afternoon looking for the rest of the body but found nothing but a piece of lung. The next afternoon at 12:15, Sergeant James Hogan located the two forearms with the hands attached, making identification through fingerprinting at least a possibility. The hunt went on for at least another week; the right

On July 6, 1937, the National Guard joined Cleveland Police along the Cuyahoga River in a search for parts of victim no. 9's body. *Plain Dealer* Collection, Cleveland Public Library.

upper arm turned up on July 10, the right lower leg on July 14. The head was never found.

On the evening of July 6—before pathologist Reuben Straus had performed the formal autopsy—Merylo brought Dr. Hubert S. Reichle, head of pathology at City Hospital, to the morgue. A tip, picked up in a downtown restaurant and passed on to Merylo by a patrolman, had led the investigation back to City Hospital—back to Edward Andrassy and someone he may have known during his employment as an orderly. With Coroner Gerber's and Straus's permission, Merylo wanted Dr. Reichle to examine the remains so far recovered to see if there was anything about the style of dismemberment that he could recognize as unique to his department or, better yet, unique to someone in his department. After carefully examining the grisly pieces, Reichle declared that his department never dissected a body in such a manner, but whoever had made the incision in the lower trunk clearly knew something about anatomy.

Pathologist Straus began examining the pieces at 2:00 A.M. on July 7, presumably dealing with the rest of the body as investigators pulled the parts from the river. The victim was a well-built man about forty years old, between five feet eight and five feet ten, weighing somewhere between 150 and 160 pounds. The killer had left the genitals intact, just as he had with the tattooed victim no. 4. The only distinguishing features Straus noted on the body were two old scars on the right thumb and a cross-shaped, blue scar on the left leg.

As before, the dismemberment demonstrated the killer's familiarity with the landmarks of the human body; but for the first time, Straus observed signs that the Butcher's level of violence and sheer savagery were increasing. He had sliced open the lower half of the torso and wrenched everything from the abdominal cavity; he had similarly split the chest and removed the heart "by a clean incision across the base of the aorta." (None of these missing organs would ever be recovered.) The pathologist also noted external lacerations on the right hand and internal ones on the diaphragm. At the neck, he encountered "considerably more hacking than seen in the previous torso cases." Multiple hesitation marks were everywhere, and some of the cut surfaces suggested that the killer's knife might have been getting dull. According to Coroner Gerber, death had occurred at least forty-eight hours before pieces of the body were discovered, but Straus was unable to determine the cause.

At the Scientific Investigation Bureau, David Cowles dried out the burlap sack that had contained the upper half of the torso for further examination and comparison with the one in which the skeletal remains of the victim tentatively identified as Rose Wallace had been found the previous month. He proudly informed the press that he was also employing a newly developed technique, an ultraviolet ray, in an attempt to detect the murderer's fingerprints on the newspapers that had been wrapped around the torso half. Back at the morgue, Gerber took a set of the victim's fingerprints, and the police asked both state and federal identification bureaus to check them through civilian and military records.

As Straus and Cowles worked on this ninth victim—the tenth, according to the *Press's* and *Cleveland News's* numbering—the police continued their search for the killer. The *Plain Dealer* reported that on the night of July 6, the day the first pieces of victim no. 9 had been hauled from the river, a fifty-four-year-old drunk alarmed customers at a bar near East 9th and Hamilton by loudly insisting that he knew "all about the torso murders" and was adept at "cutting people up." Three terrified women contacted Gerber, who, in turn, called the police. They dutifully arrested the intoxicated former ambulance driver, though they were sure he was "talking through his hat." On July 8, Detectives Carl Zicarelli and Robert Carter drove to a blackberry patch near Short and State Roads in Parma—a suburb on Cleveland's west side—where three mushroom gatherers had spotted a small trunk wrapped tightly in wire the day before. Alarmed by the foul odor, the trio had called the police. When Zicarelli and Carter arrived, the mysterious trunk had vanished leaving nothing behind but its imprint in the ground. In Akron, an industrial city thirty miles south of Cleveland, a former railroad worker who enjoyed watching animals die in slaughterhouses barged into the police station with a bloody razor in his hand. Considerably more intriguing was the sighting of a large, middle-aged man dropping a bundle into the river from the West 3rd Street bridge. But police could never locate him.

In late August, between one hundred and two hundred coroners from all over the country attended the convention of the National Association of Coroners at Cleveland's Carter Hotel. Coroner Gerber submitted an anatomical survey of all the torso killings to the participating coroners and then asked for their individual analyses on the off chance that one of the attendees might detect a pattern that had so far eluded local investigators. Gerber and Reuben Straus treated their assembled colleagues to slides of the victims and a huge display of morgue photographs, but apparently nothing useful came from their presentation.

On October 17, the magazine *Official Detective Stories,* a national publication with offices in Chicago and Philadelphia, promised a five-thousand-dollar reward for information leading to the arrest and conviction of Cleveland's torso killer—so long as the magazine enjoyed exclusive rights to the informant's story. It was the first time a bounty of this sort had ever been offered by a national magazine in a multiple murder case. Predictably, tip letters of every description began pouring into Cleveland from all over the country. Many were thoughtful; many were not. "I believe," declared one writer from Detroit, "that this killer is a woman a sexually infected prostitute an asiatic [*sic*] or a negro [*sic*] claiming to be an American Indian claiming to be an herb doctor and vending a line of patent medicine's [*sic*] of her own preperations."

In the year following the discovery of victim no. 9, Merylo and Zalewski pursued suspects who fell into three broad categories: odd characters loitering in the Kingsbury Run area, specific individuals whose names were brought to their attention, and doctors whose behavior was in some way suspicious. Based on the traditional assumption that a killer always returns to the scene of his crime, the pair of detectives frequently canvassed the Run and the adjacent neighborhoods looking for anyone who seemed out of place or was acting strangely. They invariably conducted their sweeps toward the end of the day when they had finished checking more solid leads.

The second category was by far the largest; potential leads came from everywhere: anonymous phone calls, letters signed and unsigned, tips from informants, and information passed on by colleagues working on other cases or through Eliot Ness's office. Everything, no matter how improbable or downright idiotic, had to be thoroughly checked. Sorting through it all was a staggering, time-consuming task; Merylo once estimated the department would receive as many as fifty tips in one day. In response to a lengthy, well-intentioned tip letter from Howard C. Smith of Samson, Alabama, Merylo wrote, "We have received thousands of different suggestions from various parts of the world, and some of the suggestions are reasonable and others would not have any bearing in this case. . . . Many persons offering the suggestions do so merely on the basis of the stories they have read in newspapers which are not always the true facts that we found in our investigation." And, indeed, tips ran the gamut from frivolous to frightening. On the one hand, there was the call from a woman who refused to give her name but insisted that Porter J. Norris of Lakewood (a buyer for Halle Brothers department store) was the killer. On the other hand, there was the woman who reported that a man calling himself a police officer had taken her from a cafe on Payne Avenue, torn her clothes, burned her repeatedly on the breasts and in the pubic area with a cigarette, and raped her anally. All of these potential leads ended in disappointment.

A man later identified as Phillip Russo was seen on Jackass Hill suspiciously surveying Kingsbury Run through a pair of binoculars before Edward Andrassy's murder in September 1935. Initial attempts to locate him apparently failed, and the elusive Mr. Russo fell through official cracks. When someone reported seeing him again in the Run almost two years later, this time with a telescope, Merylo and Zalewski launched a doggedly determined, ultimately successful search that lasted four months. They could not, however, implicate Russo in the killings.

In August 1937 Merylo and Zalewski picked up a lead on an individual whom Merylo dubbed the "sadist." He described the unidentified man in his report of August 11 as "a likely and best suspect in the torso murders." Acting on a legion of tips from prostitutes and street informants, they doggedly pursued their quarry all over the county for more than a month. They finally tracked down a rather pathetic man who lived on West 23rd and had spent nine years of his life in a Columbus, Ohio, school for the feeble-minded. At the age of twenty-five, he had been stirred sexually by the sight of a female poultry shop clerk slicing off the head of a live chicken. Ever since that defining moment, he had bought a chicken every week or so and gone to a whorehouse, where he paid a prostitute anywhere from a dollar to two dollars to cut off the bird's head while he masturbated. Once he had

Lloyd Trunk (*left*) of the Scientific Investigation Bureau with Detective Merylo. Merylo maintained an active interest in all aspects of police work, including forensic science. Courtesy of Marjorie Merylo Dentz.

even asked that the bloody knife be rubbed along his neck. Even granting that these women had probably seen every perversion imaginable, such bizarre and sadistic sexual behavior alarmed even the cheap prostitutes whom he routinely frequented. When Merylo showed the man crime scene photographs of some of the Butcher's victims, he winced. Such graphic horrors could make him faint, he complained. He insisted "that he never could watch or permit 'any human hurt.'" After fingerprinting and photographing their onetime prime suspect, Merylo and Zalewski let the man go.

In November 1937 the pair turned their attention to a religious cult in the East 40th area called the Moriab High Science (or perhaps Seance) Temple. They learned that the secretive organization practiced voodoo and was headed by a black man named Dorsey Wade, the same "voodoo doctor" implicated in a 1928 murder-decapitation. From then until December 1938, when references to the group in their daily reports cease, the cult and the mysterious Mr. Wade became a prime focus in their investigation.

In early August 1938, the police suddenly and inexplicably were swamped by a flood of accusations concerning a number of city undertakers. A tip letter from an out-of-state embalmer spelled out in compelling, terrifying detail why hunting for the Butcher among the ranks of those who worked with the dead made perfect sense. "We have many of the same instruments as a surgeon," the writer asserted. "We are taught to make clean incisions and are masters with a scalpel as well as Mr. Surgeon. Disection [sic] is one course any college trained embalmer learns." "We have The [sic] most logical way of disposing of the bloody mess" the writer assured Cleveland police. "As for transportation of—say a messy corpse—well any undertaker is equiped [sic] with rubber sheets, leather lifting harness, etc." Perhaps most frightening of all, undertakers would have easy access to the sort of human targets the Butcher favored, since "Hundrest [sic] of down and out men to [sic] come to such places looking for clothes—and food." It seemed an extraordinarily promising lead. "However," Merylo lamented in his report of August 9, "we did not have any definite information with which we were able to approach any of the undertakers mentioned by our informants."

Many of the tips regarding suspect physicians seemed much more promising, and when they ultimately led to dead ends, the frustration and disappointment must have been particularly vexing. For seven months Merylo and Zalewski hunted a mysterious Dr. Hawk, a rumored drug addict and onetime resident of the Jackass Hill area who had apparently lost his license, only to find a weak and broken man near seventy in a ward at Charity Hospital. They unsuccessfully pursued leads about a heavy-drinking doctor who showed up at the Florida Grape Juice Winery in the Great Lakes Exposition every Thursday and Saturday night. One evening he offered a young man twenty dollars to go away with him; the pair vanished into a chauffeur-driven black Packard, never to be seen again. They sought information about a certain Dr. Dabney who had been committed to a hospital for the criminally insane in Lima, Ohio, for cutting off a patient's head during an operation performed in Cuyahoga Falls. "We received information regarding a doctor, with an office on Woodland Ave., whose name we do not wish to mention at this time, that his professional clients are questionable characters," Merylo wrote in his report of October 1, 1937. The pair checked into some information "concerning two prominent physicians" passed on to them directly by Eliot Ness's office. In late April 1938, Deputy Inspector Costello passed Merylo some information concerning a doctor—no longer allowed to practice—named Kern, who lived close to the Andrassys on Fulton Road. There was a tantalizing lead on May 4, 1938, about a doctor "who was taking narcotic treatment in the workhouse, who always wore gloves and never wanted to remove the gloves from his hand." The very next day, an informer named Harry Harper directed Merylo's and Zalewski's attention to a mysterious "Dr." Tom Baker—he was actually a male nurse—who worked at the Wayfarer's Lodge. Harper described Baker as "a vicious type pervert and a dope fiend." According to Merylo's report of May 5, "He [Harper] also stated that this man is an associate of a man by the name of Bates, who at present is employed at the County Morgue; he also mentioned another doctor who at the present time is in politics, and I prefer not to have his name mentioned at this time; supposed to be connected in one group."

A handprinted note dated October 17, 1937, 8:00 P.M., proved particularly intriguing. "The ten men killed by 'the butcher of Kingsbury Run,'" read the strange piece of correspondence, "6 ft. high—200 lbs doctor Liesness [sic] no JO 494. JO 495 Plymouth Watch this man." The tip led Merylo and Zalewski to one Dr. Nemecek of 5454 Broadway, an exceptionally powerful man who did, indeed, stand at six feet four and one-half and weighed 220 pounds. But this lead, like so many others, was a dead end. In his report of November 4, Merylo dismissed Dr. Nemecek as a suspect with a refrain that would echo through the entire investigation with depressing regularity: "we are satisfied that he had no connection with the Torso Murders."

NOTES

The account of Cleveland's labor troubles in the summer of 1937 is taken from Van Tassel and Grabowski, eds., *The Encyclopedia of Cleveland History*.

Cleveland's three daily papers covered the discovery of victim no. 9 and subsequent phases of the investigation, July 7–August 3, 1938.

Police reports from Sergeants James Hogan and Glenn A. Rogers, and Detectives Emil Musil, Carl Zicarelli, Robert Carter, and Theodore Carlson—July 6–8 and 13–14—are part of case no. 47125 and are on microfilm at the morgue.

All anatomical findings are from the autopsy protocols, case no. 47125.

Peter Merylo chronicles the investigation in his daily reports, July 1937–August 1938, his memoirs, and the Otwell/Merylo manuscript. He describes his interrogation of the "sadist" in his report of September 17, 1937.

The following items are among Peter Merylo's personal papers: the tip letter from Detroit suggesting the killer was a woman, the tip letter from the out-of-state embalmer, the letter from Howard C. Smith of Samson, Alabama, a copy of Merylo's response to it, and the strange note identifying Dr. Nemecek as a potential suspect.

April 8, 1938
DRUGS AND THE MAIDEN

Joe Perry noticed the black Lincoln sedan immediately because it was so out of place in an industrial area such as the Flats. Perry, foreman of the Booth Fisheries Company, and another employee, Sam Bosak, watched curiously as the relatively old car—they judged it be a 1932 model—cruised slowly north on Merwin Avenue at 6:10 P.M. on Thursday, April 7. Inside two well-dressed men between forty-five and fifty seemed to be scanning the river. Perry and Bosak grew increasingly suspicious when the Lincoln appeared again the next day at noon, moving in the same direction, the same two men again searching along the riverbanks and studying the buildings in the area. A month earlier at 8:40 P.M. on March 3, James Macka, an attendant at a Sohio refinery pumphouse, had seen a similar automobile pull out on the Jefferson Street bridge and stop. A man had gotten out of the car and tossed a large, heavy bundle into the river. When, following up on Macka's sighting, police searched the area the same night, they found a huge dent in the corrugated tin roof of a shanty underneath the bridge, apparently caused by something falling from above. When they dragged the river the next day, they found nothing.

The labor agonies of the previous summer had passed, and work routines had returned to normal in the Flats. For Charles F. Stock, bridge tender for the B&O Railroad, life was again lazy and uneventful. On Friday, April 8th, he occasionally scanned the river absentmindedly during his 7:00 A.M. to 3:00 P.M. shift but saw nothing unusual. At 2:15, however, Steve Morosky, a thirty-five-year-old WPA worker, strolled down the hill at the end of Superior Avenue to visit Joe Sovan, a shanty dweller living along the Cuyahoga River. About three feet from a sewer outlet, he noticed a white object floating among some old pier pilings that he at first thought was a

The storm drain at the foot of Superior Avenue in the Flats where Steve Morosky found a piece of victim no. 10's leg. The discovery led to a bitter clash between Coroner Gerber and Ness assistant Robert Chamberlin. Courtesy of Marjorie Merylo Dentz.

dead fish. When he poked it with a stick, he realized, to his horror, that it was the lower half of a human leg, amputated at the knee and ankle.

To David Cowles of the Scientific Investigation Bureau, the discovery of a severed limb meant that the mysterious Butcher, who had been inactive for nine months, had struck again; he immediately responded to the call, joining Detective Joseph Sweeney and others along the Cuyahoga's shore in the Flats. It was not entirely apparent to Cowles whether the limb belonged to a man or woman or even if it was a right or a left leg. The skin, however, was white and delicate, the curve of the calf distinctly feminine. During his initial examination, Cowles also found six long, blond hairs sticking to the leg, perhaps from the head of the victim. Despite the location where the limb had been found, Sweeney did not think it had floated through the nearby storm sewer because of the shallowness of the water and the lack of abrasions on the skin.

By the time Detectives Orley May and Emil Musil arrived at 4:15, a sizable contingent of law enforcement personnel had gathered at the scene and Cowles had already taken the leg to the morgue. The two men knew the drill. Just as they had the previous July, when pieces of victim no. 9 began to appear, May and Musil spent the remainder of their shift cruising up and down the river in a borrowed boat, carefully searching the waters and both banks in a fruitless attempt to find more of the body. The two detectives questioned everyone they found along the river, but no one had seen anything or anyone suspicious. At the end of the day, they made arrangements with the harbor master's office to continue their search with the city launch the next morning.

Cowles arrived at the morgue with the leg at 3:15, and Coroner Gerber immediately declared it to be the work of the Kingsbury Run Butcher. "Crude knife marks indicate the slayer was in a hurry," he told the *Plain Dealer* on April 9. From the lack of decomposition, he guessed the limb had been in the water for not more than seventy-two hours and that the person to whom it belonged had not been dead for more than a week. Though he awaited official confirmation through X-rays, he was convinced it was the left leg, belonging to a woman about five feet two inches tall and between twenty-five and thirty years old.

Early the next morning, April 9, the police returned to the banks of the Cuyahoga. They combed the entire area from the mouth of the river to Scranton Road and searched through the hobo shanties along the riverbank. They even returned to Stone's Levee, where the skeletal remains of victim no. 8, the woman tentatively identified as Rose Wallace, had been found the previous June—all to no avail. The only probable lead came from John Mokris and Frank Skrovan, who reported seeing a heavyset man enter a storm sewer under the High Level Bridge, close to the spot where the piece of leg was first discovered.

A week later, detectives were following up on a tip from a pair of truck drivers from Middlefield, Ohio, who had picked up a young hitchhiker heading toward Elyria on April 7, the day before the piece of leg had been discovered. The stranger identified himself as a sailor on Lake Erie and then suddenly predicted that "there will be another torso murder within 72 hours." By the end of the month, Ness's personal assistant Robert W. Chamberlin and David Cowles were cooperating with New York state police lab technicians in trying to determine if a woman's dismembered body found in Lake Ontario was part of the Cleveland series. The body bore evidence of having been burned or treated with chemicals and, at one point, wrapped in cheesecloth or burlap and buried for a short time before being tossed into the lake. According to the *Plain Dealer* on April 27, Dr. Bradley H. Kirschberg, director of the New York state police scientific laboratory, hinted darkly in his preliminary report that the absence of certain organs pointed to "the possibility of operation by a sex maniac either before or after death."

Deep cracks began to develop within the ranks of the investigators. Merylo and Zalewski had been working on the case exclusively for almost two years and had put in countless hours of overtime. The pair had diligently followed every lead, no matter how trivial; they constantly revisited reports and retraced their investigative steps to make sure they had not missed something significant. Their determined digging had taken them repeatedly to the most depressing and dangerous sections of the city and brought them into continual contact with a never-ending parade of lunatics, deviants, and criminals. Overwhelmed by frustration and fatigue, the seemingly inseparable pair allowed a minor disagreement over whether a former acquaintance of Edward Andrassy's should be questioned or simply kept under surveillance to erupt into a full-blown quarrel. Zalewski asked to be taken off the case, and though he ultimately remained with the investigation and continued to work with Merylo, their relationship was irreparably damaged.

Ness precipitated an equally serious breach when he suddenly disclosed to the press that his personal assistant, Robert Chamberlin, had been working on the case behind the scenes with the full blessings of the safety director's office and had met with Sweeney and Cowles on the night of April 8 after the limb had been discovered. Although he made no comment at the time, the next day Chamberlin dropped a personal bombshell by telling the *Press* that he wanted experts from either City Hospital or Western Reserve University to double-check Gerber's conclusions about the piece of leg. "I mean no reflection on the coroner," he insisted, "but since there is a possibility this might even be the missing leg of the 10th [*sic*] victim found last July, the time of death is very important and I thought Dr. Gerber wouldn't mind other experts corroborating his findings."

Whether Chamberlin was speaking for himself or for Eliot Ness, the ill-timed, ill-considered announcement roused the coroner's ire. It was not just a matter of a Republican safety director intruding on the turf of a Democratic coroner; a man far less touchy than Sam Gerber would have taken personal offense at such an inexplicable and public questioning of his professional competence. First of all, it would hardly take a forensic genius to tell the difference between a relatively fresh limb and one that had presumably been stuck in the mud at the bottom of the Cuyahoga for the better part of a year; second, Straus's autopsy protocols on victim no. 9 contain detailed descriptions of both lower extremities. To what "missing leg" was Chamberlin referring? The discovery of a fresh victim would undoubtedly draw renewed public attention to the stalled investigation, and this may have been a ploy by Chamberlin—or Ness—to avoid some of that pressure. Gerber stood by his medical judgments about the leg and adamantly refused to surrender it to "other experts." According to Ness authority Paul W. Heimel, the outraged coroner even went so far to protect his domain as personally guarding the door to the morgue. The ultimate irony in the entire confrontation rests with the fact that a year before, Peter Merylo—the legendary bull in the china shop—had been diplomatic enough when bringing in Dr. Hubert S. Reichle, head of the Pathology Department at City Hospital, to examine the remains of victim no. 9 to avoid rousing the coroner's wrath. On April 11, however, Gerber submitted a piece of muscle to William Hay at the Department of Health for analysis. Whether he did this on his own or was goaded into it is unclear, but those tests found no "hypnotic or narcotic drugs" in the tissue.

Within a month, the question of whether this was or was not a part of a new victim would become irrelevant. At 2:00 A.M. on May 2, Sergeant James Hogan, Lieutenant Steve Tozzer, and Detective Walsh responded to a call from Oscar Meister, bridge captain on the upper West 3rd Street bridge. He and Albert Mahaffey had seen a human thigh floating in the river fifty feet east of the bridge. The officers pulled it from the water and searched under the bridge, locating a burlap sack at the south end whose inscription alleged that it contained one hundred pounds of Wheel Brand potatoes from Bangor, Maine.

The discovery of another severed body part was potentially significant enough to bring Coroner Gerber to the scene. His preliminary examination of the bag revealed that it contained both halves of a headless torso, another thigh, and a left foot, all sufficiently decomposed as to make immediate determination of the sex impossible. By 2:45, Gerber had returned to the morgue with the burlap sack and its grim contents.

From the surviving protocols, it is not clear who performed the official examination, but some of the wording suggests that it was done by someone other than Gerber. The parts were, indeed, female, and the foot matched the month-old lower leg. The abdomen bore a superficial nine-centimeter scar, as well as a thirteen-centimeter laparotomy scar, possibly indicating a cesarean operation. The sloppiness which Straus had observed in the disarticulation of victim no. 9 was present here as well; according to the protocols, all the cut surfaces showed multiple hesitation marks. "These are more numerous and irregular than seen in the previous 'torso murder.'" The same viciousness noted in the previous victim was also apparent here: there were lacerations on both thighs, and the killer had snapped the back ribs with his bare hands. Gerber's initial speculations about the height and age of the woman proved accurate, and her weight was now put at about 120 pounds. For the first time in the series of killings, drugs were detected in the system; examination of tissue from the liver and the lungs revealed the presence of enough morphine to cause unconsciousness, perhaps even death. She was judged to have been dead for a month, and though the exact cause of death remained undetermined, the lack of blood in the heart suggested "probable laceration anterior aspect neck with secondary hemorrhage."

While police focused their attention on a neatly wrapped bundle of women's clothing found on East 65th back in January—the small garments could conceivably fit the latest victim, the search for the rest of the body continued. Detectives May, Musil, and Joseph Horazdosky found a piece of lung tissue in the Cuyahoga, and two men in a motorboat came across a grotesque mass of intestines floating in Lake Erie close to the mouth of the

On May 2, 1938, police pull out of the Cuyahoga River a burlap sack containing additional pieces of victim no. 10's body. *Plain Dealer* Collection, Cleveland Public Library.

river: both ultimately were judged nonhuman. Tugboat captain William Atwood reported seeing two burlap bags bobbing in the river near a dock south of the Jefferson Avenue bridge on April 26. When he and his crew sighted the pair of sacks again a few days later, they tried to snag at least one of them but failed. Merylo assumed one of the bags had been found on May 2 by Oscar Meister; the other sack, he reasoned, probably contained the head. As in previous torso cases, investigators regarded finding the head as one of their best chances to learn the identity of the victim, so they mounted a diligent but unsuccessful search for that elusive second sack.

On May 5, Merylo tried a scientific experiment with a ten-pound ham. In slightly less than a year, the Cuyahoga had yielded up dismembered pieces of two different bodies, some of the parts in burlap bags. Merylo wondered what the rate of decomposition would be in the water. How long would the pieces of a body stay submerged before bobbing to the surface? Where would the currents take them? How quickly? At 2:45 P.M., at a point close to the Jefferson Avenue bridge, Merylo dropped the ham into a burlap sack, marked it with a metal identification tag, and heaved it into the river. By May 9, it was seen floating about one thousand yards north, just a couple of hundred yards away from the West 3rd Street bridge, where the first piece of victim no. 9 had appeared in July 1937. When the shifting winds carried the sack and its contents back up the river, Merylo retrieved it and repeated the experiment.

On May 8, William Mayhue, a forty-two-year-old laborer, snagged his line on something while fishing in Lake Erie, presumably close to his home on West 81st. When he yanked it free, he discovered four strands of a woman's hair tangled on his hook. By May 18, the story had reached Merylo. Mayhue showed him the spot in the lake where he had been fishing, and, after conferring with Chief Miller of the Lakewood Police Department, Merylo called in the Coast Guard to search the area. They found nothing.

† † †

Day after day, curious onlookers stalked the police search from the banks of the river. "It doesn't take much to collect a crowd these days," remarked Assistant Harbormaster Henry Silverthorn to *Cleveland News* reporter Howard Beaufait. "If you just stand and look in the water a lot of others will soon gather around and look, too."

None of the other body parts would ever be found; the woman would remain unknown. On May 3, Gerber received a poignant telegram from Florence Akers of Kennett Missouri: "Wire description of body found May 3 [sic] might be my daughter Kay Akers." His reply the next day was professional, dispassionate, and terse: "From Fair to medium color of skin. Medium Brown Hair. Approximately 5' 5" tall Weight 115–125 Age from 25–30. Old operative scar mid line of abdomen 6 inches long. Old scar on right side of abdomen 4 inches long. Might have worn 5 to 6 shoe. Head both arms and hands/Right leg and foot still missing. Dr. Gerber Coroner."

NOTES

Reports from Detectives Orley May and Robert Carter and Sergeants George Zicarelli and James Hogan document the discoveries of April 9 and May 2. All are part of the coroner's files, case no. 48176. By this time, stories about the torso killings appeared in city papers almost on a daily basis. The events surrounding victim no. 10, related police activities, and other developments in the case were covered by the three Cleveland dailies, April 9–May 5, 1938.

All anatomical findings are from the autopsy protocols, case no. 48176.

Peter Merylo deals with victim no. 10 in his official reports (April–December 1938), his personal memoirs, and the Otwell manuscript.

Henry Silverthorn's comments to Howard Beaufait are from an undated newspaper clipping in Peter Merylo's files.

The correspondence between Florence Akers and Dr. Gerber is in the coroner's files, case no. 48176.

August 16, 1938
DOUBLE MURDER AGAIN?

The most grotesque public spectacle the city had seen since Sergeant James Hogan led the unsuccessful search for the arms and head of victim no. 6 in Kingsbury Run two years before, began to unfold in the late afternoon of August 16. James Dawson, Edward Smith, and James McShack, African Americans who eked out a meager existence by scavenging for reusable scrap and junk they could sell to dealers, were searching through a dump close to the southwest corner of the newly completed Lake Shore Drive and East 9th where much of the refuse from the Great Lakes Exposition had been discarded. At about 4:00 in the afternoon, Dawson left his companions to get a truck. "I was getting ready to gather some of the iron together so we could sell it to a junk yard," he told the *Plain Dealer* on August 17, "when I passed a little gully and saw what looked like a coat sticking out of the rocks."

As Dawson descended into the five-foot depression, stumbling over pieces of broken concrete, he realized that the coat was actually a bundle covered with a neat pile of rocks. Alerted by the buzz of flies circling the area, he pushed aside some of the rocks and concrete debris, then recoiled from the putrid smell. He called for his two companions to join him, and as he carefully began removing some of the rocks from the bundle, Smith saw what looked like human bones.

The three men scrambled out of the gully and hailed the first policeman they saw—Patrolman Martin Conners doing traffic duty near the Lake Shore-East 9th intersection. At 4:30 Conners put in the call to the Detective Bureau, and within minutes, a sizable contingent of police, including James Hogan and Peter Merylo, as well as Coroner Gerber, gathered at the trash dump. Even to these veterans of the torso investigation, the grisly scene at the corner of Lake Shore and East 9th must have come as a shock. Under a small pile of rocks and chunks of concrete lay a human torso wrapped first in the sort of heavy brown paper used by butchers (perhaps a grim joke), then in a man's torn, striped summer coat, and finally in a tattered, colorful, homemade patchwork quilt. Jammed among the rocks under the torso rested a package wrapped in the same brown paper containing the thighs held together with a rubber band. Five feet away lay a similarly wrapped package containing a severed head with some matted, silky, light brown hair about six inches long still attached to the scalp. Strangest of all, police

Inspector Charles Nevel and Sergeant James Hogan search the rubble at the East 9th-Lake Shore dump site where victims no. 11 and no. 12 were found, August 16, 1938. Police made no attempt to cordon off the crime scene. Courtesy of Marjorie Merylo Dentz.

located the arms and lower legs in a brown cardboard box fashioned from two different containers—one from the Independent Biscuit Company of Cleveland, the other from the General Seafoods Corporation of Boston, Massachusetts. For the first time since victim no. 5, the killer had left the entire body behind. The makeshift box looked new and clearly had not been exposed to the elements for very long. In stark contrast, the enclosed limbs and the rest of the corpse were in such an advanced state of decay that Gerber could not be sure whether the internal organs had been removed or had simply decomposed. Parts of the skin appeared mummified, and the coroner even wondered if some of the body pieces had been frozen. He judged the remains to be those of a female. As usual, the police uncovered tantalizing but inconclusive bits of evidence—two burlap bags, a label from the coat, and a page from the March 5, 1938, issue of *Collier's Magazine.*

To homebound commuters on Lake Shore Drive late that afternoon, the sight of so many uniformed and plainclothesed police officers combing through the rocky, trash-strewn field while others photographed the area could only mean that the Butcher had struck again. Many slowed down as they passed; others stopped to join a steadily growing crowd of onlookers. According to the *Plain Dealer* on August 17, a couple hundred people, many of them women, followed as Gerber and county undertaker Frank G. Nunn conveyed the remains to the morgue. By the next afternoon, the crowd of curious spectators had grown so large that attendants called the police to disperse them.

Patrolman Barret of the Identification Bureau tried, apparently unsuccessfully, to take a print of the left thumb before County Pathologist Reuben Straus began the formal autopsy at 6:00 A.M. The only clues to the woman's identity that he could offer the police were a porcelain Davis Crown pivot tooth in the upper jaw and an irregular, even deformed, big toe nail on the left foot. Otherwise there was little for him to report, and he spelled out his concluding observations with stark simplicity.

White female torso, 30–40 years of age, 64 inches tall, dead about 4–6 months, weighing during life about 120–125 pounds.

Head disarticulated at the level of the third intervertebral disc, with knife marks on dorsum of third cervical vertebra.

Extremities disarticulated at all the major joints, with knife marks on the articular surfaces.

Bobbed (?) slightly brown or blond hair on head.

Straus left the official cause of death undetermined but judged it a probable homicide.

Although some officers continued to canvass the dump into the early evening, Hogan had left, probably about the same time Gerber and Nunn drove to the morgue, and the official language of the report he turned in to Inspector Charles Nevel masks the deep frustration he must have felt over a case in which bodies accumulated as quickly as leads disappeared. There is no record of exactly when Straus finished his grueling examination of victim no. 11. The day, however, was not over for him or for James Hogan and Sam Gerber.

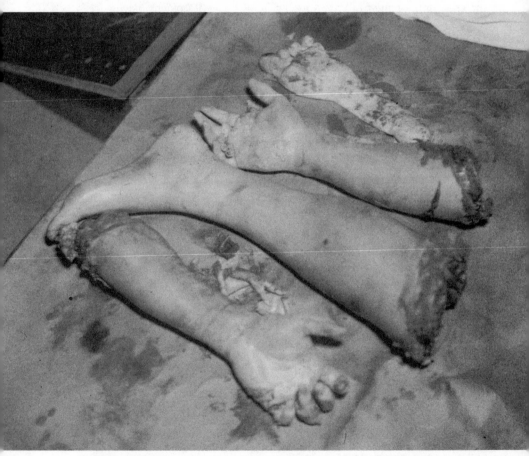

This photograph is undated, but the condition of the body parts shown matches the anatomical descriptions of victim no. 11. Courtesy of Marjorie Merylo Dentz.

At 5:30, Tod Bartholomew, a thirty-nine-year-old machinist at the Clark Manufacturing Company, and his wife, Cecelia, passed by the dump site on the way to their East 36th Street home and noticed the crowds still milling in the area. Within the next hour he learned of the new torso discovery (Hogan's report says he read about it in a newspaper, but it seems highly unlikely that any large, metropolitan daily could get out an edition that quickly) and returned to the scene close to 7:00 with his wife and a friend, Jennie Talas of Payne Avenue. Bartholomew parked his car behind a billboard, and the trio joined the onlookers near a large pipe. At about 7:30, as darkness descended, he became increasingly aware of a foul odor emanating from a nearby shallow depression in the ground. When he looked down into it, he saw human bones—victim no. 12.

At this point, the time element becomes confused. According to official reports, Hogan and Gerber were notified at 8:30 and 8:45 respectively. The two men returned to the dump; an obviously posed *Press* photograph shows them examining the bones with Inspector Charles Nevel. But the coroner's documents state that the autopsy was performed at 9:00. Clearly the bones could not have been gathered up and dispatched to the morgue in only fifteen minutes, and with police still on the crime scene, a delay of an hour in informing their superiors seems inconceivable if not totally impossible. In all likelihood the police reports are in error. Dr. Straus would have checked and recorded the official time when he began the autopsy; officers on the scene would not have had the opportunity to write their reports until later in the evening or the next day.

The suddenly renewed search proceeded through the descending darkness. As Gerber gathered and examined the bones, a weary Sergeant Hogan picked up a large, round can to put them in. The report he submitted later that night mutes the nasty shock he received: "found the pelvis bones, ribs and vertabraes [sic] of a human being lying on the ground next to a can, and in the can found a human skull." At first, Gerber incorrectly judged the bones to be African American; he could not determine the sex or even tell if the skeleton was complete.

Back at the morgue, all the bones and refuse judged to be significant were laid out on a large sheet, like pieces of a ghastly jigsaw puzzle awaiting assembly. At some point, either that night or the next day, Gerber posed with some of the bones for a stilted *Plain Dealer* photograph, but Reuben Straus performed his second difficult autopsy of the evening. His conclusions were even less detailed than they had been with no. 11.

Incomplete white male torso, 30–40 years of age, 66–68 inches tall, weighing during life about 135–150 pounds, dead about 7–9 months.

Head disarticulated at the level of the third inter-vertebral disc, with knife marks on dorsum of second and third cervical vertebrae.

Extremities disarticulated at all the major joints (?)

Long dark brown coarse hair on head.

The hair was a clue of sorts. During the autopsy, Straus judged it to be too short for a woman and too long for a man. Other than that, all he could offer the police to aid the identification process was a good set of teeth, evidence of a broken nose, and several small pieces of newspaper apparently from May issues of the *Cleveland News*. He concluded that some charred bones brought in with the skeleton were nonhuman, and when David Cowles of the Scientific Investigation Bureau found six additional

Coroner Gerber examining the skull of victim no. 12. Note that he is not wearing gloves. Courtesy of Marjorie Merylo Dentz.

bone fragments on the crime scene the next day at 3:15 P.M., Straus was not sure whether they belonged with the skeleton. As with victim no. 11 earlier in the evening, Straus judged the death a probable homicide.

Abandoned pieces of clothing and pages from newspapers and magazines had been common features of most of the torso killings. This time the murderer had left behind three unique and potentially significant bits of evidence: the homemade box fashioned from two cartons that contained the extremities of no. 11, the colorful quilt that had been wrapped around her torso, and the large tin can that held the head of no. 12.

The can proved the easiest to check. The label, Bako Brand Plum Butter, sent Merylo and Zalewski to the the Weideman Company at 1240 West 9th, where sales manager Elmer W. Nobis stated that in 1937 the firm had produced and sold between three and four hundred forty-pound cans of plum butter to bakeries all over the city. Given the sheer number of containers and bakeries involved, Merylo reasoned in his report of August 17 that tracing a single can would be impossible.

Both the box and the quilt were considerably more problematic. Police learned that the portion of the box from the General Seafoods Corporation originally had held frozen haddock fillets and had been shipped to Jake Katz in the Central Market in June. Katz told the police that he always threw empty boxes on the curb outside his Bolivar establishment where anyone could have picked them up. A nineteen-year-old market clerk reported to Merylo that he had seen a strange, middle-aged man called Gus carry away some of the discarded cartons several times in the past few months. In the stifling morning heat toward the end of June, the man appeared wearing a heavy rubber coat and rubber boots. "I'm believing it's cool outside, and that keeps me cold," he explained. "In the winter I go without a shirt sometimes and believe it's hot, and that keeps me warm."

On the evening of August 16, police called Nathan Robb, manager of the Independent Biscuit Company on Lakeview, to the morgue to identify the part of the makeshift box that came from his company. From the serial number and other markings, he judged the container to be about a year old but promised to double-check with the company that manufactured it in Grand Rapids, Michigan. The next day Detectives Musil and Zicarelli followed up on the lead with Robb at the Independent Biscuit Company. The box, which had originally contained Royal Tea Cookies from the Veltman Cookie Company of Grand Rapids, had been shipped to Cleveland via the Nickel Plate Railroad on June 17, 1938; the shipment had arrived, been unpacked, and stored in a company warehouse on June 20. The cookies had been distributed on July 15 to a couple of west side five-and-ten stores and the Central Market. Unfortunately, the company kept records only on the number of cartons sent to a given customer, so there was no way to trace a specific box. Musil and Zicarelli checked into the Independent Biscuit Company personnel but found that all "had been employed there at least two years, were all married men, and bear a good reputation."

The information about both boxes raised as many questions as it answered. The cartons had been in the city only since midsummer, yet victim no. 11 had been killed in the spring. Had the Butcher left her pieces in the dump when she was murdered or, as the history of the boxes would indicate, several months later? If the latter, where had he kept the decomposing corpse until disposal? Had he transported the pieces in the two burlap bags found on the scene? When both victims no. 11 and no. 12 had lain undiscovered so long, was it even conceivable that the Butcher had returned to the dump site to repackage some of his handiwork to make their presence more obvious? If someone had been at Lake Shore Drive and East 9th at the right time of night, would he have seen a dark figure silently picking his way across the rocky mounds of trash with his homemade box under his arm?

The history of the colorful quilt was equally perplexing. The *Press* published a photograph of it, and Charles Damyn, a barber, identified it as one he had sold to a junkman in early July. From Damyn's remarkably detailed description, Detectives Theodore Carlson and Herbert Wachsman tracked down Elmer Cummings, who insisted that he had sold the quilt to the Scovill Rag & Paper Company at 2276 Scovill Avenue—in the same seedy neighborhood from which Flo Polillo and Rose Wallace had disappeared and tantalizingly close to the spot where the first set of Polillo's remains was discovered in January, 1936. The company owner, William Blusinsky, told the detectives that he had been stockpiling rags in his warehouse and had not been burglarized. The quilt, which no one there could remember seeing, could have left the premises only if one of his employees, all of whom he vouched for, had taken it or if someone had stolen it from the receiving platform. Carlson and Wachsman played by the book. They searched the premises of everyone involved in the quilt's odyssey, questioned their family members and neighbors, and checked into the backgrounds of their employees. They came up empty and were left with one seemingly unanswerable question: when any old rag would have served the Butcher's purpose, why would he risk detection by stealing such an identifiable quilt from the Scovill Rag & Paper Company?

Early on the morning of August 17, Acting Detective Inspector Charles Nevel told assembled lawmen that solving the torso killings was the single most important job facing the department. A little later, Hogan returned to the dump site leading a force of eighteen detectives, as many uniformed officers as the department could spare, and about one hundred volunteer "torso detectives" in a careful exploration of the entire area between East 9th and East 26th, the Pennsylvania Railroad and the lakeshore. Though Hogan remained, as always, the complete professional, he had become so pessimistic about the case that he told newspaper reporters before the operation began that he doubted they would find anything. "He's changing his technique," Merylo told the *Press*. "Why, I don't know. But for the first time since the two bodies we found in September, 1935, he has left two victims together. And, again changing his method, he left heads of these last two."

Suddenly, additional clues seemed to come from everywhere. A week before the discovery of the bodies of no. 11 and no. 12, on August 16, Edward Bruhn had found a tangled mass of light brown hair, similar to victim no. 11's, in a black tin box in a field on Coit Road near Euclid Avenue. On August 16, George Brennels came across a woman's stained dress, slip, stockings, and underwear close to East 83rd. Neither man had given a second thought to his odd discovery until victims no. 11 and no. 12 appeared. Cowles tested the hair while Gerber dealt with the clothing. The dress could fit the victim, the coroner declared, but the underwear was too large for her. More seemingly bloodstained clothing, belonging to a missing nurse, Anna Miller, turned up near a quarry south of Berea. After tracking down the forty-one-year-old woman in Toledo, the relieved authorities learned that the garments had been stolen from her several weeks before she moved.

The city received yet another nasty jolt when the body of an armless and footless nude male washed ashore at Gordon Park—an area along the Erie north coast from roughly East 72nd to East 88th—raising the possibility of a third torso victim within two days. But Gerber immediately quashed such speculations by pointing out that the man's arms and feet had been knocked off from floating in the lake for at least a year and that the unidentified male had not been dismembered.

Police returned to Kingsbury Run to search unsuccessfully for pieces of yet another potential victim when an informant told authorities that on Sunday, August 14, he had watched a man get out of a green coupe on Bragg near Jackass Hill and toss a bundle into the gully.

In the midst of this chaos, the *Press* chose to raise the level of apprehension in the city. On August 17, under a page 1 headline that asked, "This Torso Killer—What Sort of Madman Is He?" the paper proclaimed: "A cunning madman with the strength of an ox. That's the torso killer—the madman who has ruthlessly slain 13 [*sic*] men and women, then dismembered their bodies and hidden the parts in lonely places. He's as regular, as coldly efficient and as relentless as an executioner when the mood to kill comes over him. Never has an intended victim escaped his relentless knife, never has a 'friend' lived to tell the tale."

† † †

Ohio anatomical law mandated that all unclaimed bodies from Cleveland hospitals, the morgue, funeral homes, and city jails be turned over to the Western Reserve University Medical School and Dr. T. Windgate Todd—an active participant in Pearce's September 1936 conference and a consultant on the autopsy of victim no. 8 in June 1937. After the professor and his assistants had photographed and measured the remains, they were turned over to anatomy classes for dissection. The unidentified remains from the torso killings also went to the medical school but apparently were kept rather than being handed over to the medical students. Since storage facilities at the morgue were limited, both former coroner Pearce and Gerber were probably just as happy to have somewhere else to store them.

In due course, the pieces of victim no. 11 found their way to the medical school and Dr. Todd. Then David Cowles of the Scientific Investigation Bureau received an urgent call from Todd asking him to stop by the college on his way to work. The professor showed him the remains of no. 11 and dropped a bombshell. He had serious doubts that they actually belonged to a legitimate torso victim because he believed they had been embalmed. Unlike the Chamberlin-Gerber "missing leg" flap over a year before, Todd's findings, if correct, raised serious questions about the competence of Reuben Straus, who performed the autopsy, and Coroner Gerber, who signed off on his results. Cowles later reflected, "He [Todd] said, 'You come here whenever you want and take portions of that body and have it examined,' which I did." The ramifications of Todd's allegations were enormous. If not a murder victim, where had the body come from? Was someone playing a joke on the police? Could that someone actually be the killer? Unfortunately, the results of Cowles's subsequent examination, like so much else connected with the case, have not survived. This potentially explosive disagreement never hit the papers, but Gerber learned about Cowles's actions and, in a burst of possessiveness, accused him of stealing. (Someone let Merylo in on the secret, however, for he dismisses no. 11 from the list of the Butcher's victims in his memoirs because of the embalming.)

Almost a year later, in May 1939, Gerber asked for the return of victims no. 10 and no. 11, and in July he requested Flo Polillo's remains. The coroner may simply have been exploring some new angle of investigation, or perhaps he was still smarting from what he saw as betrayal by Todd and Cowles. Records in the coroner's files document the transfers but provide no reasons for them.

With the discovery of two new victims, no. 11 and no. 12, every bit of potential evidence, every shred of information—no matter how small—seemed to become front-page, headline news, and every revelation or speculation concerning the case stretched the already taut public nerves a little more and increased the pressure on the beleaguered police department. The inevitable explosion came in the early morning hours of August 18.

NOTES

Police reports from Sergeants James Hogan and William N. Miller, Detective Emil Musil, and an unknown officer cover the discovery of victims no. 11 and no. 12 and the events that immediately followed. They are contained in the coroner's files, case nos. 48621 (no. 11) and 48625 (no. 12). Peter Merylo deals with subsequent phases of the investigation in his daily reports (August–December 1938), his memoirs, and the Otwell manuscript. Cleveland's three daily papers reported on the discovery of the bodies and the subsequent investigation, August 17–29, 1938.

All anatomical findings are from the autopsy protocols, case nos. 48621 (no. 11) and 48625 (no. 12).

Dr. T. Windgate Todd's revelations about victim no. 11 are recounted by David Cowles in a taped interview conducted in September 1983.

August 18, 1938
A DESCENT INTO HELL

Eliot Ness had had enough. Egged on by a flurry of sensational front-page newspaper coverage, public agitation had soared over the appearance of two more mutilated bodies at the Lake Shore Drive-East 9th dump. Within a couple of days of the terrible discovery, it became obvious that the police were rapidly running out of leads, just as they had in all the previous killings. The safety director decided that a dramatic response was required—something akin to Coroner Pearce's "torso clinic" of two years before. At 12:40 A.M. on August 18 an assault team of twenty-five detectives and uniformed policemen—including Ness's assistant Robert Chamberlin and David Cowles of the Scientific Investigation Bureau—pulled up to the Central Viaduct firehouse in eleven automobiles, then listened while the safety director mapped out a strategy for systematically raiding the hobo jungles that spread out below in Kingsbury Run.

Shortly after 1:00 A.M., Sergeant James McDonald led a grimly silent squad of ten men down the Eagle Street ramp into the blackness. They took up positions to block any escape from the main shantytown huddled on the hill at Commercial and Canal Roads. Toting an ax handle, Ness followed, leading the main raiding party that was armed with hammers, clubs, flashlights, and acetylene lamps borrowed from the fire station. The group moved through the darkness as quietly as their numbers would allow. As they neared the sprawl of dilapidated hovels, a few stray cats hissed and scurried for cover; the mingled stink of boiled chickens and cheap whiskey hung in the air over the tangled mass of cardboard boxes and corrugated metal.

Suddenly the sound of furious knocking on the door of one of the makeshift shelters broke through the heavy silence. With military preci-

Eliot Ness (*left of center*) with some of the vagrants rounded up during the shanty-town raid of August 18, 1938. *Cleveland Press* Archives, Cleveland State University.

sion, Ness led the raiders from shack to shack, rousing the startled, angry inhabitants with violent banging. If an indignant squatter were so foolish as to deny the police entry, he had his door bashed in and found himself being vigorously hauled into the nighttime darkness. Gradually Kingsbury Run echoed with a cacophonous thunder of barking dogs, wood banging on wood or metal, loud shrieks of protest, and angry swearing. Flashlight beams cut through the air, momentarily illuminating and freezing a squalid dwelling or an uncomprehending, red-eyed face. Some of the men seemed lost in a drunken stupor and had to be carried from their hovels. As Ness led a search of the thirty-some huts, a fire truck, presumably at the top of the incline or on a bridge, illuminated the entire area with the fierce glow of an arc light. Even at such a late hour, curious spectators and passersby slowly gathered to watch the unfolding spectacle that, according to the *Press* on August 18, reminded one policeman of a Mississippi-style manhunt through the swamps.

At 1:45 A.M., the raiding party split up, part of it heading west to the Lorain-Carnegie Bridge, the other moving farther east. The transients who gathered in the shantytown under the bridge's huge arching span that linked the east and west sides of the city were considerably less destitute than their counterparts at Commercial and Canal. One even protested to the *Press* on August 18 that he would lose the job he had finally found if police detained him. Northeast of the bridge, the police lined up on the rim of the hill at East 34th. Below them the rapid transit and train tracks stretched out in the blackness, and farther off stood the stagnant waterway where authorities had searched unsuccessfully for the head and arms of victim no. 6 two years before. Slowly they descended the steep, grassy slope, flashlights searching through the sumac bushes for the dirtiest, the most down and out of the hobo population. But cold fear of the Butcher had already done its work; the usual inhabitants had deserted the area, save for a dozen sleeping on the concrete ledges under the railroad bridge at East 36th.

At Commercial and Canal, wardens from the Animal Protective League passed through in the wake of the police, rounding up the cats and dogs some of the men had kept as pets. Behind them came the scavengers—neighborhood boys who picked through the rubble for whatever small treasures they could find. The police transported the sixty-some vagrants who had been corralled in the triple-pronged raid to the Central Police Station; like an invading army, Ness and his men left nothing behind. Finally, two companies of firemen under Battalion Chief Charles Rees dragged the remnants of the shantytown to the base of the hill, soaked them with coal oil, and set them ablaze.

At the station, the police fingerprinted everyone caught in the roundup to aid in identification should any of them later fall under the Butcher's knife. About a dozen were found to have criminal records; none could provide any useful information on the murderer. Since only two of the Butcher's victims had ever been positively identified, authorities assumed he picked his targets from the transient populations in Kingsbury Run. "Then too," Ness told the *Press* on August 18, "the contents of the stomachs of some of the victims have been mostly fruit and vegetables, indicating they live off refuse picked up around the markets." He justified the raid as an attempt to deprive the killer of his prey. "Henceforth," Ness went on, "such men will have to stay at the [Wayfarer's] Lodge, where there are ample facilities for them."

Ness had always enjoyed good relations with the city newspapers. He courted members of the press, and they willingly showcased his initiatives as safety director. But if he expected the same favorable press treatment of his shantytown raid that Pearce's torso clinic had enjoyed, he was deeply disappointed. Press reactions ran a gamut from neutral to hostile. Though Ness maintained it was his concern for the welfare of Kingsbury Run's transients that motivated his actions, the *Press* chastised him. "But the Commercial Hill dwellers are not thanking Mr. Ness for his concern about their remaining unidentified if their heads should be chopped off," the paper insisted on August 18. "Nor do they thank him for burning down the village." (A *Plain Dealer* account of the raid on August 18 indicated that the authorities marked each shack so that the dweller could later claim his belongings, but that seems not to have happened.) "The net result of the director's raid seems to have been the wrecking of a few miserable huts and

The hobo jungles of the Flats and Kingsbury Run go up in flames on August 18, 1938. Courtesy of Marjorie Merylo Dentz.

the confinement of the occupants, along with jobless men seized in similar raids, at the Workhouse," proclaimed a *Press* editorial on August 26. "As we said a week ago, we can see no justification for the jailing of jobless and penniless men and the wrecking of their miserable hovels without permitting them to collect their personal belongings."

Four days later, on Monday, August 22, Ness launched an equally draconian operation of questionable legality. Exercising his authority as safety director and acting on the long-held assumption that the Butcher and his "laboratory" must be somewhere in the neighborhoods bordering Kingsbury Run, Ness dispatched six two-man search teams of detectives and fire wardens into a ten-square-mile area from the Cuyahoga River to East 55th to Prospect Avenue. Wardens could enter and inspect a dwelling without a search warrant, so under the guise of conducting routine fire inspections the police could look for signs of the Butcher's activity. Among the detectives systematically exploring every house and building were Orley May, Emil Musil, Peter Merylo, and Martin Zalewski—men who had worked the case the longest, knew its details the most intimately, and felt the frustration of their failure the most deeply. Authorities kept the entire operation secret from the general public and the press so as not to alert the killer.

Five days later, on Friday, August 26, with only one section of the huge block of land remaining to search, the press broke the story as Acting Detective Inspector Charles O. Nevel conceded that the well-planned, well-executed operation had turned up nothing. The papers treated Ness and his barely legal searches far more kindly than they had his shantytown raids of the previous week, primarily because—although no clues to the murders came to light—the systematic search focused renewed public attention on the terrible living conditions in the downtown area. The teams uncovered hundreds of people living in appalling fire traps without toilets or running water, entire families crowded into single dingy rooms and sleeping on the floor. "Big rats ran from under the flooring in some of the huts," Merylo recalls in the Otwell manuscript; "the stench was nauseating; the meanest flophouse looked good by comparison." The interests of social reform had been served even if those of law enforcement had not.

As a last resort, authorities turned to talk of a reward, just as they had in the summer of 1936. Coroner Gerber thought that if the promised sum were large enough, the Butcher might try to collect it by pointing the finger at someone else. Ness endorsed the idea of a joint city-county reward. Councilman Harry Marshall suggested five thousand dollars—a huge sum in Depression-era America—and county commissioners president John F. Curry thought the county would probably match it, bringing the proposed reward to a staggering ten thousand dollars. Criminals and other questionable types who would usually avoid the police, authorities reasoned, might be tempted to tell whatever they knew because of the sheer size of the reward, and even though countless money-hungry amateur detectives undoubtedly would burden police with worthless tips, something useful might turn up.

August 1938 would mark a major turning point in the career of Eliot Ness. From then on, his star faded in Cleveland. The torso killings had terrorized and fascinated the city for four years, and after four years of work, the most massive and intense police investigations in city history—two of them under the direct leadership of one of the country's most famous lawmen—had failed to find the killer. The pressure on Ness was enormous and intense. Whether his actions in the final weeks of August were the knee-jerk responses of a man desperately in need of results or the appropriate, well-planned measures of an accomplished professional seems to be a matter of personal interpretation, not to say prejudice. In either case, there remains something both wonderfully heroic and perhaps sadly anachronistic in the image of the onetime G-man standing resolutely in Kingsbury Run, ax handle in hand, overseeing his men on their methodical march of destruction through the shantytowns.

Somewhere in the city there was still an unknown phantom. Perhaps he coldly surveyed all the attention he was getting from the police and the press. Perhaps he reveled in it; perhaps he was simply indifferent. But August marked a turning point for him as well. The investigation would continue for years, but history says that in that month he stopped. But did he? History also maintains that Eliot Ness never caught or even identified him. But did he?

NOTES

All three Cleveland dailies reported and commented on Ness's shantytown raid as part of the ongoing newspaper coverage of the torso killings that began with the discovery of victims no. 11 and no. 12 on August 16, 1938, and continued until the end of the month.

Although Merylo discusses his participation in the systematic search of the squalid inner city in the Otwell manuscript, he has little to say about the shantytown raid. Apparently, he was not involved in the events of August 18.

MURDER, MUTILATION, AND MAYHEM

On December 29, 1938, a Cleveland postal inspector called Detectives Merylo and Zalewski to his office and handed them a letter, addressed to Cleveland chief of police George Matowitz and dated December 23, 1938, that had been found in the dead letter office.

Chief of Police Matowitz,
You can rest easy now, as I have come out to sunny California for the winter. I felt bad operating on those people, but science must advance. I shall astond [sic] the medical profession, a man with only a D.C.

What did their lives mean in comparison to hundreds of sick and disease-twisted bodies? Just laboratory guinea pigs found on any public street. No one missed them when I failed. My last case was successful. I know now the feeling of Pasteur, Thoreau and other pioneers.

Right now I have a volunteer who will absolutely prove my theory. They call me mad and a butcherer [sic], but the truth will out.

I have failed but once here. The body has not been found and never will be, but the head, minus the features is buried on Century Boulevard, between Western and Crenshaw. I feel it my duty to dispose of the bodies as I do. It is God's will not to let them suffer.

X

At this point, Cleveland police had been deluged with about eighteen hundred pieces of correspondence dealing with the mysterious killer. A copy of this letter was dispatched to Los Angeles police, and officers in California launched a futile search of the area the writer specified.

Initially, an ecstatic Peter Merylo told the local press on January 7, 1939, he felt the letter was genuine and one of the best solid leads authorities had in the case, but within a year he dismissed it as the ravings of a crank. By mid-1942 California investigators tentatively identified a quack doctor, one Charles August DiVere, as the probable author of the letter, but they could not establish any link between him and the Cleveland butcheries.

† † †

In December 1938, Cleveland police responded to reports that human bones had been found in a clogged sewer pipe on McBride Avenue and in a basement on Addison Road. The first set, discovered by a couple of plumbers, was quickly identified as sheep bones, and the second group turned out to be a collection of chicken bones and spare ribs.

In that same month, Earl Carl Harris, a black man arrested in Highland Park, Michigan, for multiple murder, attracted Merylo's attention—not as a viable suspect in the torso murders but because of his alleged ties to voodooism. The specter of voodoo had hovered over the investigation into the Cleveland killings virtually since the beginning because of Edward Andrassy's supposed links with a shadowy cult operating in the East 49th area. "It has long been suggested to us," Merylo wrote in his report of December 15, "that Voodooism may have been responsible for these killings. However, we were never able to learn its operation or its rules or bylaws due to the fact that any person we may approach to question in connection therein were [sic] apparently too frightened to reveal all the data that we endeavored to learn from them." Merylo hoped Highland Park police could press Harris for details about voodoo practices and asked his superiors to make the formal request.

Although the pace of the investigation slackened in 1939 and early 1940, Merylo and Zalewski continued their hunt for the killer. In February they responded to a cleaning woman's hysterical story about one Dr. Antonio Longoria and a bloody bed with electrical wires attached, only to find a serious but unorthodox scientist doing cancer research. In April they checked out a dump at East 72nd and Kingsbury Run when the owner, Al Goodman, found a human right foot with one toe burned away—apparently cut from the leg with a saw about three inches above the ankle—on his property. In June they were thirty miles south of Cleveland in Akron questioning a pair of Hudson doctors who allegedly performed abortions. In August the investigation reached across the Atlantic; Merylo requested information from the police of Leeds, England, about a woman's torso found there in early June. In October they were back on the outskirts of New Castle, Pennsylvania, looking into the discovery of a decapitated, decomposed male corpse. In March 1940 the pair pursued a man who supposedly had driven a needle into a woman's breast and sucked her blood.

On May 3, 1940, the Kingsbury Run murders again hit the front pages of Cleveland's newspapers. A string of old boxcars was waiting for the scrap heap at a Pittsburgh & Lake Erie railroad yard in Stowe Township, Pennsylvania, a suburb near Pittsburgh. The derelict cars had stood abandoned for a year in Youngstown, Ohio, before being moved first to Struthers, Ohio, on April 19, and then finally to Stowe Township two days later. Yardmen were apparently running a random check before the cars were demolished when one of them opened a car and found the dismembered corpse of a man—the head missing, the body parts wrapped separately in burlap. In another car, searchers found a similarly dismembered, similarly wrapped body—head also missing. In a third car lay the decapitated, decomposed body of a third man—intact except for the head—the word "NAZI" with an inverted "Z" cut deeply into the chest. The victims had been using newspapers as mattresses, and the killer apparently tried to burn the bodies by setting the papers on fire. According to Dr. P. R. Heimbold, a coroner's physician in Pittsburgh, the bodies had been cut "by an expert who had some knowledge of anatomy or was a butcher." All three were naked, short, and stocky, between thirty and forty years old, and had been dead for about two months, indicating they were probably killed in Youngstown. None of the missing heads were ever found. Police turned up a bloody footprint on one of the papers, a blood-encrusted marijuana cigarette, between fifty and seventy-five dark hairs probably belonging to the victims, and a single blond hair, possibly the murderer's. Official checks of missing person reports in Struthers and Youngstown turned up nothing. One of the victims was identified through his fingerprints, however, as James Nicholson, a twenty-nine-year-old drifter with a record of homosexual activity, trespassing, and burglary.

The chilling, eerie echoes of the Cleveland killings—the naked, burlap-wrapped bodies, the missing heads, the skillful dismemberment, the desolate crime scenes flanked by railroad tracks and hobo jungles—were sufficiently strong to take Merylo, Zalewski, Ness's assistant Robert Chamberlin, David Cowles, and Lloyd Trunk (the latter two of the Scientific Investigation Bureau) to Youngstown and Pittsburgh. Cowles was cautiously inclined to link the mutilated trio to the Cleveland Butcher, and he took samples of the spinal columns to compare the cut marks with the Cleveland victims. Merylo, too impatient to wait for test results, told Pittsburgh reporters he had no doubts that a single perpetrator bore responsibility for all the Cleveland, New Castle, and Youngstown killings. He now put the body count at twenty-three.

By carrying all these reports of murder and dismemberment from the entire Ohio-Pennsylvania-New York area, Cleveland newspapers effectively transformed the city's elusive killer into a mysterious plague, inexorably and silently spreading out in all directions. Anxious and murder-weary Clevelanders scanned the daily papers for any familiar, telltale sign that the Butcher, who had not killed in the city since August 1938, had returned: an abandoned pile of clothing in a deserted field, a mysterious automobile cruising the Flats, any unexplained disappearance, any unusual nighttime activity in the city's industrial neighborhoods.

Mutilated bodies continued to accumulate outside the city for years. In late 1939 the headless corpse of Wallace Lloyd Brown, a recent parolee, had been found in a dump along the Monongahela River. On May 31, 1941, a couple of amputated male legs floated down the Ohio River near Pittsburgh, and on June 21, 1942, the decapitated body of a man ultimately identified as Ernest Alonzo was hauled out of the Monongahela. In mid-1945 two headless male bodies in burlap bags turned up in the Hudson River near New York City, and in October of the same year the headless, mutilated body of Lydia Thompson was found in a swamp near Pontiac, Michigan.

For Cleveland police, any discovery of a dismembered body part beyond city borders seriously complicated an already difficult investigation. Were these murders all the work of one man? Was that man Cleveland's notorious Butcher? At one extreme stood the deeply frustrated and cautious Sergeant James Hogan, always reluctant to credit the Butcher with another victim; at the other end of the scale was Peter Merylo, willing to add any newly found body part or severed bone to the killer's total.

Merylo had always accepted the Pennsylvania killings as the work of the Cleveland Butcher; in July 1937 he had spent his two-week vacation prowling the dismal New Castle swamp in the company of Constable Walter Bannon, a local man in his fifties whose firsthand knowledge of the city's

decapitation killings stretched back to the first case in 1921. When he returned to Cleveland, Merylo told Chief Matowitz he was more convinced
than ever that the killer rode the rails and performed his butcheries in
empty boxcars.

Since the day Matowitz had assigned him to the torso killings in September 1936, Merylo had unsuccessfully lobbied his chief to allow him to
go undercover disguised as a bum for an extended period. Finally, in June
1940, Matowitz granted the long-standing request, and Merylo prepared
to join society's outcasts and ride the rails between northeastern Ohio and
western Pennsylvania in search of the Butcher. His partner, Martin Zalewski,
declined such unorthodox and potentially unpleasant duty—as did every
other police officer Merylo approached—invariably citing either an unwillingness to upset their wives or a reluctance to get "tangled up with a lot of
perverts and screwballs" as the reason. Finally, Merylo recruited Patrolman
Frank Vorell to join him on his railway odyssey. Since Youngstown would

Detective Peter Merylo, preparing to go underground, with an unidentified transient. Courtesy of Marjorie Merylo Dentz.

serve as the hub of their activity, in mid-July Merylo alerted Youngstown police chief Turnbull about what he and Vorell would be doing and emphasized that no one was to know they were operating in the area.

At 6:00 A.M. on July 14, the now unshaven and shaggy-haired pair dressed in dirty, ragged clothes and quietly disappeared into the hobo jungles and railroad yards of Youngstown, Ohio. The next morning at 7:30, they hopped a freight on its way to New Castle. Running alongside train No. 96 as it slowed for a bridge, Merylo and Vorell swung themselves up on the rungs of the ladder at the side of a huge oil tanker and moved cautiously out on the catwalk near the top of the car. Their grips tightened on the handrail as the fast freight picked up speed and thundered over the twenty miles of uneven track at seventy miles per hour. Twenty minutes later, as the train slowed down on the outskirts of New Castle's notorious Murder Swamp, the pair dropped from the car and began hunting for the city's hobo jungles. At about 8:00 P.M., they boarded No. 97 back to Youngstown, jumping off the train with three other riders in the railroad yards outside the city.

Merylo understood the desperate men on society's fringes very well. Clannish, private, and deeply suspicious of strangers, they would not easily share their experiences with an outsider; Merylo knew he would have to live, travel, sleep, and eat with them for weeks to gain their trust. For a man as neat and clean in his personal habits as Peter Merylo, this was rough duty. At times he simply could not bring himself to eat the disgusting daily fare served up around the campfire, and he quietly took out a room in an inconspicuous Youngstown boardinghouse where he could at least shower on a regular basis.

From July 14 until August 5 Peter Merylo and Frank Vorell rode the freights across eastern Ohio and western Pennsylvania seeking out small pockets of hoboes and jobless men; they moved through a depressing and dangerous twilight world of tramps, marijuana pushers, prostitutes, and railroad cops in a quest for viable leads. At one point, a Republic Steel Corporation policeman arrested Merylo for trespassing when he inadvertently blundered on to a private railroad siding belonging to the company. Merylo remembered the bloody marijuana cigarette butt police found in one of the boxcars outside Stowe Township, Pennsylvania, and wondered if the local Youngstown pushers might lead to the Butcher. By posing as a heavy user on the prowl for a "reefer," Merylo managed to make a couple of contacts among area pushers, but nothing useful materialized other than a couple of drug busts. On August 5, Chief Matowitz got word to the pair through

A candid photograph of Merylo riding the rails somewhere between Cleveland and New Castle, Pennsylvania. Courtesy of Marjorie Merylo Dentz.

Youngstown police that Frank Vorell's father was seriously ill and called them back to Cleveland.

As Merylo and Vorell searched for clues in the railroad yards and hobo jungles of Ohio and Pennsylvania, other elements of the Cleveland police force quietly began to return to other duties. When Merylo returned to Cleveland, he found that Martin Zalewski—nearing the end of his stint on the force—had been pulled from the torso murders and placed on less demanding duty. Now lacking a steady partner, Merylo worked with whoever his superiors assigned to him until the official investigation ended.

The search for the killer ground steadily on through 1941 and 1942, though new leads were few and unpromising. Other officers in the department passed on to Merylo their official reports of virtually every sex offender and deviant they picked up. In February 1941, he checked on a man in Akron who gave away women's clothes and ran a rooming house—from which it was rumored women suddenly disappeared—only to be confronted by sixty-nine-year-old, feeble-minded Henry Potter, who greeted him at the front door in a boxer's stance.

Tip letters continued to pour in. But for every one that offered solid information, there were a legion of useless but well-meaning bits of correspondence describing chance encounters, some of them years old, with suspicious characters all over the Northeast. Psychics offered advice based on their visions; cranks described their dreams of murder and dismemberment. Some letters were simply crazy, such as one from "B. L." in January 1942 that proclaimed: "I have long suspected Brandt, president of the Brandt Co, located at 427 Bolivar as the Torso murderer for reasons so ridiculous when I see them on paper that I won't mention them here." One deranged woman ended her incoherent diatribe with: "Cleveland police is always drunk lazy dizzy good for nothing whey does the got wish such woe on me St. Lukes Hospital do the killing grief—shaken sister."

Since sensational stories about the Cleveland Butcher and his activities graced the pages of the nation's true crime magazines, Merylo and his fellow officers endured a never-ending flood of letters from would-be detectives all over the country looking for pen pals in the Cleveland Police Department. Robert Hull from Jackson, Michigan, produced such a flow of what Merylo described as "unbelievable and fantastic stories pertaining to our so-called Torso Murders" that he decided the writer was "suffering from a mental disorder" and asked his superiors to alert the local chief of police. "We wish to advise the Michigan Police," he wrote in his reports, "that we have received a seven page letter and a cheap writing tablet full of sketches and retracing of various human heads, drawings and other fantastic literature which does not make any sense." Closer to home, Pete Diehl, a resident of the Sandusky Soldiers and Sailors Home, kept up a similar epistolary stream to Merylo for at least three years. In one letter, dated February 13, 1939, Diehl voiced his suspicions about another resident, a man he referred to simply as "our Doc." With so many people crying wolf so loudly and so frequently, it was perhaps inevitable that a potentially valuable piece of information would slip by unnoticed in an undermanned, overworked police department. A doctor at the Sandusky home had, indeed, already attracted the attention of David Cowles and Eliot Ness.

† † †

In 1942, Merylo began pursuing what would turn out to be his last reasonably solid lead in the case. The brief, crudely lettered note arrived in late January.

A killer, at large
Albany N.Y.
Saturday Jan 24
Sir
Is their any reward for the so called mad butcher of Kingsbury Run if so rit at once
Norman Carter
Railroad YMCA
607 Broadway
Albany New York

Something about the formation of the letters—especially the "A"—attracted Merylo's attention; they bore a strong resemblance to the word "NAZI," with its inverted Z, carved into the chest of one of the three Stowe Township victims. He managed to trace a black man named Norman W. Carter—born in Corning, New York, on June 16, 1905—to the Albany terminal of the Railway Mail Service where he once worked as a laborer, but there the trail became hopelessly tangled. Carter's former employer vouched for his dependability, and none of the various home addresses Merylo unearthed panned out. Either someone else was using Carter's name or Merylo was trailing the wrong Norman Carter.

For Merylo the on-again, off-again support of his superiors became a draining frustration. He argued that he could not make progress on the torso murders when he was being constantly pulled from the case and given other duties. "I advised him [his commanding officer] that I cannot meet the citizens and make them believe that I was going to clean up this crime, when the true fact is that I never had time to even make a thorough investigation," he complained in his memoirs. The years of intense work were also taking their toll. He constantly revisited old reports, searching for a clue that had previously eluded him. He slept poorly. He dreamed about the case. At times an idea would jolt him from his fitful slumber, and he would go out into the darkness alone to pursue a new lead. Merylo's nephew Allen P. Pinell, a former social worker and therapist with the Veterans Administration, remembers his uncle as moody and restless, sometimes preoccupied or ill at ease at family gatherings. "There was a dark side to Uncle Pete," he reflects.

The time Merylo could devote to the case dwindled steadily as higher-ups assigned him to other duties more and more frequently because of manpower shortages. Finally, Chief Matowitz took him off the case entirely on October 1, 1942. No bodies had turned up in Cleveland since August 1938, he explained, and there were newer cases far more pressing. And, after all, he reasoned, the victims were just bums.

On March 15, 1943, Merylo turned in his final report on the Kingsbury Run murders to his immediate superior, Lieutenant Harvey Weitzel—a detailed eleven-page summation of his work on the case. He listed all the victims found in the northern Ohio-western Pennsylvania area, traced the paths his investigations had taken, outlined procedures for others, should the hunt continue, and discussed some of his major suspects. Toward the end of this document, Merylo pointed proudly to his and Martin Zalewski's arrest record while working the case—an impressive tally of 350 felony and 665 misdemeanor arrests, not counting juvenile offenders, all but 22 convicted. Merylo closed his report by thanking all those who had assisted him over the seven-year span of the investigation and vowing to continue. "I will never give up my work on these Torso Murders, as long as the killer is still at large, he will be arrested," he wrote. "[The] Torso Murders Investigation had developed into a habit with me, I will continue on this investigation, regardless what my other assignments may be, I will continue to work on my day off and my vacations as I did in the past."

NOTES

Copies of the tip letter from Los Angeles are in Peter Merylo's files.

The leads checked from January 1939 until May 1940 are recorded in Merylo's official reports from that period.

Cleveland and Pittsburgh papers covered the discovery of the three Stowe Township victims on May 3, 1940. Merylo deals extensively with this aspect of the case in his reports, his memoirs, and the Otwell manuscript.

Merylo provides extremely detailed narratives of his and Patrolman Frank Vorell's underground activities from mid-July to early August 1940 in his official reports, his memoirs, and the Otwell manuscript. His account of how Patrolman Vorell ultimately became his partner is from the Otwell manuscript. Merylo chronicles the steps in his investigation after returning to Cleveland in his official reports, August 1940–March 1943.

All the tip letters specifically referred to in the text are from Merylo's files. Though some of Robert Hull's letters to Merylo are among his papers, the cheap writing tablet of drawings to which Merylo refers has not survived. Pete Diehl's letter alerting Merylo to "our Doc" is among his papers. Merylo's files also contain the note from Norman Carter, various pieces of official correspondence with authorities in Albany, New York, and his reports on the hunt for Carter to his superiors in the Cleveland Police Department.

Merylo's daughter Marjorie Merylo Dentz and his nephew Allen P. Pinell provided the descriptions of the impact the investigation was having on him in formal interviews and conversations.

July 22, 1950
AN ECHO FROM THE PAST

Workmen called him the sunbather. He was curiously, even comically out of place in the sprawl of industrial wasteland and run-down housing close to East 22nd and the lakeshore, an area frequented by hoboes and transients. Yet the heavy, fiftyish-looking man with thinning gray hair came to Norris Brothers Company, movers, at 2138 Davenport Avenue every day for six weeks and sunbathed for about twenty minutes on a year-and-a-half-old pile of steel girders at the west end of the company's property. Then, one day, he stopped coming—just about the time some Norris employees began to notice sickening odors, apparently carried by the shifting winds, while they were cleaning up the yards near some hoisting machinery and the sunbather's heap of girders.

On that warm July 22 afternoon, Mike Jaratz and John Cooper, residents of the Wayfarer's Lodge on Lakeside, were walking through the neighborhood close to Davenport Avenue when they suddenly came upon a partly decomposed human leg in a field. When the police arrived, they immediately checked the area around the huge mound of steel where workmen had first detected foul odors two weeks before and discovered the dismembered torso of a white male, both arms, and one leg, all in an advanced state of decomposition, on the ground beneath the pile. A dog, they surmised, must have dragged the other limb into the field where Jaratz and Cooper found it.

It had been a dozen years since the torso murders stopped; the chilling echoes of Kingsbury Run, however, were not lost on either Detective Captain David E. Kerr, head of homicide (he had been on the force a little over a year when the murders started), or Detective Lieutenant James Dodge: a naked, dismembered corpse, a head missing, no sign of blood on the scene, sports pages from a May 1949 issue of the *Cleveland News*

Norris Brothers at 2138 Davenport Avenue, where Robert Robertson's dismembered body was found in July 1950. *Cleveland Press* Archives, Cleveland State University.

under the body, and abandoned bits of clothing nearby—though it was not clear any of it belonged to the dead man. This time, however, there was something new: two pages from a phone book covering the letter K.

Based on the missing head and the naked state of the corpse, Dr. Gerber, still Cuyahoga County's coroner, declared the death a homicide while on the scene; the man had been dead, he reasoned, for between six and eight weeks (nowhere near as long as the newspaper pages found underneath would suggest but close to the time the mysterious sunbather began his ritualistic appearances). Back at the morgue, Gerber determined that the victim was a shade under six feet tall and that the right arm had been severed from the torso, though the rest of the pieces had deteriorated too much to be certain. The next day he confirmed that the dismemberment had been carried out with a sharp instrument; he later put the man's age close to forty and estimated he weighed about 160 pounds. The city papers were quick to draw parallels with the Kingsbury Run slayings—similarities that Gerber admitted, though he insisted there was no proof that Cleveland's notorious Butcher had dispatched this latest victim.

On July 26, Gerber returned to the discovery site, along with some entomologists, to gather soil and bug samples. While they combed the area, the missing head turned up wedged in a pile of lumber about twenty feet away from the heap of steel girders where the rest of the body had been found on July 22. The coroner's preliminary examination disclosed no injury to the skull, four missing teeth (though those remaining were in reasonably good shape), evidence of an overbite that could possibly result in a protruding upper lip, small ears, and brownish hair—newly cut—streaked with gray. After soaking the head in trisodium phosphate for three days, Gerber was able to add a mole or skin tumor close to the middle of the forehead and evidence of an old nose injury to the description.

From late July through early August, city papers ran artists' renderings of the victim based on these details and a photograph of Gerber's reconstruction of the man's face. "Torso Victim: Know Him?" asked a *Press* headline on August 8. Three hundred letters from as far away as Alabama, New Hampshire, and North Carolina—each containing a description or photograph of a missing loved one—poured into Cleveland.

The police finally identified the dead man in late August through old-fashioned drudgery. Detectives John Sullivan and Robert Schottke were making a routine check at the Wayfarer's Lodge on July 26 when they learned that someone had phoned to ask if Robert Robertson was still a resident. Robertson had checked into the facility in February 1949 but had disappeared on June 12, 1950—exactly when Gerber estimated the victim had been killed. A search through between three and four thousand fingerprints on file turned up a Robert Robertson who had been jailed in the Warrensville Workhouse for intoxication a few days in December 1949. Meanwhile, Gerber had finally obtained some usable prints from the partly decomposed hands of the victim, and, on August 28, Sergeant Robert Blaha matched the two sets of fingerprints.

In one sense, Robert Robertson fit the Kingsbury Run victim profile perfectly: a forty-four-year-old, unemployed, single male originally from Boynton, Pennsylvania, who had chalked up a dozen arrests for intoxication since 1949. He had suffered a stroke in 1943 that left him with a paralyzed right arm and a speech defect. His downward-spiraling work history in Cleveland included stints at GM's Fisher Body Division, Park Drop Forge Company, a Shaw Avenue cafe, a Kresge five-and-ten store, and the old Court House cafe on Lakeside near Ontario Avenue. A onetime resident of a rooming house on East 124th, Robertson had been evicted two years before by his landlady, Betty Austin, because of his heavy drinking.

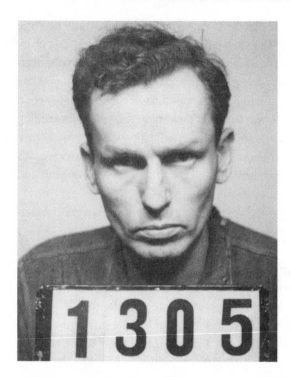

Robert Robertson fit the down-and-out profile of the Butcher's targets perfectly. Robertson may have been the Butcher's final Cleveland victim. *Cleveland Press* Archives, Cleveland State University.

Unlike the majority of the torso victims, however, Robertson had been identified and had relatives in Cleveland who would presumably miss him. His contacts with his brother and three sisters, however, turned out to be few and fleeting; one had not seen him since the death of their mother two years before, and none had seen him since Easter. The police rounded up Robertson's siblings and took them to the morgue, where they identified their brother's gruesome remains but, curiously, refused to sign an official affidavit verifying the body as his.

The investigation into Robert Robertson's murder quickly became a frustrating echo from the mid-1930s: even with a name to work with, the trail that took police through a blighted landscape of broken neighborhoods peopled with derelicts simply petered out. As with Edward Andrassy, Flo Polillo, and Rose Wallace, authorities could follow Robertson's movements only up to the point just before he met his killer; then the tips and leads stopped, and Robert Robertson vanished.

If the police thought there was any connection to the Kingsbury murders, that assumption is not reflected in the surviving file on the Robertson case. Authorities treated his death as an isolated crime. The killing captured the attention of city newspapers for over a month, and, unlike the police, they assumed there must be a link to the torso butcheries of a dozen years before. (Even today photographs and clippings relevant to Robertson's murder are filed with the Kingsbury Run material at the Cleveland Public Library and in the *Press* archives at Cleveland State University.) The heavy contemporary coverage treated readers to a 1943 photograph of the victim, an outline of his body indicating its distinctive features, and many drawings of his head. By September, however, Robertson had slipped from both the pages of Cleveland dailies and the minds of the city's residents. Shortly thereafter, the police investigation ended. History now recognizes two endings to the Kingsbury Run murders—one in August 1938, the other in July 1950.

NOTES

Cleveland's three daily papers devoted an enormous amount of space to the Robertson killing, July 23–August 30, 1950.

The steps in the investigation are contained in the official file on Robert Robertson's murder at the Cleveland Police Department.

Portrait of a Killer

With the forensic techniques available today, could Ness and the police have caught the Butcher? This fair but difficult question is one that I am invariably asked whenever and wherever I speak on the Kingsbury Run murders. Indeed, the almost total lack of hard evidence that could implicate any suspect remains one of the most puzzling, even remarkable, aspects of the case. If such forensic specialists as A. J. Pearce, Sam Gerber, and David Cowles had enjoyed the benefits of modern crime-solving techniques, their chances of catching their elusive quarry certainly would have improved greatly. But the investigators, everyone from the police to the scientific experts, were hobbled as much by their 1930s crime-solving techniques, the restrictions under which the police department operated, and their preconceptions about the killer as they were by their relatively primitive forensic science.

Chief Matowitz put Merylo and Zalewski on the case full-time in name only, and the support they received from higher-ups was hardly exemplary. The most casual glance at Peter Merylo's reports shows that his superiors constantly assigned him and his partner to other duties, especially when the heat from press coverage of the killings abated. Even when the murders were headline news, Merylo often had to spend his mornings in court attending to other cases before he could follow up on torso tips. If he wanted to leave the county to pursue a lead, standard procedures forced him to ask and wait for permission—sometimes for days—to do so. During the investigation he begged his superiors for an official car, arguing that he had to rely on his own.

Modern police officers would be horrified at the casual manner in which their predecessors conducted a crime scene investigation. In those days, authorities never made any attempt to cordon off the area; police and curious onlookers wandered at will, destroying potential evidence beneath their feet. Walter Piszczek, then sixteen, and his older brother watched as police combed the ground in the evening twilight on Orange Avenue where the second set of Flo Polillo's remains was found in February 1936. Today, he marvels that any clues survived such a stampede.

For much of the investigation, the police had no clues about the murderer they were hunting. The circumstances surrounding the death and disposal of the Lady of the Lake in late 1934 proved so baffling that, as far as one can tell from newspaper accounts, no one speculated on the nature of her killer. A year later, authorities saw the double murder of Edward Andrassy and his never-identified companion as simple, though starkly brutal, crimes of passion, and given Andrassy's reported exploits with women both single and married, it did seem logical to assume that some bizarre love-betrayal-revenge scenario lurked behind the killings. But his alleged ties to and brushes with the underworld also pointed to gangland payback, so the police searched for the murderer among the ranks of outraged husbands or boyfriends and low-level hoods. Four months later, they stalked Flo Polillo's killer through her ugly twilight world of pimps, prostitutes, bootleggers, drug pushers, and drunks. In both cases, authorities operated on the long-held assumption that murder victims were dispatched by people they knew for such basic motives as greed or revenge.

All that changed in the summer of 1936, when three headless corpses turned up in as many months. The entire city began to realize that what had previously been regarded as isolated acts of butchery were, in fact, linked. From then until the investigation ended, two widely contrasting profiles of the Butcher dominated the hunt. The first image came from the local media, which painted him in vocabulary drawn from pulp fiction and Hollywood horror movies: monster, fiend, maniac, insane butcher. The second image had begun to crystallize out of the accumulated observations and speculations in Reuben Straus's autopsy protocols and achieved its final form during Coroner A. J. Pearce's groundbreaking "torso clinic" of September 1936. In what must be regarded as one of law enforcement's first attempts at modern profiling, police, pathologists, mental health professionals, and medical men came together and fashioned a remarkably detailed portrait of the killer: a large, powerful man who lived near Kingsbury Run, possessed considerable anatomical knowledge, may not have been previously acquainted with his victims, and, though probably insane, functioned well enough to hold a job and appear outwardly normal.

The first and most lurid of these images captured the public imagination, and all three papers kept city residents abreast of all the colorful and seriously deranged unfortunates snared by the police for questioning. It would be unfair to characterize isolated aspects of the investigation based solely on the newspaper coverage, but in spite of the conclusions reached by the participants at Pearce's clinic, the police did seem to show continued interest in such wild characters even though most of them hardly fit the conference's profile of the Butcher. According to one story, for example, Petey Scalzone—a violently sadistic mob enforcer dubbed the Turkey Man—was dragged in by the police for questioning a total of eighty-eight times. As late as February 1939, police hauled in a twenty-nine-year-old tramp who lived in a wooded area on the west side simply because he carried a small hatchet in a burlap bag.

After Pearce's torso clinic, the most clearheaded, thoughtful, and detailed speculations about the killer came from Sam Gerber. The official series of twelve victims had already run half its course when he was elected coroner in the fall of 1936. He familiarized himself with all the case records from Pearce's tenure, consulted with other experts at the Western Reserve Medical School and the city's Department of Public Health and Welfare, and even solicited aid from a national conference of coroners meeting in Cleveland in the fall of 1937.

"He may have been a doctor or medical student sometime in the past," Gerber wrote, "butcher, osteopath, chiropractor, orderly, nurse or hunter in order to be able to accomplish the dissection with such perfect finesse." The coroner further speculated that the Butcher was probably right-handed and dismembered his victims with a large, heavy butcher knife. He may have once belonged to what Gerber termed "the upper strata of life" but had fallen to the lower-class level of his victims through unknown and unfortunate circumstances.

He is a person of more than average intelligence, with definite professional knowledge of anatomy but not necessarily a man of surgery. He is large and strong. He probably lives in the section bounding Kingsbury Run where he comes and goes without attracting attention. In all probability he belongs to a higher social stratum than his victims, but can mingle with vagrants without arousing their suspicion. His murders are committed mostly in a laboratory near the Run. He is a pervert who sometimes drugs his victims and may lead a normal life when not absorbed with his sadistic passion.

Gerber went on to break murderers down into three general categories—truly insane (including schizophrenics), borderline insane, and feeble-minded—and suggested that the Butcher may have belonged to either of the first two groups. Gerber was not a psychiatrist and had little on which to base his speculations, so his categories remain necessarily vague.

Because the police were able to positively identify only two—three if Rose Wallace is included—of Cleveland's officially recognized twelve victims, the coroner assumed that "these victims were all of the lower stratum of life with little or no family ties, possibly vagrants, prostitutes, perverts, and the like, living in or frequenting the vicinity of Kingsbury Run." He further concluded: "To associate with such a group, without arousing suspicion, the murderer must be of the same physical make-up, that is, a white person (most likely male), probably a known frequenter of the same regions, well-developed and strong enough to do the heavy work involved in his type of murder and disposal of the victims, and about the same age groups (thirty to forty years)." From arranging the murders in the order they were probably committed and adding in the dates bodies were discovered, Gerber speculated that the murderer ceased his activities if a victim was found soon after disposal but kept on killing if his handiwork lay undiscovered.

Peter Merylo's theories about the killer were considerably less technical and far more blunt. "I am of the opinion," he wrote in his unpublished memoirs, "that the murderer is a sex degenerate suffering from necrophilia, aphrodisia, or erotomania, who may have worked in the pathology department of some hospital, morgue or some college where he had an opportunity to handle a great number of bodies, or may have been employed in some undertaking establishment, and that he had a mania for headless and nude bodies." He further reasoned "that the murderer procured his [sexual] gratification while watching the blood flow after cutting the jugular vein of his victim." In one of his most fascinating speculations, he wondered if "this may be a case of infatuation for statues, the kind with the head and limbs broken off." He cited the case of Carl Tansler Van Cosel, a hospital worker living in Key West, Florida, who had become so obsessed with a sculpture he had seen in Rome that he stole a woman's corpse from her tomb and slept with it for seven years simply because she reminded him of that statue.

Some of Merylo's judgments were as astute as those of any medical expert who worked on the murders. In late 1938, he carried on a brief correspondence about the case with Howard G. Smith of Samson, Alabama, who had written him a very long, thoughtful letter about the killer. On October 7, 1938, Merylo replied:

> In our investigation during the past two years, we have checked on all the phases mentioned in your letter. Also have gone back into History in an effort to locate a parallel to the Torso Murders being committed in this area but were unable to locate any similar type of crime. In your letter you mention Jack the Ripper in London, but this killer only committed his crimes upon one sex, while the Torso Murderer has changed from one sex to the other, apparently without discrimination. Therefore we are of the opinion that we have to deal with a person whose mental processes are so far unknown to scientists.

† † †

Bizarre theories about the killer came from everywhere. Edwin J. Creel, a self-described criminologist from Washington, D.C., wondered if all the victims might have belonged to a suicide club headed by some thrill-seeking sadist. A mysterious Susan V. Gill from Brighton, Illinois, wrote to Cleveland police insisting that they would find the killer if they investigated a certain "Dr. Quinzer" who had organized a "society of Mafia and trained its members in terrible surgery." Even the police—including Merylo himself—were not immune to such inventive flights of fancy. Merylo, for example, once speculated that the red corpuscles in the killer's blood were being destroyed because of trypanosoma (a flagellate infusorian) infection and that he "might possibly seek to replenish his blood supply along vampire lines."

Other general observations about the killer may be relevant. He butchered all his female victims in the extreme, cutting the arms and legs into several pieces and sometimes bisecting the torsos themselves—Rose Wallace and no. 11 being exceptions. He tended to leave his male prey intact, however, except for decapitation and emasculation: Edward Andrassy, as well as victims no. 2, no. 4, and no. 5. But does this indicate a pathology—a virulent hatred of women, for example—or did he simply tend to dispose of his male victims in locations close to his base of operation? It would have been simpler to transport remains over a great distance if the body were cut into manageable pieces. Such considerations invariably lead to the question of whether he owned or had access to an automobile—hardly a foregone conclusion at the height of the Depression. If the Butcher did own a car, that would support Coroner Gerber's contention that he came from the upper levels of society. In the early summer of 1936, he killed victims no. 4 and no. 5—both males and intact except for the heads—outside on the spots where the bodies were found; he murdered all the others in an unknown location and discarded the bodies or the pieces somewhere else. In the early days of his murderous activity, he seemed concerned with bizarre displays of his handiwork: he buried the heads of Andrassy and no. 2 close to their bodies, carefully rolled up the head of no. 4 in his pants and placed the bundle under a bush, packed the newspaper-wrapped parts of Flo Polillo's body in two produce baskets and left them in the snow behind Hart Manufacturing. But in the later phases of the series, he seemed to lose interest, casually dumping remains in the Cuyahoga River, in other waterways, or, in the case of Rose Wallace, under a bridge. Both the sheer level of his violence and the degree of mutilation he inflicted tended to accelerate; he cut out the heart and emptied the abdominal cavity of no. 9 and left deep gashes in the thighs of no. 10. He also placed some of the remains in burlap bags before disposing of them. But again, is there some pathological explanation for this or are the reasons purely practical? Until paranoia ultimately gripped the city, who would look twice at someone in Kingsbury Run or the Flats carrying a burlap produce bag over his shoulder?

Today it is clear that the Kingsbury Run Butcher was a serial killer—arguably one of the first documented appearances of the breed—who kept Cleveland on edge during his three-to four-year rampage. In the 1930s, no one in law enforcement knew what a serial killer was. They did not understand that particular pathology, nor did they even know the term. It would be another forty years before Robert Ressler of the FBI's Behavioral Science Unit in Quantico, Virginia, created that label to describe a particular kind of murderous activity. The purpose of profiling is to simplify an investigation by focusing specifically on a particular type of individual associated with a particular sort of crime. In the absence of such techniques, the hunt for the Kingsbury Run Butcher was rendered almost impossible from the start. Law enforcement personnel simply had no tools for narrowing the search. As the investigation proceeded, in fact, the range of suspects broadened; every lunatic and deviant, every person acting strangely, was fair game.

The restricted resources of an undermanned police department were no match for the task.

The FBI's serial killer profile emerged slowly from detailed analyses of countless crime scenes and extensive interviews with as many jailed perpetrators as Ressler and his associates could gain access to. In 1988, during a well-publicized TV demonstration of how their methods worked, Agent John Douglas attempted to profile and then identify Jack the Ripper through crime scenes analyses, detailed consideration of the medical reports, and a careful survey of all the identified potential suspects.

The typical serial killer is a white male between the ages of twenty-five and thirty-five who violently murders either total strangers or people with whom he is only minimally acquainted, driven by some terrible inner rage or lust. Though a long period, even years, may pass between one killing and the next, a serial killer will continue in his murderous ways until he is stopped by incarceration or death. In his memoirs Peter Merylo intuitively insisted, "I believe that this man would not stop the killing as long as he is at large, and alive." Serial killers fall into two broad categories—either "disorganized" or "organized." Generally, those in the former group are poorly educated, socially inept, slovenly, unskilled or jobless loners of slight stature and below average intelligence who live close to their crime scenes and select their victims from purely chance meetings. An organized killer, on the other hand, is usually well-groomed, powerfully built, and of above average intelligence. Outwardly, he is successful and seems normal. He is charming socially, holds a good job, and may be married with a family. He picks his victims with greater care than his disorganized counterpart, often selecting people he can impress or dominate. (In a unique deviation from the general serial killer profile, the Kingsbury Run Butcher crossed both racial and gender lines when selecting his victims.) He will play cat-and-mouse games with the authorities, following the progress of the official investigation in the media and taunting police with their inability to apprehend him. The conclusions arrived at during Pearce's torso clinic and Sam Gerber's detailed descriptions clearly point to an organized killer; indeed, both sets of speculations come remarkably close to the official FBI portrait.

With a serial killer, murder is preceded by what is termed a "pre-crime stressor"—a series of events that may include financial reverses, loss of job, or a marital breakup. This trigger may be an overwhelming reflection of a dimly remembered or totally forgotten matrix of disturbing childhood situations and their attendant emotions that jolt the perpetrator over the edge. He may be aware of his rage or anger but not entirely sure of its exact causes.

The questions of "how" and "where" are as perplexing as the question of "who." The first issue did not receive much serious, detailed attention in city newspapers; rather, the press was content to parrot police spokesmen who tended to speak darkly but vaguely of the killer "overpowering" his victims. Exactly what that may have meant was never very clear. On one hand, there was the unspeakable horror of Edward Andrassy with rope burns on his wrists, perhaps conscious and struggling violently as the Butcher's knife cut deeply into his neck; on the other hand, there was victim no. 10 with enough drugs in her system to cause unconsciousness, if not death.

Where did the Butcher meet his victims? On the street? In the dark, isolated areas of the Flats or Kingsbury Run? In bars, hotels, or flophouses, perhaps even whorehouses? Victims no. 4 and no. 5 had been butchered on the lonely spots where their bodies were later found. Had the killer been riding the rails with his intended targets, as Peter Merylo believed? Did he use sex as the lure to draw them to the remote areas where he killed them, or did he merely encounter them there by chance? All of these questions again raise the issue of whether the Butcher knew his victims before he killed them. Were they all strangers to him; did he know any of them?

Where had the Butcher killed and dismembered his prey? Did he have a single base of operation somewhere in the city, or did he take advantage of whatever derelict buildings may have been nearby? For the general public during the 1930s, any talk of a "laboratory" would have conjured up images of *Frankenstein* or any of a host of other mad doctor movies from Hollywood studios; but the Butcher's lair did not have to be that large or elaborate. He would have needed no more than enough space to spread out a body and work comfortably. Decapitating someone, however, whose heart was still beating—whether that person was conscious or not—would produce a geyser of spurting blood, and the whole process of murder and dismemberment would have created a terrible mess. While it is tempting to think that a bathtub would have solved that problem, it is difficult—

even comically grotesque—to imagine the Butcher trying to maneuver the dead weight of a human corpse in the narrow confines of a bathtub so as to cut with surgical precision. An undertaking establishment or a medical facility would have provided both the necessary space and the means of cleaning up the mess, but the privacy to work would have been a major problem—unless the Butcher had some connection with the establishment and enjoyed after-hours access.

Rebecca McFarland (former vice president of the Board of Trustees of the Cleveland Police Historical Society, librarian/historian, and expert on Eliot Ness) suggested one of the abandoned breweries along the Cuyahoga River as a possible site for the Butcher's laboratory—an intriguing idea that, to my knowledge, the police never looked into. The floor of a brewery is sloped to allow for drainage, which would make using the building for anything else extremely difficult. Each brewery was also constructed with a tunnel down to the Cuyahoga River so that ice could be easily dragged into the facility to keep the beer cold. Most brewery owners at the time expected that Prohibition would be short-lived, so plants were guarded or regularly checked even if closed. Brewers who were in financial trouble, however, and who did not have the resources to ride out Prohibition, had no choice but to abandon their plants permanently. A derelict brewery would provide the Butcher with the necessary space and privacy to work; the sloped flooring would solve the blood problem; and the tunnel could account for how some victims (no. 9 and no. 10, for example) wound up in the river without anyone seeing anything.

For Peter Merylo, however, there was no question: the bloody footprint in one of the Stowe Township boxcars confirmed his long-held suspicion that the Butcher rode the rails, picked his victims from among the ranks of the hobo populations with which he traveled, and carried out his murder-dismemberments in railroad cars. These assumptions about the killer would determine the focus of his investigation until the day he died.

NOTES

Walter Piszczek recounted his memories in a series of telephone interviews with the author. September 1998.

The story of Petey Scalzone, the mob enforcer arrested eighty-eight times, was given to me by Bill Redmond during a telephone interview.

Coroner Gerber's speculations about the Butcher appear in both Howard Beaufait's "Kingsbury Run Murders" and John Bartlow Martin's "Butcher's Dozen: The Cleveland Torso Murders."

Detective Peter Merylo spells out his theories about the Butcher in his unpublished memoirs. Some of his ideas are also quoted in John Bartlow Martin's "Butcher's Dozen: The Cleveland Torso Murders." Howard G. Smith's letters to Merylo and copies of the detective's answers to them are in Peter Merylo's files.

George Condon discusses Edwin J. Creel's notion of a suicide club and Merylo's theory of the Butcher suffering from a blood disorder in "The Mad Butcher of Kingsbury Run." The letter from Susan V. Gill is referred to in a newspaper clipping on the case dated 1960.

The discussion of serial killers and their behavior is drawn from Robert H. Ressler and Tom Schachtman's *Whoever Hunts Monsters* (New York: St. Martin's, 1992) and John Douglas and Mark Dishaker's *Mind Hunter: Inside the FBI's Elite Serial Crime Unit* (New York: Pocket Star, 1995).

Rebecca McFarland shared her ideas about the city's abandoned breweries in a series of conversations.

SUSPECTS

It can be argued powerfully that he was the most remarkable
murderer of all time.
—John Bartlow Martin, "Butcher's Dozen:
The Cleveland Torso Murders"

Today, more than seventy years after the Kingsbury Run murders were committed and in the absence of most of the police files, there is no way to tell how many viable suspects authorities may have had. After the legions of bizarre characters cataloged by the press are discounted, few potential candidates remain. Who were they, and under what circumstances did they come under suspicion? Did any of them fit the profiles established by either Coroner A. J. Pearce's "torso clinic," his successor Dr. Samuel Gerber, or Peter Merylo? Did any of them have the opportunity to murder and dismember all the victims attributed to the Butcher?

And exactly how many people did the Butcher kill? The problem of attribution remains the greatest obstacle in decisively placing a bloody knife in anyone's hand. Today, it is not even clear that a single perpetrator was responsible for the deaths of the twelve victims commonly recognized and accepted by both popular tradition and history. If Dr. T. Windgate Todd's observations about no. 11 being a previously embalmed body are correct, that would remove her from the Butcher's total. And if no. 11 is discounted, should no. 12—found in the same location at the same time—be taken off the list as well? People who have studied the case invariably question one or more of the twelve canonical victims, often for reasons no stronger than an educated hunch. Andrew Schug, former member of the Board of Trustees of the Cleveland Police Historical Society and my longtime research partner, has doubts about no. 5, the only victim discovered outside of Cleveland on the west side. Marilyn Bardsley, who has studied the case since the early 1970s, is inclined to dismiss no. 8, the skeletal remains found in a burlap bag under the Lorain-Carnegie Bridge and tentatively identified as Rose Wallace.

That other butchered victims were found in the Cleveland area complicates the picture even more. Should the Lady of the Lake, discovered on the Erie shore in September 1934, be included? Her partial remains turned up a full year before Edward Andrassy and no. 2 were murdered, but they were discovered in the same general area as the upper torso of victim no. 7 two and a half years later. Cleveland's three dailies were divided on the issue. The *Press* and *News* confidently credited the Butcher with the Lady of the Lake's death and referred to her, rather than Andrassy, as victim no. 1; the more reticent *Plain Dealer* lumped her together with the other victims but refused to alter the traditional numbering to accommodate her. Detective Peter Merylo accepted her as a legitimate torso victim (he refers to her as "Murder #1" on a list of victims he prepared on June 30, 1942); Coroners Pearce and Gerber were inclined to dismiss her. Should Robert Robertson, found and identified in July 1950, be added to the list? It had been twelve years since the Butcher's activity had ceased; but the dismemberment clearly recalled his previous victims, and Robertson certainly fit the victim profile. Without ever definitely attributing Robert Robertson to the Butcher, all three Cleveland newspapers commented on the familiar "Kingsbury Run technique."

The moment speculations move beyond Cleveland's "Butcher's Dozen," the Lady of the Lake, and Robert Robertson to include all the dismembered bodies found in the south Michigan–northeast Ohio–western Pennsylvania and New York area, questions of attribution become virtually unanswerable. Should the three Stowe Township, Pennsylvania, victims, found in 1940 in abandoned boxcars, be included? What about the dismembered bodies that turned up in New Castle, Pennsylvania, during the years 1921–34 and 1939–42?

These are not just abstract academic questions. To link any potential suspect to a crime, it is necessary to show that he had the opportunity to commit it. If, for example, all the New Castle victims are credited to the Butcher, then at least one prime candidate is disqualified from consideration because of lack of opportunity. Unfortunately, none of the newspaper accounts or surviving official documents make it clear exactly what Eliot

Ness, David Cowles, James Hogan, Sam Gerber, or any of the other major investigators thought about those dismembered bodies found outside of Cleveland. Were they to be added to the Butcher's tally or not? Cleveland authorities treated all such out-of-state reports seriously, and they investigated them carefully and thoroughly. But when dealing with the press, they refused to commit themselves and spoke guardedly about probable or possible links to the local butcheries.

Only Peter Merylo refused to equivocate in public; as far as he was concerned, all the Cleveland, Stowe Township, and New Castle killings were the work of the same man. And that man remained elusive. The police certainly did not lack suspects. The number of people investigated and discounted was astronomical. The phrase "may be a good suspect in our Torso Murders" occurs over and over again, with numbing regularity, in Merylo's official police reports. "I roughly estimate that we have checked approximately 7300 suspects in connection with these crimes," he speculates in his memoirs, "and it is very doubtful whether the real torso killer was ever amongst them." But was he?

NOTE

Peter Merylo's memoirs are included in his case files.

FRANK DOLEZAL

Frank Dolezal always looked the same. In photograph after photograph his expression never varied—neither angry nor scared but strangely vacant and bewildered. All his neighbors agreed there was something weird about his eyes. "He seemed just as normal as you or I, but his eyes seemed to stare right through you," remarked the employment manager of the United States Aluminum Company to the *Press* on July 8, 1939. "They were like Svengali's eyes in the movies." "The only strange thing about him was his eyes," agreed a bartender. "They were queer."

As the only man actually arrested and charged in the torso killings at the time they occurred, Frank Dolezal achieved instant celebrity. Reporters hungering for sensational news in a sensational case eagerly passed Sheriff Martin L. O'Donnell's daily updates about his suspect to a populace frightened, fascinated, and weary of the Kingsbury Run murders. For both press and public, Frank Dolezal represented closure—the long-awaited coda in an anguished, endless symphony.

In the summer of 1938, while Eliot Ness was torching the shantytowns and conducting an organized, systematic sweep of the neighborhoods bordering Kingsbury Run and the Central Market area, a private investigator named Lawrence J. "Pat" Lyons studied all the police and coroner's reports—though how he gained access to them is unclear—and then began quietly pursuing his own theories about the murders. Like Ness and members of the police department who had worked on the case, Lyons deduced that the killer must have some sort of easily cleaned "laboratory" close to the Run that probably contained refrigeration and storage facilities. Since he lacked the authority to carry out an official search for such a murder site on his own, Lyons took his ideas to former mayor Ray T. Miller. Miller was a Democrat, and, in a move that was probably political, he sent Lyons, not to Eliot Ness, an appointee of Republican mayor Harold Burton, or the police, but to a fellow Democrat, Cuyahoga County sheriff Martin L. O'Donnell. City police had worked on and agonized over the Kingsbury Run murders since they began; they had conducted their investigation in a public spotlight and had endured the heat for their failures. The county sheriff had contributed little if anything to the investigations and had watched from the sidelines while Ness and his forces took all the pressure. This was more than simple competition between two law enforcement agencies; Sheriff O'Donnell remained a staunch political ally of Democratic congressman Martin L. Sweeney, who ferociously attacked the Republican administration of Mayor Harold Burton over its inability to catch the Kingsbury Run Butcher. O'Donnell gave Lyons the official blessing he needed and assigned Chief Deputy Sheriff John Gillespie and Deputy Sheriff Paul McDevitt to work with him.

Over a period of months, the three men passed through the broken-down neighborhoods but enjoyed no greater luck than Eliot Ness had in August 1938. Disappointed but undaunted, the trio changed tactics and began exploring the possibility that the two (three if Rose Wallace is included) identified victims may have known each other—ties which the Cleveland police had already struggled to establish—and, further, that their murderer could be found by systematically investigating any of their mutual acquaintances. Eventually, their investigation took Lyons, Gillespie, and McDevitt to a sleazy bar at the corner of East 20th and Central, and there among the prostitutes and bums, the separate pieces Peter Merylo had struggled with unsuccessfully for so long suddenly seemed to come miraculously together. They learned not only that Flo Polillo and Rose Wallace had been regular customers of the bar but that the two women knew each other well. Even more intriguing, Edward Andrassy's orbit often brought him to the rundown establishment as well. Better yet, all three belonged to a group of regulars who frequently came together to drink.

Ultimately, all their tips and leads pointed to a mysterious "Frank," who not only possessed a stockpile of butcher knives but, according to rumors, liberally threatened imagined transgressors with his large, wicked blades whenever they annoyed him. The three investigators finally identified the man as Frank Dolezal, a fifty-two-year-old Slav immigrant who earned a living as a bricklayer but had at one time worked in a slaughterhouse. Now a resident of East 22nd, he had once lived in a dilapidated apartment building at 1908 Central, close to Hart Manufacturing on East 20th—where the first set of Flo Polillo's remains had been discovered in produce baskets—and the Scovill Rag & Paper Company, the supposed source of the quilt in which the torso of no. 11 had been wrapped. Dolezal also frequented the neighborhood bar at East 20th and Central where the pitiful lives of Andrassy, Polillo, and Wallace had intersected. (On July 8, the *Press* printed a large composite photograph of this seedy neighborhood surrounding Charity Hospital to illustrate how close to each other all these relevant sites were.) When Lyons, McDevitt, and Gillespie gained access to the shabby four-room apartment Dolezal had once occupied, they discovered dark stains on the floor of the bathroom and in the tub. Could the long-sought, fabled Butcher's laboratory really be nothing more exotic than a dingy bathroom in a decaying apartment building? Lyons scraped samples from the floor which he passed on to his chemist brother G. V. Lyons for analysis.

In mid-June Pat Lyons got careless, and Merylo picked up his trail. Lyons began frequenting the Forest Cafe, a neighborhood dive at East 19th and Central that catered primarily to the black prostitutes and pimps who lived and worked in the area. One night he flashed a gold badge, bragged that he was an investigator from the *Chicago Herald* working on the torso killings, and proudly displayed a briefcase filled with newspaper clippings and photos of the murder victims. Proprietress Helen Merrills grew alarmed at the intoxicated Lyons's obnoxious behavior toward her clientele and contacted Merylo. His immediate reaction was to add the mysterious drunk to his list of potential suspects, but when O'Donnell's office learned that Merylo had gotten wind of Lyons and his activities, the sheriff moved quickly and arrested Frank Dolezal at 6:00 in the evening on Wednesday, July 5, 1939.

Two days later, following what must have been a horrendous interrogation—during which Dolezal was denied food and rest periods longer than ten minutes—Sheriff O'Donnell called a press conference and announced, with appropriate fanfare, that the long-hoped-for break in the torso killings had finally come. At 2:00 that afternoon, County Detective Harry S. Brown had gotten their prisoner to admit to the murder and dismemberment of Flo Polillo in January 1936. Under O'Donnell's initial questioning before lunch that day, Dolezal had admitted drinking with Polillo in his apartment on the Friday night before her partial remains were discovered. He said he had quarreled with her because she had tried to take some money from him, but he insisted he had not killed her. In the afternoon after lunch, Detective Brown took over the interrogation, and under the intense pressure of his questioning, Dolezal finally broke, stating that he had hit Polillo sometime between 2:00 and 4:00 A.M. on January 26 as she came at him with a butcher knife. When she fell and hit her head against the tub, Dolezal's confession went on, he assumed she was dead, so he hoisted her body into the bathtub and sliced off her head, legs, and arms—in that order. Some of her clothes he burned; the others he left behind Hart Manufacturing in the snow along with the two baskets containing pieces of her body. Then at 4:00 that morning, Dolezal packed the remaining body parts in baskets and carried them out into the zero-degree weather and headed for Lake Erie three miles away. On the shore close to East 49th, isolated in the vast empty blackness, he silently dropped the last pieces of Flo Polillo's butchered corpse into the frigid waters.

O'Donnell proudly displayed his prisoner to the assembled newsmen like a prize trophy. Unshaven and dressed in a badly rumpled, sweat-stained shirt, Frank Dolezal sat quietly in a chair flanked by the sheriff's men. Seemingly almost oblivious to his surroundings, he met the scrutiny of curious newsmen and the photographers' exploding flashes with the same blank but penetrating stare everyone who knew him had described.

Suddenly, almost miraculously, crucial bits of evidence substantiating Frank Dolezal's guilt seemed to flood in from all sides. Two of the four butcher knives the sheriff and his men had seized at Dolezal's current East 22nd address bore mysterious dark stains. Dolezal refused to comment about a scrapbook found in his possession from which some photos had apparently been ripped out. Lyons's chemist brother maintained that the stains on the bathroom floor were, indeed, blood. Dolezal had abruptly and suspiciously left his Central Avenue apartment in August 1938, just as Eliot Ness was leading his massive, intensive search of the area. Dolezal had once lived with Flo Polillo and had even been seen with her on the night of Friday, January 24, 1936, a mere two days before some of her dismembered body parts turned up behind Hart Manufacturing. The sheriff showed reporters a ominous-sounding letter from Nettie Taylor of Wheaton, Illinois, who claimed to be Dolezal's sister-in-law. The letter related that Dolezal's sister Anna Nigrin, had been killed in July 1931 on a Geauga County farm near Chardon. When the dead woman's son Joseph came to Cleveland to settle his mother's estate, he disappeared—never to be seen again—after moving in with his uncle Frank Dolezal. The sheriff and his men tore out the bathtub at Dolezal's former Central Avenue aparartment and uncovered more blood-like stains on the wall and floor. Some of Dolezal's former neighbors had seen Polillo, Rose Wallace, Edward Andrassy, and an unidentified sailor (perhaps the tattooed victim no. 4?) in his apartment. A neighbor at his former address on East 19th reported that Dolezal went out nights and brought homeless men he had picked up at Public Square back to his apartment. The informant further assured the sheriff that Dolezal had a violent temper and had once threatened a woman with a knife for spying on him; he had frequently seen both Edward Andrassy and Flo Polillo, as well as many others, in Dolezal's company. Lillian Jones, a twenty-two-year-old black prostitute, insisted that Dolezal had attacked her with a knife while she was in his apartment and that she had escaped certain death by leaping from his second-story window. According to the *Plain Dealer* on July 7, O'Donnell said her allegation "strengthens my suspicions that Dolezal was connected with other torso murders." (The woman produced her shoe with its broken heel as proof of her ordeal but offered no explanation as to how she managed a jump from such a height without breaking anything else.) Harold Kiersner, a recently released convict who had lived with Dolezal in the weeks before his arrest, authored a lurid tabloid article for the *Press* on July 8 alleging that the suspect drank at least twenty bottles of beer a day, turned violent when drunk, and indulged in frequent crying jags. Finally, Chief Jailer Michael Kilbane told the *Press* on July 8 that Dolezal had balked at the suggestion that he return to the alleged crime scene with the sheriff's men because he was afraid of "seeing Mrs. Polillo's 'ghost.'"

Frank Dolezal was arrested and charged with the murder of Flo Polillo. This *Press* photograph was probably taken on July 7, 1939. *Cleveland Press* Archives, Cleveland State University.

O'Donnell's dramatic coup had as much to do with politics as law enforcement. Now county Democrats could gloat that one of their own had triumphed where the handpicked darling of the Republican administration had failed. Eliot Ness was gracious in seeming defeat; Peter Merylo was not. "The sheriff is to be commended for his investigation," the safety director declared to the *Plain Dealer* on July 8. "The leads he has uncovered will, of course, be followed up to see what possible connection the Polillo case may have with any others. My department and I stand ready to make available to the sheriff any information or facilities that he might feel could be of assistance."

Merylo, on the other hand, was outraged. He felt that the sheriff was intruding on his territory, and he stormed into Chief Matowitz's office and contemptuously dismissed the notion that Dolezal could be the Butcher. He had checked the bricklayer out thoroughly twice, he fumed: first as far back as November 1936 and again in August 1938 after the discovery of victims no. 11 and no. 12. (According to Merylo's comments in the Otwell manuscript, the sheriff had explained to the press that he had not passed on the information about Dolezal that Lyons had brought to his attention because he knew city police had previously questioned and released him.) "I had been working on this case for years," Merylo declares in Otwell. "The sheriff and his men had been in it only a few weeks. I thoroughly questioned Frank Dolezal on two occasions. I had questioned the women and the men who were his companions. I had him under surveillance a long, long time. I used orthodox and unorthodox police methods on this man and I was as thorough as possible."

Though Merylo and other members of the force regarded Frank Dolezal as a deviant and had watched him make repeated advances to men in the city parks, police officers who knew him well judged him a simple, honest man. "The kids liked him; he bought them ice cream cones and candy," Merylo reflects in the Otwell manuscript. "The neighbors liked him, too. He'd buy a lot of steaks and some wine and have in a gang for an evening. . . . He was gregarious as they come. He liked to have people around." Chief Matowitz cautioned the angry detective against any public outbursts or interference in the sheriff's investigation; politics dictated that O'Donnell and his office be given a free hand in building their case.

It is not clear whether Merylo contacted the press or reporters called him, but, with the understanding that he must remain anonymous, Merylo effectively torpedoed the sheriff's case. He pointed out that no matter what he was alleged to have said in his so-called confession, Dolezal could not have disposed of Flo Polillo's head in Lake Erie because the water was frozen well beyond the breakwall on the night of January 26, 1936. A simple check with the U.S. Weather Bureau substantiated Merylo's claim. "This was my first experience where a man is making a confession to a murder or any other serious crime," he wrote in his memoirs, "and does not know the details of the crime which he is alleged to have committed."

Then, as quickly as the case against Frank Dolezal had come together, it began to crumble. If he had disposed of some of Flo Polillo's clothes behind Hart Manufacturing, why hadn't the police found them? If he had tossed parts of her body into the lake, how did some of them later turn up in a shallow depression on Orange Avenue? How could any of this have happened on the night of January 25–26 when then Coroner Pearce was certain she had been dead for at least two days when her body was discovered? Coroner Gerber subtly suggested that Dolezal's confession to Flo Polillo's murder was meaningless unless he admitted to the other killings as well. "Our records show some slight differences in the manner in which Mrs. Polillo's body was dismembered and the manner in which others were," he told the *Plain Dealer* on July 8, "but I still feel that the murderer of Mrs. Polillo is responsible for all the crimes." In the July 14 edition of the *Press,* Dr. Enrique E. Ecker of Western Reserve University dropped a forensic bombshell by denouncing the stains in Dolezal's bathroom as nothing more than "plain dirt." And Edward Andrassy's father, Joseph, weakened a possible connection between Dolezal and his son when he denied recognizing the suspect's photograph. "I never saw that fellow in my life," he insisted to the *Press* on July 8.

On Saturday, July 8, Dolezal obligingly retracted the initial account of his nocturnal journey to the lake and the disposal of Flo Polillo's head. Now, he insisted, he was on his way to work at the American Steel and Wire Company. "I took it [the head] out on E. 37th Street. I poured a gallon of coal oil over it [burned it] and buried it. I can take you to the spot," he declared to Deputy Sheriff Michael English, according to the *Plain Dealer* on July 9. Merylo sank this second confession almost as effectively as he had the first; Dolezal had never been employed by American Steel and Wire. To verify Dolezal's claim, however, O'Donnell bundled him into a car, along with Detective Harry S. Brown and Deputies Michael English and George Butler, and headed for the spot his prisoner had described. It was ominously close to where police had searched for pieces of no. 6 in September 1936. The men cleared away the weeds and began digging. Curious spectators began to assemble, and Dolezal pathetically tried to hide from their scrutiny by bending over and covering his face with his hands. After a half-hour search, the men had found nothing, save for a few bone fragments that Gerber later identified as cat, dog, or sheep bones. The frustrated sheriff was convinced that Dolezal did not want to reveal his disposal site because he realized authorities would locate the other missing heads there.

An eager press reported every new development in the ongoing Dolezal saga to a public desperately hoping that the murders were over. But from the beginning, Dolezal had steadfastly, even violently, maintained that he had nothing do with any of the other torso killings, and now rumors began to circulate in the press that he had retracted his second confession as well.

On Monday, July 10, O'Donnell ceremoniously transported his suspect to East Cleveland and the only lie detector, a Keeler polygraph, in the entire northeast Ohio area. Observers noticed bruises on Dolezal's nose and right eye as he left his cell. His shirt was ripped, and he complained that his ribs hurt. "When a reporter asked what was wrong with his ribs," Merylo recounts in the Otwell manuscript, "Harry Brown, county detective, told the reporter, 'You ought to have your jaw punched.'"

At 3:30 in the afternoon, East Cleveland police chief L. G. Corlett escorted Dolezal to a soundproof room in the basement of the police station, where Paul F. Beck, a recent graduate of the Western Reserve University Law School, conducted the tests. According to Beck, the polygraph indicated that Dolezal had, indeed, killed Flo Polillo. Curiously, Beck did not ask him about discrepancies between his confession and the police reports regarding her death, nor apparently did he inquire about Dolezal's possible involvement in the other torso murders.

During his ordeal, Dolezal complained bitterly that he had been beaten repeatedly by the sheriff's men and then offered yet a third explanation as to the fate of Flo Polillo's head. "I was working on the Shore drive project," the *Press* quoted him on July 10. "The morning after I killed Flo. . . . I took the head and went down to the project at 6 A.M. before the other fellows got there. The steam shovel was there. I got alongside the steam shovel and threw the head in a ditch where I knew the steam shovel was going to throw dirt. Then I covered the head with dirt so no one could see it." (Even though Frank Dolezal had been a resident of the United States since 1903, when he was sixteen years old, family members report that he spoke broken English. The *Press* was apparently according him a fluency in the language that he did not possess.) O'Donnell declined launching a search for the head because odds weighed so heavily against success.

At 3:30 the next afternoon, six days after his arrest, Frank Dolezal was formally arraigned on first-degree murder charges before Justice of the Peace Myron J. Penty. (One of those present, State Senator and Justice of the Peace William J. Zoul, had been previously touched by the case; did he remember that he had married Edward Andrassy and Lillian Kardotska almost ten years before?) Fearing his prize might try an insanity plea, O'Donnell arranged for psychiatrists K. S. West and S. C. Lindsay to examine the prisoner for an hour and a half before the arraignment. They judged Dolezal sane. At the conclusion of the court proceedings, O'Donnell announced that Dolezal had finally signed a third confession, which, unlike his earlier admissions, he felt was true.

Merylo, however, regarded this new confession as bogus as the other two, and again, working anonymously from the sidelines, he directed

The search for Flo Polillo's head along East 37th in Kingsbury Run, July 8, 1939. Cuyahoga County sheriff Martin L. O'Donnell (hands behind his back) stands in the foreground. Frank Dolezal is to the left in the rear (beneath the arrow) trying to cover his face. Courtesy of Marjorie Merylo Dentz.

newspapermen to the WPA office where Dolezal's time card showed he had been making repairs at East Technical High School on January 26, 1936, and had never been assigned to the Lake Shore Drive project. "This same record was open to inspection to the Sheriff or any member of his staff, but no such attempt was made to examine those records," Merylo charges in his memoirs.

Suddenly, the entire weight of America's traditional beliefs in justice, fair play, and civil liberties crashed down on O'Donnell and his department. In the days following his arrest, Dolezal's brother Charles had obtained an attorney for him. Fred P. Soukup had not been allowed to see his client before the arraignment and was not even present at the formal proceedings because Penty failed to inform the defendant that he had a right to a lawyer. Now he launched a public probe into whether Dolezal had been mistreated during his six-day incarceration in the county jail without formal charges; the Cleveland chapter of the American Civil Liberties Union began a similar investigation to determine if the sheriff's department had violated Dolezal's civil rights; and the civil liberties committee of the American Bar Association weighed in with a request that O'Donnell present himself at its noon meeting on July 12 at the Hotel Allerton and explain, according to the *Plain Dealer,* "why the usual procedure of preferring charges against confessed criminals had not been followed in this case." The county prosecutor summoned the sheriff to his office and demanded to know what kind of case he actually had against Dolezal. Who were his witnesses? Where was his evidence? Common Pleas judge Frank S. Day overthrew the July 11 arraignment because Dolezal had been denied counsel. In the midst of this legal chaos, Dolezal retracted his more recent confession, at first alleging he was "in a daze" when the sheriff extracted it from him, later insisting it was beaten out of him.

The *Press,* which up until this point had remained reasonably neutral in its reporting, turned against the sheriff. On July 11, reporter William Miller pointed to the problem areas in O'Donnell's case against his suspect and asked, "Is Frank Dolezal the torso murderer? Or is he a harmless psychopath who has been forced into admitting a crime he did not commit?" An editorial in the same issue questioned both the sheriff's conduct and his intentions. The beleaguered sheriff remained obstinate. "I am convinced that the newspapers intend to misconstrue everything I say," he declared to the *Press* on July 13. "I will have nothing more to say on the case until the Grand Jury takes action." He had not sought any help from the police or their voluminous records on the murders and now insisted he would present the case against Frank Dolezal to the grand jury without any assistance from the prosecutor's office.

By July 18, however, the sheriff had apparently softened his position, for Acting County Prosecutor John J. Mahon announced publicly that he would personally comb through police records looking for miscellaneous bits of information that would strengthen the murder charge against Dolezal. If O'Donnell had indeed relented, it may have been owing to prevailing legal opinions that a first-degree murder charge would be difficult to sustain because of Dolezal's statement in his confession—which he had retracted anyway—that Polillo had come at him with a knife.

The county prosecutor, apparently growing increasingly wary about the whole Dolezal business, called in Peter Merylo and asked if he had anything to add to the case. "I advised the Prosecutor that I had this man in custody on two different occasions, that if I had a case against him I would never have turned him loose," Merylo wrote in his memoirs. When informed he would no doubt be subpoenaed to appear before the grand jury, Merylo declared that he could not offer anything more than he already had and strode angrily out of the office, taking a parting shot at O'Donnell as he went. "Whenever I arrested any criminal charged with an offense I never had to subpoena the Sheriff to the Grand Jury to help me to make the case."

At a second arraignment on July 21, Frank Dolezal was bound over to the grand jury on a reduced charge of manslaughter. *Press* photographs of the high-profile proceeding in the archives of Cleveland State University show a packed court right out of Hollywood—every seat taken, people standing all over the crowded room. A close-up reveals Dolezal's brother Charles, stone-faced and grim, sitting beside his obviously worried wife, Louise. More panoramic shots catch the defendant slumped over at the table, trying to hide his face behind his hand. Dolezal sat passively through the proceedings, but, according to Merylo's recollections in the Otwell manuscript, when deputies tried to escort him out of the courtroom, he suddenly rolled up his shirtsleeve and held up his bruised left arm. "They said they didn't beat me," he cried to the still crowded courtroom. After almost two weeks of intense interrogation, a trio of retracted confessions, and three different tales of the whereabouts of the head, the long-hoped-for break in the torso case had dwindled to a single charge of manslaughter.

† † †

Whatever happened in the county jail on the afternoon of August 24 will likely remain a mystery. Dolezal actually had all of Cellblock B-4 to himself, where, according to reports, he spent most of his time with his rosary in prayer. Two guards watched him constantly, and to foil any possible suicide attempts, the door to Cell 4-A, which housed him, was kept unlocked. On that afternoon, Deputy Sheriffs Hugh Crawford and Adolf Schuster were on duty in B-4. Sometime before 1:45, Schuster left the block to escort some visitors downstairs. Crawford later testified that at the same time he also left the block to tell three visitors in another cell on the same floor that their time was up. Dolezal was then pacing up and down the runway that connected the cells. At 1:48, Crawford returned to find Frank Dolezal, reportedly still gasping for breath, hanging by a makeshift rope of cleaning rags from a coat hook in Cell 11. Sheriff O'Donnell and Assistant Chief Jailer Archie Burns answered Crawford's desperate call for help. "We found Dolezal hanging limply against the wall with a rag wrapped around his neck," the sheriff told the *Plain Dealer* on August 25. "I took my pocket knife out and gave it to Burns, who cut the rag while Crawford held Dolezal. We called for the male nurse and the fire rescue squad [at 1:52]." Help arrived and administered both oxygen and an insulin shot within five minutes, but Frank Dolezal was dead.

At 3:00 in the afternoon, veteran torso investigators Sergeant James Hogan and Inspector Joseph M. Sweeney, along with Coroner Gerber and Dolezal's attorney Fred Soukup, arrived at the jail to look into the suspicious death. In a fury that he had not been called earlier, Soukup, according to the *Plain Dealer* on August 25, blasted Deputy Sheriff Clarence M. Tylicki. "I had a hunch something like this would happen before he ever went to trial," he roared. "What kind of jail are you running here, anyway?" If the two homicide detectives took any pleasure from the sheriff's embarrassing predicament, they apparently did not show it, but they did require O'Donnell and his personnel to make their statements at Central Police Station. Gerber judged the death a suicide resulting from asphyxiation by strangulation.

Having already expressed its skepticism over the entire Dolezal affair in an editorial on July 11, the *Press* explored his death in gruesome detail. The paper printed a large photograph of a cadaverous-looking Coroner Gerber holding up the makeshift rag noose in both hands. Beside it were a shot of the death cell and a disturbing police photo of the dead man lying on a bunk.

Immediately holes opened in Crawford's and O'Donnell's chronicle of events. Dolezal stood at five feet eight, yet he allegedly had hanged himself from a hook that was only five feet, seven inches off the ground. "O'Donnell said Dolezal had used a piece of towel to hang himself. Mike Kilbane [chief jailer] said he had used bed clothing," Merylo asserts in the Otwell manuscript. Who were the visitors that the deputy said he had gone to inform they had to leave the jail? O'Donnell required all those visiting prisoners to sign a register, yet those names had not been turned over to city police. Adolf Schuster, one of the two deputies guarding Dolezal and—one assumes—an ally of the sheriff, wondered why a man planning suicide would eat all his lunch beforehand. Crawford swore he had not left his post for more than three minutes, but Gerber insisted that it would take twelve to fifteen minutes for asphyxiation to occur. The time discrepancies bothered William E. Edwards, director of the Cleveland Crime Commission, so he ordered the coroner to perform an autopsy—something Gerber had initially seen no reason for since he regarded the death as a simple suicide.

Was Gerber dragging his feet? Surely he was aware that his judgment that it would have taken at least twelve minutes for Dolezal to die conflicted with Crawford's contention that he had left the prisoner alone for only three minutes. Wouldn't a time discrepancy this large over such a significant point as time of death have prompted the coroner to conduct an autopsy? Or is this simply another example of Samuel Gerber reacting with the subtlety of a pit bull when he thought his judgment was being questioned—just as he had when Ness's assistant, Robert Chamberlin, wanted an outside expert to examine the lower left leg of no. 10, and as he had when he learned that Dr. T. Windgate Todd of the Western Reserve University Medical School had turned over pieces of no. 11 to David Cowles for further tests? "In view of all the street corner rumors and other reports of brutal treatment of Dolezal," Edwards declared to the *Plain Dealer* on August 25, "I think it only fair to the sheriff and the public to make as thorough as possible an investigation to ascertain the truth or falsity of these reports."

Given the suspicious nature of Dolezal's death, the intensity of public and press interest, and the persistent rumors of mistreatment, this was a high-profile procedure—reputations potentially rode on the results. Dolezal's younger brother Charles gave the necessary family permission for the autopsy to proceed; and at 6:30 A.M. on August 25, Drs. Gerber, Reuben Straus, and Harry Goldblatt, an assistant professor of pathology at Western Reserve University, went to work. Though the results of lab tests on the internal organs would take days, the immediate disclosures were shocking. Frank Dolezal had six broken ribs, three on each side! The degree of healing indicated the fractures could be anywhere from two months to two years old, but attorney Fred Soukup harbored no doubts that Sheriff Martin L. O'Donnell ultimately bore responsibility. "It is absurd to imagine that he could do the work he did [bricklaying] if he had received the fractured ribs before he went to jail," he angrily declared to the *Plain Dealer* on August 25.

Gerber convened a public inquest into Frank Dolezal's death at 10:30 A.M. the next day. He issued subpoenas to twelve individuals, including

The inquest into Frank Dolezal's death. *Left to right:* county prosecutor John Mahon (standing), John R. Hart (hand under chin), Sheriff Martin L. O'Donnell, former common pleas judge David Hertz, Dolezal family attorney Fred Soukup, and (possibly) William Edwards, head of the Crime Commission. *Cleveland Press* Archives, Cleveland State University.

Sergeant James Hogan, Sheriff O'Donnell, Chief Jailer Michael F. Kilbane, as well as Crawford and Schuster, the two deputies on guard duty when the "suicide" occurred. Tensions and animosities seethed beneath the surface in the hot, stuffy room from the start of the proceedings. Lined up on one side of the table were Dolezal family attorney Fred Soukup, William Edwards, director of the Crime Commission, and former common pleas judge David R. Hertz; on the other side sat Sheriff O'Donnell and his men. "The hostility was almost a solid wall between them," Merylo recalls in the Otwell manuscript. O'Donnell and Edwards had been long-standing political enemies, ever since the Crime Commission had tried to get the sheriff booted out of office over his alleged failures to enforce gambling laws.

The proceedings quickly turned into a barrage of charges and counter-charges. William Edwards led off, testifying that he had information alleging that Dolezal had been blindfolded, gagged, and beaten into unconsciousness. He also understood that Dolezal had asked for and been given some medicine: what was it, he wanted to know (O'Donnell thought it was aspirin), and why, he wondered, would someone contemplating suicide ask for medicine? When Fred Soukup demanded to know how Dolezal got the rags with which he hung himself, one of the sheriff's deputies insisted that the prisoner had asked for something to do and had been given rags to clean his cell. (No one at the inquest seems to have questioned this explanation.) Soukup supported William Edwards's allegations and insisted that Dolezal had complained of having been blindfolded, beaten, and kicked. O'Donnell, Kilbane, and Brown testified that he had not been touched. If anything, O'Donnell stoutly maintained, Dolezal had been treated too well. The visible injuries to his face and upper arm, as well as the broken ribs, he argued, resulted from two previous botched suicide attempts, both of which had been reported in the press.

At one point, Gerber lost control and the official proceedings nearly collapsed into a fistfight among the sheriff, Deputy Clarence Tylicki, and William Edwards. No sooner had the coroner managed to restore order when the angry sheriff turned on him and demanded to know if the Soukup-Hertz camp had supplied him with the questions he was asking—an allegation Gerber hotly denied.

When David Hertz testified, he backed up the allegations that Frank Dolezal had been severely mistreated and added an explosive detail of his own: Dolezal had maintained, he charged, that when the beatings were over, a white-haired man entered his cell and questioned him. It was surely not lost on anyone in that room that Sheriff O'Donnell was crowned with a full head of snow-white hair.

At the end of the day, Gerber called for a recess until August 29. Peter Merylo left two written accounts of what happened next and what was said—the Otwell manuscript and a special report, dated April 2, 1940, prepared at Eliot Ness's request—and in both documents he levels some extraordinarily serious charges. Frank Dolezal's alleged suicide took place on August 24; in his report to Ness of April 2, 1940, Merylo recounts that "about a week later" (which would seem to place events on August 27, the day after Gerber recessed the inquest), police arrested three black prostitutes in connection with a robbery. Merylo recognized one of them as the same Lillian Jones who had previously claimed that she had jumped from Dolezal's apartment window when he came at her with a butcher knife. When Merylo pressed her on her story, she confessed it was a lie, fabricated to satisfy and get rid of the obnoxious private detective Pat Lyons. In a sworn affidavit she further alleged that when Dolezal was arrested, Lyons had, in her words, bragged, "We have got him in jail and [he] will never get out of there," and "We will get it out of him, knock it out of him, he will never get out of there alive."

Lillian Jones and her younger sister Ruby (whether Ruby was one of the three prostitutes arrested by the police for robbery is not clear) were both subpoenaed to appear before the coroner's inquest when it reconvened on August 29. Only Lillian answered the summons. She testified that her sister had been intimidated, though by whom she apparently did not say, and was afraid to show up. According to Merylo in the Otwell manuscript, William Edwards then stated that Ruby had overheard unnamed sheriff's deputies in a bar saying, "Dolezal is the right man and we're going to beat the hell out of him until he confesses." The next day, Ruby appeared before the inquest and substantiated Edwards's claims.

There is obviously some confusion about who said what to whom and whether it was said directly or simply overheard. Both Merylo's report to Ness of April 2, 1940, and his comments in the Otwell manuscript agree on one point: Lillian Jones signed a sworn statement retracting her charge that Frank Dolezal had come at her with a knife, further insisting she had been pressured into making the allegation either by Pat Lyons (Merylo's report to Ness) or unnamed sheriff's deputies—which could still have been Pat Lyons (the Otwell manuscript). But whether Ruby Jones overheard Pat Lyons (or someone else) make the damning statements about beating a confession out of Frank Dolezal or whether Pat Lyons made them himself directly to Lillian Jones is unclear. Granted, the two accounts are not necessarily mutually exclusive; both versions of the story could be true. Ruby could have overheard Pat Lyons talking to her sister Lillian. But given the extremely serious nature of the charges, the seeming confusion is unfortunate.

On September 5, two months after Frank Dolezal had been arrested by the sheriff and two weeks after his suspicious death, Gerber handed down his official verdict on the death—an uneasy, politically sensitive compromise that solved little and probably satisfied no one. Dolezal had, he maintained, died by his own hand, but his injuries had, indeed, been sustained while in the sheriff's custody—perhaps from beatings, perhaps from the alleged suicide attempts, maybe from a combination of both. Throughout the whole affair, O'Donnell tried to avoid any blame and put a positive spin on events. "All I can say," he mused to the *Plain Dealer* on August 25, "is that he must have been afraid to face the grand jury. I am sure we had the right man. We did all we could on the case. We got a confession from him, and we were close to tying him up with another of the torso murders."

Merylo's report to Eliot Ness of April 2, 1940, dealing with Lillian Jones's arrest and her allegations concerning Pat Lyons, needs further comment. As contemporary police reports go, it is a rather long document—three single-spaced, typewritten pages. At the top of the first page, Merylo has typed, "Report requested by Eliot Ness, Director of Public Safety." Why would Ness be so interested in the events surrounding the Dolezal affair eight months after the fact? Why would he want to have all of this information legally verified in an official report? He may have been taking a hard look at the conduct of everyone involved in Dolezal's arrest, for it is certainly no coincidence that a few days before, on March 27, Frank Dolezal's younger brother Charles filed two petitions in the court of common pleas. In the first suit, embracing seven causes of action, he charged Pat Lyons and Sheriff O'Donnell, as well as deputies Kilbane, Gillespie, Brown, and English, with everything from false arrest to mistreatment of their prisoner. No doubt Gerber's suicide verdict rankled Charles Dolezal, but for legal purposes he accepted the judgment and sued the sheriff in a second petition for failing to prevent it. During the drawn-out legal sparring that ensued, Martin L. O'Donnell suddenly died of a heart attack in June 1941. Eight months later both petitions were "settled and dismissed at defendants' cost"—though exactly what that means is not specified in either court document. By then, however, the Kingsbury Run murders had faded from Cleveland headlines and the fate of Frank Dolezal was very old news; this glimmer of vindication for the Dolezal family passed by unnoticed.

Today, no one familiar with the case believes Frank Dolezal was guilty. No matter what mistreatment he had been subjected to while in the sheriff's custody, he vehemently refused to admit to more than Flo Polillo's murder. Pat Lyons even suggested to the press that Flo Polillo did not belong with the other murders—in spite of Gerber's assertions to the contrary—and that his extensive investigation had snared only her killer, not the Kingsbury Run murderer. Dolezal was also a relatively small man. At five feet eight, it does not seem likely he would have been capable of overpowering the larger Edward Andrassy (who stood at five feet eleven and carried an ice pick), nor does it seem plausible he could have possessed the strength to carry Andrassy's corpse down the sixty-foot slope of Jackass Hill. The assembled experts at Coroner Pearce's torso clinic in September 1936 concluded that the murderer probably led a normal life and appeared sane; the sheriff apparently based part of his case on the fact that Dolezal's behavior was not normal. Last, serial killers do not stop until they are stopped in some way. There had been no new murder-dismemberments for well over a year when O'Donnell had Dolezal arrested in July 1939, as Gerber pointed out. "The arrest of Dolezal didn't stop the murders; they had already stopped."

† † †

"Whenever anyone asks me about my background, I tell them I have a mass murderer and a nun," jokes Dolezal's great-niece Anne Louise Dolezal. But according to her sister Mary, the ugly incident continues to haunt older generations of the family—those who remember the man and still feel lingering resentment over his mistreatment and the sting of embarrassment brought to the family name. The police once arrested Charles Dolezal for getting into a fight on the street—probably in defense of his brother's blackened reputation.

Former Clevelander Mary Dolezal Satterlee now resides in Los Angeles. She readily concedes that her family never discussed any of this openly or completely. "It was taboo to talk about it," she remarks. She has, however, developed an interest in her great-uncle Frank and has extensively researched his life and the grim circumstances surrounding his death. "He was one of ten children. Only three of them came to the United States," she muses. "Everyone says he was the gentlest, sweetest man." She reflects wistfully on her grandmother's wedding photo, which shows a Frank Dolezal very different from the unshaven, unkempt, haunted man the newspapers presented—the only Frank Dolezal Cleveland ever saw. But the steel enters her voice when she recounts the fate of the troubled man she never knew. "Let's be clear about this! He was murdered!" Strong words! But discoveries over the past ten years have more than validated her charge.

The first inkling that Gerber's verdict of 1939 was questionable came in the early summer of 2000. Andrew Schug and Rebecca McFarland, both on the Board of Trustees of the Cleveland Police Historical Society at the time, gained access to some of the torso records at the morgue. The three of us were gathering material for a display on Eliot Ness and the Kingsbury Run murders to be set up in the Playhouse lobby during the September–November 2000 run of a new musical covering Ness's years in Cleveland. Because of my teaching schedule and my assumption that there was probably nothing significant there that I had not already examined, I did not accompany them. Both reported back that they had seen a series of poster-sized, terribly disturbing autopsy photographs of Frank Doelzal, at least two of which clearly showed the scar on his neck supposedly left by the makeshift noose. What they found most compelling about the grisly pictures was that they showed the mark around Frank Doelzal's neck to be a deep, piano-wire-thin scar. "I'm no pathologist," Rebecca McFarland reflected, "but I don't see how a noose made of rags could have made that mark"—an opinion with which Andrew Schug concurred. David Satula, a fellow researcher into the Kingsbury Run murders, saw the same photographs, independently of McFarland and Schug, a couple of years before, and he wholeheartedly supports their judgment. In one of those wonderful, unpredictable serendipitous occurrences, he read about the kind of bruises (or scars) hanging leaves on the neck the day before he saw the photographs in the morgue. His source (the name of which he could not remember) described the characteristic V-shaped mark around the upper part of the neck, caused by the upward pull of the rope; the scar marking Frank Dolezal circled the middle of his neck with no indication of the telltale V shape. "It looked more like strangulation than hanging," he told me.

I did not get a look at those photographs until 2003 or 2004. By then I had teamed up with documentary filmmaker Mark Stone, and we were at the morgue revisiting a lot of the material associated with the Kingsbury Run murders, including the death of Frank Dolezal. As we studied those revealing photographs that McFarland, Shug, and Satula had seen three to four years before, we began to experience the same nagging doubts about

Coroner Geber's 1939 suicide verdict that they had expressed. Granted, we were amateur sleuths with no training in the forensic sciences, but things just did not look right: that thin mark on his neck! How could that scar be reconciled with the bulky-looking noose apparently fashioned from cleaning rags with which Dolezal allegedly hanged himself and that Gerber had so accommodatingly displayed to press photographers? And then there was the question of the time element! According to his jailers, Dolezal had only been left alone for a few minutes: perhaps long enough to die by asphyxiation as Gerber had insisted in his official verdict, but could a mark that thin and deep be caused by thick rags in so short a time?

Then in the fall of 2004, the archivist at the morgue unearthed the complete transcript of the inquest into Frank Dolezal's death that Gerber had somewhat reluctantly convened—an imposing document of well over two hundred pages. It took several careful readings to fully digest the weighty tome, but it gradually became clear that the seeming formality of the proceedings masked all sorts of serious issues: blatant contradictions, obvious personal agendas, hostility, evasions, and—in at least one instance—an outright refusal to answer the question. At the very least, Gerber's suicide verdict seemed highly questionable; but Mark and I needed more professional help than we were able to access in Cleveland to substantiate our suspicions. Even though the torso murders and the death of Frank Dolezal had occurred nearly seventy years before, local officialdom seemed strangely reluctant to revisit anything that had to do with that infamous case. At the recommendation of a forensic anthropologist at the Smithsonian in Washington, D.C., we were able to secure the cooperation of the faculty and student body of the Applied Forensic Sciences Department of Mercyhurst College in Erie Pennsylvania. Over a period of several months in the latter half of 2004, we presented our material to classes in the forensic sciences and conducted interviews with a number of noted experts in the field who served on the faculty. In a unanimous opinion, everyone declared that Frank Dolezal's death could not have occurred in the manner that Sam Gerber's autopsy protocol insisted it did: there were just too many inconsistencies and contradictions as to the sequence of alleged events in the official inquest testimony. The wound on Frank Dolezal's neck was simply incompatible with the official assertion that he had died of asphyxiation when he hanged himself with a makeshift noose of toweling. Understandably reluctant to offer definitive judgments based on a study of old and fragmentary evidence, however, everyone carefully avoided uttering the damning word "murder"; but under the circumstances, no other option appeared possible.

Unfortunately, Frank Dolezal died in legal bureaucratic limbo. Since his death occurred before his scheduled appearance before a grand jury, the question of his guilt or innocence was never publically resolved. Perhaps due to a simple lack of money or worry that a gravestone might be vandalized by Clevelanders who accepted the notion of his guilt, the family had Frank Dolezal quietly interred in an unmarked grave in West Park Cemetery on the city's west side. In the summer of 2010, my research team, members of the board of trustees of the Cleveland Police Historical Society, and other interested parties raised the necessary funds to pay for a simple stone marker from Milano Monuments in Cleveland. According to Mary's wishes, besides the almost obligatory birth and death dates, the stone simply reads "Rest Now." On Sunday, August 24, 2010—the seventy-first anniversary of Frank Dolezal's death—members of his family, individuals in law enforcement, and others who had donated funds for the stone gathered at the cemetery for a simple commemoration ceremony. Frank Dolezal was as much a victim of the Mad Butcher as any of the individuals that fiend killed, decapitated, and dismembered outright; and now after more than seventy years, the clouds of doubt and suspicion that have swirled around him have been cleared away, and his family has finally been granted vindication and closure.

NOTES

The events surrounding and including Frank Dolezal's arrest, as well as the details of his alleged confessions and his arraignments, were covered by all three Cleveland dailies, July 6–14, 1939. Dolezal's death and the inquest into it were covered August 23–September 5,1939.

Peter Merylo gives an account of how he got involved with Pat Lyons and the subsequent arrest of Lillian Jones in his special report to Eliot Ness dated April 2, 1940. Merylo relates how he led the press to question Frank Dolezal's "confessions" in his memoirs. He describes the inquest into Dolezal's death in the Otwell manuscript. All three documents are in his personal files.

The records of Charles Dolezal's two court actions against Sheriff O'Donnell and others in the sheriff's department are archived in the Court of Common Pleas, case nos. 496329 and 496330.

Coroner Gerber's statement about the killings having stopped before Frank Dolezal's arrest is taken from John Bartlow Martin's "Butcher's Dozen: The Cleveland Torso Murders," 68.

Anne Louise Dolezal discussed her great-uncle with me in a phone interview. I have had the privilege of knowing Mary Dolezal Satterlee since the summer of 1997. She provided me with the details of her great-uncle's background and shared her family's reactions to his arrest and death in lengthy conversations.

For a full account of Frank Dolezal's arrest and death, an examination of the coroner's inquest that followed, and a discussion of the modern day CSI-like procedure that led to the conclusion that he was most likely murdered by person or persons unknown, see James Jessen Badal's *Though Murder Has No Tongue: The Lost Victim of Cleveland's Mad Butcher* (Kent, Ohio: Kent State University Press, 2010).

WILLIE JOHNSON

On June 28, 1942, a fourteen-year-old girl watched curiously as a tall, powerfully built black man got out of a cab along Kingsbury Run, struggling with a heavy trunk and a small satchel. Even though there had been no torso killings since August 1938, an air of mystery and terror still haunted the Run, and almost any activity just slightly out of the ordinary was bound to attract attention. When the young girl saw the man slowly descend the steep slope lugging his burdens, she grew alarmed and alerted the police. (Almost exactly six years before, Gomez Ivey and Louis Cheeley had found the head of the tattooed victim no. 4 wrapped in a pair of pants and deposited under a small tree near East 55th.) Later that same day, in a scene eerily reminiscent of those June 1936 events, three young black boys from the nearby neighborhood—Jimmy Wright, Charles Boyde, and Theodore Burns—went down into the Run to play. The trio came upon the trunk under the Sidaway Bridge, near Kinsman and East 55th, resting in the tall weeds like a pirate's abandoned treasure chest. Their spirit of adventure kindled by the unexpected find, the boys opened their prize only to discover it contained the limbless and headless torso of a black woman. The arms and head had been tossed into nearby bushes; only the legs were missing. Ultimately, police identified the victim as a nineteen-year-old prostitute named Margaret (Marie) Frances Wilson.

When the cab driver identified Willie Johnson as the man he had driven to Kingsbury Run, police arrested him at his East 97th Street rooming house. The thirty-six-year-old Helena, Arkansas, native had worked at a series of low-paying jobs, including farmhand and porter at a barbershop, and had had several serious run-ins with police. In 1933, he had served a term in an Arkansas workhouse for highway robbery and had been fined for carrying concealed weapons. In the same year, Fort Wayne, Indiana, police questioned him in a local murder investigation, and in 1940, he shot a man during a fight in the same city. He had first come to Cleveland sometime in 1936.

At first, Johnson insisted to the police that he had nothing to do with the gruesome murder-dismemberment, and he defended himself with a tale so outlandish it must have jolted or amused even those jaded cops who thought they had heard it all. When Wilson had attacked him with a knife during a fight over money, he said he had knocked her unconscious to the floor and then simply gone to bed! He awoke later and was, according to the *Press* on June 30, 1942, "mystified to find her lying in pieces all over the floor." He jammed her body parts into the trunk and satchel, and then, incredibly, went back to bed. When he awoke for the second time, he decided to "get rid of this stuff," hence the disposal in Kingsbury Run. On the morning of June 30, Johnson admitted the killing when Detective Sergeant Martin F. Cooney confronted him with Wilson's butchered remains at the morgue. At the end of July, police recovered the victim's missing legs, along with a piece of drapery from Johnson's room, near the streetcar tracks on Cedar Hill.

In the meantime, Cleveland police had uncovered some links, ranging from tenuous to solid, between Johnson and the Kingsbury Run murders. Detective Sergeant Cooney declared that the suspect had once lived in a place frequented by Flo Polillo, and two witnesses placed him with Rose Wallace, victim no. 8, in the days before her disappearance in August 1936. Charles Sadoti, a onetime bootleg joint operator, identified Johnson as a regular at his Charity Avenue establishment and the man whom he had seen there with Rose Wallace around August 15, 1936. When Johnson allegedly began to beat Wallace in a lot next door, Sadoti maintained that he broke up the fight and sent them on their separate ways. By the end of that August, Rose Wallace had dropped from sight; ten months later, Russell Lauer discovered what might have been her partial skeletal remains in a burlap sack under the Lorain-Carnegie Bridge. Johnson angrily insisted he had never known Rose Wallace and grew so enraged at Sadoti that he tried to attack him at the Central Police Station; as three detectives restrained him, the furious Johnson threatened to kill his accuser.

At his December 1942 trial in the court of common pleas under Judge Charles J. McNamee, Johnson reverted to his original story and insisted he awoke to find Wilson's dismembered body in his room. After deliberat-

The crime scene under the Sidaway Bridge in Kingsbury Run. *Cleveland Press* Archives, Cleveland State University.

ing for little more than an hour, the jury returned a guilty verdict with no recommendation for mercy—a finding that automatically mandated the death sentence. Johnson's behavior suddenly grew so erratic that authorities sent him to the Lima State Hospital for the Insane for observation. For over a year, he wore a turban and woolen underwear cutoffs, complained of frequent headaches, and insisted his brain was "leaking." Even after five Lima psychiatrists judged he was feigning and pronounced him sane, Johnson persisted in his aberrant behavior. He wore his now familiar costume to court when Judge McNamee sentenced him to death and continued to do so after he arrived in death row at the penitentiary in Columbus.

Just before his scheduled execution in March 1944, Coroner Gerber and *Cleveland News* writer Howard Beaufait visited with Johnson for an hour and a half in an attempt to connect him with the twelve officially recognized torso butcheries. Still wearing a variation of his odd costume, Johnson smoked incessantly, complained of nosebleeds, and paced back and forth in a cell littered with Bibles and sacks of tobacco. "I didn't do it," Johnson insisted, according to Beaufait. "But I'll tell you something I have never told before. I know who killed that girl and cut up her body. I was to get $25 for carrying the body away, that's all." He then named an eastsider whom the police had previously questioned and eliminated from suspicion in the torso case. On March 10, Johnson died in the electric chair still maintaining his innocence. Though Detective Frank W. Story and former Ness associate County Prosecutor Frank T. Cullitan dismissed notions that he had anything to do with the still-unsolved Kingsbury Run murders, Gerber—along with several members of the police department—thought he might be responsible. "Willie Johnson has all the qualifications of the so-called torso killer," Beaufait quotes the coroner in a *News* article on March 9, 1944. "He is smart, strong as an ox, and entirely capable of these crimes both physically and mentally." Forty years later, Gerber curiously reversed himself. "Johnson wasn't the torso murderer," he told George Condon, author and former columnist for the *Plain Dealer,* in a torso murders retrospective published in the March 1984 issue of *Cleveland Magazine.* "Neither was Dolezal. Neither one of them committed those murders." This would not be the only time Gerber would inexplicably retract a previous statement about the Butcher.

NOTES

The best coverage of the Willie Johnson episode can be found in the *Press* clipping file at Cleveland State University and a similar file on the Kingsbury Run murders in the General Reference Department of the Cleveland Public Library.

Gerber's retraction of his previous statement about Willie Johnson's guilt appears in George Condon's "The Mad Butcher of Kingsbury Run."

THE KENTUCKY BUTCHER

In a case filled with the weird and strange, the story of the Kentucky butcher ranks, perhaps, as the most grotesque. His tale remains so incredible and terrible that, whether he ultimately had anything to do with the Kingsbury Run murders or not, it could furnish enough fodder for a host of low-budget, mad-slasher movies.

His possible connection with the Cleveland killings began in 1942, when Arnold Sagalyn, onetime special assistant to Eliot Ness, was working for the

Press. The paper sent him and writer William Miller to Maysville, Kentucky, to check out a man who had committed a murder startlingly similar in some ways to the Kingsbury Run atrocities. The killer had brutally dispatched an acquaintance because the man had refused to sell him any of his prize "coon dogs." The murderer then took the dogs, stripped the man's body, and had the victim's clothes retailored to fit him. Not content with such cold-hearted thievery, the killer decapitated his victim, placed the head on a platter, and then hacked the limbs from the corpse. He ground up the dismembered body parts and sold the meat to an unsuspecting sausage manufacturer. According to Sagalyn, people in the county at the time still talked of the sausage that burned with a strange blue flame. Not surprisingly, considering the trail he left behind him, the man was quickly apprehended, tried for murder, convicted, and sent to prison. The killer's brother, however, enjoyed ties to the governor, so in true good-old-boy fashion, the convicted man served a brief token sentence in prison and then was quietly released.

Once in Maysville, Miller and Sagalyn went to the local newspaper office not only to learn as much about the case as possible but to try to get a lead as to where the killer could be found. When the two newspapermen approached the man at the front desk and asked to speak with the editor, the man casually rose and picked up a baseball bat that had been lying on the desk. Once they had explained their mission, the man lowered his bat and introduced himself as the editor. Maysville must have been quite a town!

After the cooperative journalist had told the pair where they could find their killer, the two decided on a cover story—they were interested in the man's coon dogs. They found their quarry on his farm, vigorously chopping wood. As they cautiously approached, the man eyed them suspiciously and began nonchalantly swinging his ax back and forth. Today Sagalyn chuckles when he recalls how he and Miller had tried to gauge the distance between them and the ax in the man's outstretched arm.

After a polite but undoubtedly strained conversation on canine matters, Miller and Sagalyn ran a background check on the ax-wielding suspect and discovered, to their surprise, that the man had relatives in Cleveland and had been in the city during the period of the murders. The two men then enlisted the aid of the local barber in obtaining hair samples from the head of Maysville's most notorious resident that they could send to Cleveland to be compared with the stray strands found with some of the victims. The purloined locks were duly collected and sent north. By that time, however, Arnold Sagalyn had joined Eliot Ness in Washington, D.C., so he never learned the outcome of those tests or the ultimate fate of the notorious Kentucky butcher.

NOTE

Arnold Sagalyn discussed this episode during two telephone interviews. Andrew Schug, former member of the Board of Trustees of the Cleveland Police Historical Society, participated in the second interview.

THE NEW CASTLE RAILROAD MAN

In 1921, the corpse of an old woman lay undisturbed in her Wampum, Pennsylvania, home. She had been nearly decapitated; only a few strands of skin held her head precariously to the rest of her body. Her house had not been ransacked, nor had anything been taken. The woman's house stood close to railroad tracks that passed by a vast, desolate swampy area dubbed by New Castle locals as the Murder Swamp, or Hell's Half-Acre. Two years later, the dismembered torso of a young girl drifted down a river that ran close by the same swamp and railroad tracks. Between 1925 and 1934, outraged New Castle residents endured the discovery of four more gruesomely dismembered corpses in this isolated spot. One headless male, dead for nearly a month, sat across a narrow path with his feet pointing north, his head buried at his feet. Nearby, the skeletal remains of a second headless man rested in a similar position. Beyond these two ghastly sentinels, the dismembered remains of a third man and a woman lay scattered over the swamp. It was an extraordinarily dangerous place; only someone thoroughly familiar with such trails as existed could safely traverse the area. One false step could plunge a man up to his waist in foul muck or quicksand. In 1934, a thousand angry New Castlers scoured the putrid expanse in a determined search for any clues. They found nothing, but at least the murders stopped.

In 1939, they started up again, and by 1942, the unknown killer had added six more victims to the Pennsylvania tally. Between these two periods of murderous activity, the years 1935 to 1938 passed by uneventfully in New Castle, but were filled with horror for Clevelanders. This intriguing coincidence fascinated Robert Mancini, a truck driver from Austintown with a passion for history and TV crime shows, who once lived in Hubbard,

Pennsylvania, near the notorious New Castle swamp. In 1992, he began exploring the possibility that the Cleveland Butcher and the New Castle maniac could be the same person.

The reasonably precise dovetailing of the two sets of Pennsylvania murders with the Cleveland butcheries is certainly intriguing, and other common features such as decapitation and dismemberment, the similarity of the victims' profiles, and the isolated nature of the discovery sites remain compelling. There are also other eerie echoes between the New Castle and Cleveland killings. The manner in which the heads of Edward Andrassy and victim no. 2 were buried recalls the buried head at the feet of one of the Pennsylvania victims. The curious mixture of deliberately putting some victims on display while casually discarding others seems common to both cases. Although the word "NAZI" carved on the chest of one of the three Stowe Township victims finds no counterpart in any of the Cleveland or New Castle killings, the sheer level of frenzied violence, especially noted in the later stages of the Cleveland cycle, seems common to both as well.

Mancini was bitten by the bug. "It was like the ultimate big-game hunt," he told Brian Albrecht of the *Plain Dealer* in July 1993. Due to a work-related injury, Mancini had time on his hands, so, though he never attended college and had no practical experience in research, he began a systematic hunt for a killer. He deduced that only a railroad man would be able to travel from New Castle to Cleveland with such ease, be so familiar with the desolate and industrial areas flanking the railroad tracks in both cities, come in contact with the vagrants who became his prey, and have such easy access to boxcars in which to commit his butcheries. He focused on the word "NAZI" cut into the chest of one of the three Stowe Township victims discovered in May 1940, wondering if he might be dealing with a fanatical Nazi hater whose murderous activities ceased in the Cleveland–New Castle area because he had joined the service.

Mancini began combing through New Castle and railroad records looking for a single man of the proper age who had lived in New Castle and had worked on the railroads for at least twenty years before joining the service during World War II. Suddenly, he found his man, Thomas Hunter Perrill—a former brakeman and conductor with the necessary years of service with the B&O, originally from West Virginia, who joined the army in 1942 but met his death in an inexplicable gasoline fire in a Louisiana latrine after only six weeks of basic training. Coming from a rural background, he may have been a hunter. His father had been either killed or wounded—Mancini was never able to determine which—during World War I, which might explain a ferocious hatred for Germans.

On a Saturday in September or October 1942, a Cleveland man traveled to New Castle by train with a friend to start a new job as a cook. On Sunday morning, his decapitated corpse was found along the rails; his mysterious friend had vanished. Shortly thereafter, Mancini's man enlisted in the army at the age of forty-four. Then the terrible New Castle killings stopped.

During the final phases of his hunt, Mancini searched for the house in which his quarry had once lived. Ideally, he would have liked to have found an abandoned, derelict structure with an old attic and deserted basement to explore. Unfortunately, the house had long since been torn down.

The Cleveland authorities believed the Butcher had to be large and powerful; was Mancini's railroad man big enough to fill the bill? Curiously, Louisiana authorities initially refused Mancini's request for the man's death certificate, even though it is a public document, and remained adamant until he contacted an acquaintance at NBC's *Unsolved Mysteries* who was able to apply the necessary pressure. The document he received from Louisiana is notable for what it does not say. Everything about the deceased's parents, including their names, is left blank; neither his social security number nor his serial number appears. This was, after all, no John Doe picked up in the gutter but an army man who died of burns and resulting infection received on a military base. Wouldn't the army have far more detailed records about him? Mr. Perrill, however, turned out to be a rather slight individual, a mere five feet six—arguably not large enough to be responsible for the Butcher's work.

Whether or not Mancini's railroad man was the Kingsbury Run murderer, there is enough mystery surrounding him to suggest that he was guilty of something. "Even if I could somehow put this guy at the scene, on the right dates, it wouldn't prove anything," he confided to Brian Albrecht on July 25, 1993. "Unless you have some witnesses, you can't prove it."

NOTES

Brian Albrecht's discussion of Robert Mancini's theory appears in the *Plain Dealer*'s Sunday magazine, July 25, 1993.

Robert Mancini shared the details of his research with me in a series of telephone interviews. He also drove to Cleveland in the fall of 1997 for a round-table discussion over dinner with me and fellow researchers Andrew Schug, Don Stragisher, and Thomas Mullady.

PETER MERYLO'S MALE NURSE

The notion that Detective Merylo suspected an unnamed male nurse who worked at City Hospital has been among the more prominent solutions to the riddle of the killings, though it is difficult to ascertain exactly when this particular theory was born. Supposedly, police somehow tied this mysterious figure to the identified victims—Edward Andrassy, Flo Polillo, and Rose Wallace. Linking him with Andrassy would be easy enough considering Andrassy's on-again, off-again work history at the hospital from the mid-1920s through the early 1930s.

The primary source for this tale seems to be Gus Zukie, a member of the Cleveland police force from 1936 to 1977, who worked with and knew Peter Merylo. Zukie reports that Merylo confided in him about his suspicions and lamented he was never able to assemble enough hard evidence to warrant an arrest. Merylo also supposedly hinted that the nurse was a member of a politically prominent Cleveland family whose local clout was such that he expected his superiors to remove him from the case to preserve the suspect's identity and his family's reputation.

As a nurse, the man could be expected to possess the medical background necessary to explain the finesse of the butcheries; his job at City Hospital and his rumored links to the identified victims also make him an attractive suspect. But assuming he even existed, who was he?

On April 29, 1938, Merylo requested his direct superior, Lieutenant Harvey Weitzel, to contact Lillian (Andrassy's former wife, now remarried) in Vickery, Ohio. At this point in his investigation, Merylo was refocusing on Andrassy's known acquaintances, and he wanted her comments on a list of thirty orderlies who had worked at City Hospital during the same period she and Edward had been employed in the psychiatric ward—she as a nurse, he as an orderly. The former Mrs. Andrassy responded to these inquiries on May 2 in a letter sent to Chief of Police George Matowitz. "The name of the man who worked at City Hospital with Mr. Andrassy and seemed most close to him, was Mahoney," she wrote. There were, however, two Mahoneys on Merylo's list—John and Robby (possibly Rorry), and Lillian was not sure which one Edward knew. "The man Mahoney was quite tall," she recalled. "At the time about 30 years of age, had medium brown hair; not very nice looking, thin face and body." Merylo had tracked down and questioned John Galvin, another man on his list of orderlies who had lived with Andrassy in 1929 or 1930, but Lillian insisted that she did not know him. There is no evidence in any of Merylo's surviving reports or his subsequent actions that a likely suspect materialized from those inquiries into Andrassy's hospital acquaintances.

Of course, it is conceivable that this shadowy figure could have emerged at some point after Merylo's determined look into Andrassy's professional associates in early 1938. The rumored link to a powerful Cleveland family remains one of the most tantalizing details about the whole story, especially since Eliot Ness's secret suspect reportedly enjoyed similar ties. But neither the names Mahoney nor Galvin carried any political weight in Cleveland at the time—nor, for that matter, did any of the other names on Merylo's list. Edward Andrassy was not a nurse; he was an orderly. But he did work at City Hospital where Gus Zukie says the elusive male nurse with connections to a prominent Cleveland family was employed. Is it possible that "Peter Merylo's male nurse" is a composite of Edward Andrassy and someone else who happened to be at the hospital?

NOTES

Brian Albrecht discusses Gus Zukie and the male nurse theory in "The Terror of Kingsbury Run," *Plain Dealer,* January 8, 1989, GI.

Lillian's letter to George Matowitz is in Peter Merylo's files. It is a fascinating document for the light it sheds on Edward's relationship with her and his family. "He was not forced to marry me in any way, and I had no idea he was anything worse than a man who drank to excess. His sister Edna knows more about him than I and I am sure more than his parents too."

THE MAN IN THE HOTEL SUITE: ELIOT NESS'S SECRET SUSPECT

The legend that Safety Director Eliot Ness had a secret suspect has hovered over the Kingsbury Run mystery ever since the murders occurred. At first, the rumors of such a figure were extraordinarily vague and sketchy, but they gathered considerable force when Ness collaborated with author Oscar Fraley on *The Untouchables*—which would become the basis for the popular television show starring Robert Stack—and *Four against the Mob* in the mid-1950s. By then Ness had left law enforcement and was no longer in the public eye. He reminisced about his days in Chicago and Cleveland with Fraley, focusing mainly on his battles with Al Capone during Prohibition.

He alluded briefly to the Kingsbury Run murders during his conversations with Fraley. There was a man, Ness reflected, about whom he had grown more and more suspicious as the investigation dragged on, though how this individual had come to his attention is not clear. The man possessed the necessary medical background to perform the dismemberments and was also supposedly linked in some unspecified way to an unnamed, prominent Cleveland family. In deference to the family's feelings, Ness brought the suspect to an unidentified hotel room for a secret interrogation. A lie detector test was administered—though by whom Ness does not say—that the suspect failed. Ness called his suspect Gaylord Sundheim, a strange pseudonym for a no-nonsense lawman to use when something nondescript such as "John Doe" would have served his purpose. Ness described his suspect as a large, powerful man who treated the whole episode as a huge joke. Realizing that he had nothing solid against "Sundheim" except, perhaps, for his personal suspicions, Ness reluctantly released the man—only to learn that he had immediately placed himself beyond the law by committing himself to a mental institution.

Ness's account is as vague as the legend that it supposedly substantiates—so vague, in fact, that there would seem no way of verifying it. Those inclined to dismiss the story suggest that the onetime hero, his middle years blighted by business failures and rumors of alcoholism, could not bring himself to admit there was ever a case he could not solve and may have fabricated the encounter.

† † †

Sometime in late May 1938, one of the most crucial scenes in the city's long-running nightmare drama played out over a one- to two-week period in an unidentified suite at the Cleveland Hotel—now the Renaissance—on Public Square. In the best tradition of Greek tragedy, this climactic event unfolded behind closed doors away from public view. Twenty years would pass before Eliot Ness revealed to Oscar Fraley that the secret interrogation had even occurred, and it would be another fifteen before any of the other participants substantiated his claim and acknowledged their own roles.

Almost everything that happened in that suite more than seventy years ago remains speculation based on guesswork and fragmentary evidence, some of it hearsay, reported by those present long after the fact—the building blocks of legend. With Safety Director Ness on that first day were Dr. Royal Grossman, psychiatrist for Cuyahoga County, and David L. Cowles, head of the Scientific Investigation Bureau. The fourth man present lay sprawled on a bed, stinking drunk. At just under six feet and over two hundred pounds, his impressive bulk suggested obesity as well as strength and power. He was a known barbiturate addict and alcoholic, and, according to his former wife and county probate records, he had been treated unsuccessfully at least once for alcoholism at City Hospital in 1933. There was no way of knowing what combination of abuses had led to this particular deep stupor or how long he was likely to remain unconscious.

The official path that led him to that hotel suite remains clouded in secrecy. He had come under police scrutiny as far back as 1935, and by fits and starts an official noose had been tightening around him for three years. On those occasions when he was sober and knew he was being followed, this elusive quarry treated his would-be pursuers like Keystone Cops, making the befuddled authorities targets of a bizarre sense of humor. Once he reportedly turned on his flabbergasted pursuer, stuck out his hand, and formally introduced himself. On another occasion, he managed to shake his tail by jumping on and off streetcars, only to call police headquarters and tell the startled officer at the desk that if the young man who had been unsuccessfully following him wanted to meet with him again, he would be in the lobby of Higbee's department store at 2:00. He led one dogged pursuer all over the downtown area, ending the proverbial merry chase by going into an all-black bar and ordering a drink for himself "and my white shadow." He wickedly bombarded David Cowles with newspaper clippings about murders, directing that they should be placed "in my file." One such communication was a drawing of the county morgue with a sign on the front door reading "No More Bodies." According to Arnold Sagalyn, special assistant to the safety director, he found the experience of being a suspect enormously exciting. He even sent Ness a photograph of a lone tree in an open field marked with an X and the instructions "dig here."

There is no way of knowing exactly what chain of events brought the down-and-out character first under much tighter, more intense official scrutiny and finally to the hotel suite for a formal interrogation. All the evidence implicating him in Cleveland's series of horrible murder-dismemberments remained purely circumstantial, and Ness probably made the decision to question him in secret because of the complete lack of hard evidence against him, coupled with the potential but unpredictable consequences of hauling him in publicly.

We will never know under what circumstances the suspect was found or exactly who brought him to the hotel suite. According to Royal Grossman, the man was so intoxicated when they picked him up that it took three days to dry him out. Whether the assembled team actively tried to sober him up or simply let him sleep it off naturally remains unknown. Ness did post a round-the-clock guard outside the door, so the trio could come and go as they pleased, checking on his condition periodically.

As he slowly began to crawl out of his self-induced fog, his behavior veered wildly from comic to dangerous. He complained about his former wife and her spending habits. He worried that he could lose his job and railed loudly against a host of persecutors. Hallucinations sometimes gripped him, and he lurched violently around the room, insisting that federal agents were after him. He turned despondent and complained bitterly about painful burning sensations in his hands and feet. Was Slap-Hap McCord still following him, he wondered. At some point, while Cowles and Grossman were out of the suite, he roused himself sufficiently to glare at Ness with such penetrating intensity that the safety director moved toward the door in case he had to alert the guards outside. To his consternation, he found no one was there. The man who had tangled with Al Capone and dodged bullets from Kentucky moonshiners later confessed to his wife, Elizabeth, that he had experienced a momentary jolt of genuine fear when he realized he was utterly alone with his unpredictable suspect.

The formal interrogation probably began on the fourth day. According to David Cowles, he and Detective Ray Oldag worked on their uncooperative suspect eight hours a day for over a week—an extraordinary grilling, even in an age far less concerned with the rights of defendants than our own.

No one knows exactly when Dr. Leonard Keeler of Northwestern University arrived in Cleveland. The interrogation had been so carefully planned that it is likely that Ness brought him in just before operatives picked up their wayward target. He had invented the Keeler polygraph, reputed to be the most sensitive, and therefore the most reliable, of the early lie detectors. At the time, Keeler was regarded as the reigning authority on the device; he had refined his technique over the course of thirty thousand tests and had instructed others in polygraph use at the crime detection laboratory of Northwestern University Law School. His machine was the prototype of the modern polygraph: a rubber tube connected a belt around the chest to the machine and measured respiration while an armband monitored blood pressure. Ness needed the very best, so he called in a marker from his Chicago days, and Keeler brought his lie detector to Cleveland and personally conducted the test. The East Cleveland Police Department had begun employing Keeler's machine in July 1937, demonstrating its reliability by using *Plain Dealer* reporter David I. Rimmel as a test subject on July 26. East Cleveland city manager Charles A. Curran offered the device to other Greater Cleveland police departments, but it would be extraordinarily difficult to arrange such a loan in secret.

Dr. Grossman had observed the suspect closely during his entire period of forced incarceration in the hotel suite. As the effects of alcohol and drugs abated, did he notice signs of the progressive mental illness that had been developing for at least a decade? The man's behavior undoubtedly struck him as bizarre, even abnormal, but Grossman surely knew that the suspect had recently been subjected to two competency hearings—what the legal language of the 1930s bluntly called inquests into lunacy—in February and April of 1938. The first action had been initiated by Dr. Leonard Prendergast, a dentist and probable friend, the other by his older sister, but county psychiatrists saw no reason to commit him on either occasion.

How did the man react as Keeler began connecting him to his polygraph for the formal interrogation? Reports about his behavior suggest he either would have turned distant and dismissed the whole affair as of no interest or treated it as a game, a huge joke. According to what Ness later told Oscar Fraley, he opted for the latter course. Careful to keep his tone of voice neutral, Keeler began working methodically through the prepared list of questions, constantly checking the trails left by the delicate metal arms that recorded the suspect's reactions. Even after his long ordeal, every inquiry, no matter how insignificant, provoked a jeering, mocking retort.

"Is your na . . . ?" Keeler started to ask.

"Gaylord Sundheim!" the suspect interrupted with a roaring, boisterous laugh, obviously enjoying a private joke.

When the session was over, Keeler drew Ness and Cowles aside. In 1983, the eighty-six-year-old David Cowles reflected, "When Keeler got through, he said he was the man, no question about it. 'I may as well throw my machine out the window if I say anything else.'" In all his laboratory tests, Keeler was reputed never to have found an innocent man guilty. According to Cowles, there were other unspecified tests, some conducted by an unidentified official from the Detroit court system, all of which pointed to the same conclusion.

Within days a small crack would appear in the wall of secrecy that had been so carefully built up around the interrogation. A May 31 article about victim no. 10 in the *Cleveland News* contained a brief, passing reference to a man who had been "grilled by federal authorities [perhaps the official linked to the Detroit court system?] and police in connection with the murders," and "subjected to lie detector tests." Thus the legend of "Eliot Ness's secret suspect" was born and would haunt the city for decades.

After the lengthy interrogation, the suspected murderer began to manifest a menacing combination of amusement and anger. Knowing that he did not have a shred of hard evidence he could take to court, Ness confronted his prime suspect—standing in front of him, thumbs in his vest pockets, looking at him sternly.

"I think you killed those people," he charged.

"Think? Prove it!"

NOTES

The fullest and most accessible account of the Gaylord Sundheim episode is in Stephen Nickel's *Torso,* 202–4.

Though I have taken a few liberties in piecing this account together, the details of the narrative are firmly grounded in information gathered primarily through interviews. Marilyn Bardsley spoke with Dr. Royal Grossman, David Cowles, and Elizabeth Ness in the early 1970s; and she provided most of the details that form this account.

David Cowles's narrative of the hotel suite interrogation is from a taped interview conducted by Florence Schwein and Lieutenant Tom Brown in 1983.

Some of the descriptions of the suspect's condition before and during the interrogation come from an interview with Sergeant John Fransen and material he gathered on the murders in 1991 and 1992. Others are based on accounts given to Marilyn Bardsley forty-five years ago by individuals who knew and remembered the suspect.

Marilyn Bardsley and Arnold Sagalyn, special assistant to Eliot Ness, provided the accounts of the suspect's bizarre behavior while under police surveillance.

The brief dialogue between Ness and his suspect during their final confrontation is from Stephen Nickel's *Torso,* 202. The question-and-answer exchange between Keeler and the suspect is conjecture on my part.

"Good Cheer, the American Sweeney"

Eliot and Elizabeth Ness's adopted son Robert Eliot Ness died at age thirty of leukemia on August 31, 1976. In memory of her husband, Sharon Ness donated her father-in-law's scrapbooks to the library at the Western Reserve Historical Society the following year. The materials meticulously document the small victories and major triumphs of Eliot Ness's career through newspaper clippings, conference programs, personal letters, and official commendations.

Among the voluminous scrapbooks, however, are some remarkably strange items: a virtually incoherent letter and five loose postcards, each bearing one or more cryptic messages, weird pronouncements, and taunting jokes. The sender decorated four of the cards by pasting on pictures clipped from newspapers or magazines. These cards, all sent from Dayton in the mid-1950s to Eliot Ness's office in the Union Commerce Building, are variously addressed to *"Eliot (Esophogotic) Ness," "Eliot-Am-Big-U-ous Ness," "Eliot (Head Man) Ness," "Eliot-Direct-Um Ness,"* and simply *"Eliot-Ness."* The writer frequently underlined words or portions of them (the underlinings seem so purposeful and selective, that it is tempting to see them as a part of the writer's jokes), and often connected words through a liberal use of dashes. The messages themselves, though handprinted, are occasionally illegible: sometimes because of the quality of the printing, occasionally because other features such as stamps and postmarks obscure some of the wording.

Most of the sometimes witty and intellectual pronouncements read like highly personal but disjointed jokes, and some use verbal puns. One card pictures Dayton's Deeds Carillon—a tall, knife-blade-like structure—on the front and reads in part, *"In-das-Freudiology / this-organ-has-the-eminence-of-a-reamer. / Whether-the-chimes / peal-the-note-for- / bell-ringing-effect / or-not-is* the- / Macbethean-question" (a probable reference to the famous lines in act II, scene II of Shakespeare's *Macbeth,* "Is this a dagger which I see before me, / The handle toward my hand?"). A partially obscured message on the same card seems to say, "Be seeyn of / ya some time in / US court of peals." Another card sends *"R'gards-to / Slap-Hap / McCord,"* while another states, *"With-the-advent-of-Spring* / the Apis-Apidae-will-again / gather-the-precious-nectar / from-ye-olde-curiosity-locus." The sender has written around the printed words "post card" on the message side of one so as to read, "mental-defective / *Post Card*ed / this."

On three of the four cards to which the writer attached illustrations, he left a message under the picture. The words underneath what seems to be a vaudeville comic or movie comedian, sticking out his tongue, unfortunately are completely illegible. "Who-is-tother-guy? Your / astral-preeminence? *Wah-Hoo,"* he asks under what looks like a shot of two men behind bars from a Hollywood film. Below an ad for pansy seeds, he assures, "No nothing-xplosive-herin." He has allowed the advertisement for *"Handbook for Poisoners: A Collection of Famous Poison Stories* edited and with an introduction by Raymond T. Bond" to speak for itself.

Three of the five cards bear a name, most likely the sender's. Beside the picture of the Deeds Carillon stand the words, *"A-Signatur / The-Sweeney Boy / R-member,"* and a message next to the pansy ad reads, *"Good-Cheer / The-American / Sweeney"* (a sly reference to the English mass murderer Sweeney Todd?). Beside the ad for the poisoner handbook stands the stark pronouncement, *"F.E. Sweeney-M.D. / Paranoidal-Nemesis /* The-Better-Half of Legal-Exaction / Will-upon you one Day?"

Unlike the handprinted postcards, the letter, sent to Eliot Ness from the veterans' hospital in Dayton on February 14, 1954, is written in script: "Enclosed a few items for your, Personal Perusal, as to Hermacy Reference, 'Per Se', should all or any have no significant application—Would that you Present to Special Agent McCord for a Personal Extraction herefrom and if again in the negative, tis no doubt as of some, Perverted, information having Dominant Dwelling, *a loft* in my, 'Wind Sheets' I trust that we shall meet again Amongst more favorable 'Federal issues'?" Under the signature *"Frank E. Sweeney M D"* stands a postscript: *"P.S. 'Phony',* criminalization— Is tough, at any m*onetary Bargaining?* As well as Phony Pschotization?"

Unfortunately, the enclosed "few items" have not survived. The reference

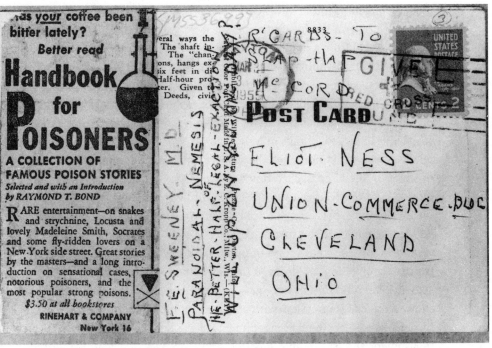

The "Paranoidal-Nemesis" postcard. This is one of the five surviving cards Francis Sweeney sent to Eliot Ness in the early to mid-1950s. It is the only one on which he identified himself with more than his last name. Western Reserve Historical Society.

to Special Agent McCord, however, is interesting, primarily because of the Slap-Hap McCord greeting on one of the cards. (There was a Walter McCord on the police force who became a detective in 1939 after seventeen years of service in the department.) For the only time on the six curious documents, the sender left virtually his full name. But who was this mysterious Dr. Frank E. Sweeney? Why would he send such incoherent ramblings to Eliot Ness? Was he as mentally disturbed as his communications would suggest? And most important, did he have any connection to the Kingsbury Run murders?

† † †

In the early 1970s, former Clevelander Marilyn Bardsley wondered if the story of Cleveland's most famous killings could be turned into a play. At the time, she knew little more about the Kingsbury Run murders than the folklore familiar to most city residents, so she began digging for information. Some coverage in the local press about her activities eventually resulted in a phone call from a man who identified himself as Dr. Royal Grossman, psychiatrist for Cuyahoga County. He confided that he had a story to tell, which he had kept secret for over thirty years. Grossman then substantiated the tale Eliot Ness had shared with his biographer Oscar Fraley just before his death in 1957 about the secret hotel suite interrogation of his prime suspect in the torso killings in May 1938. At the time, Bardsley could not tell if Grossman did not know the suspect's name or was simply unwilling to share it. She later tracked down David Cowles, living in retirement in Florida, and the former head of the Scientific Investigation Bureau confirmed Grossman's account but—citing a promise made to Ness—adamantly refused to divulge the suspect's name.

A year later, another round of publicity in city papers about Bardsley's research prompted a call from Al (actually either Alec or Alex) Archacki, a sixty-five-year-old former burglar—a bizarre but charming character who showed up for his interview with a shotgun hidden under his trench coat. In 1934, he told her, he had met a tall, well-dressed man in an upstairs establishment at East 6th and Superior, which Archacki alternately referred to as either the Eagles Club or Weber's. (There is no city directory listing for an Eagles Club, but Weber's Restaurant occupied 242 Superior.) The affable stranger flashed a roll of bills, struck up a conversation, and offered to buy Archacki a drink. Though he remained friendly and polite, the man kept asking questions such as, "Do you live around here" and "Do you have a wife?" For some reason, Archacki decided his new drinking companion was gay, so he refused to be drawn into any intimate disclosures.

He ran into the man again three years later while serving a sentence for armed robbery at the Ohio State Penitentiary in Mansfield. At the time, an arrangement between the Sandusky Soldiers and Sailors Home and the Ohio penitentiary system allowed honor prisoners from Mansfield, like Archacki, to work at the home and live in a cottage on the grounds. Archacki said he met his former drinking companion, who was a resident of the home, in the mess hall. The two men immediately struck up an ideal symbiotic relationship: Archacki supplied his new friend with liquor, and the man, who turned out to be a doctor, reciprocated by writing him prescriptions for "barbitals." Archacki recounted that he began to notice a curious pattern between the terrible killings in Cleveland and the doctor's periodic absences from the home. (Bardsley reconfirmed all the details of this story in a second interview with Archacki twenty years later in the early 1990s.) Though the doctor had initially introduced himself as Al Sweeney, Archacki insisted that his real name was Frank. Royal Grossman then admitted to Bardsley that this mysterious physician was, indeed, Eliot Ness's prime suspect, and when she called David Cowles in Florida and greeted him by simply saying, "Francis Edward Sweeney," he thundered back at her, "Who gave you that name?!"

† † †

Officially the books are never closed on a homicide, though realistically most investigative trails run cold in a matter of days. In late 1991 to early 1992, then Cleveland police chief Edward Kovacic received an official request from Los Angeles authorities to look into a possible connection between the torso killings and the murder-dismemberment of the Black Dahlia in the late 1940s. The inquiry may have been prompted in part by speculation in the popular media that the infamous Los Angeles murder might be linked to the Cleveland crimes. Kovacic handed the assignment to Sergeant John Fransen (now retired) of the Police Homicide Unit.

Though he quickly disposed of the notion that the same individual could be responsible for the murders in both cities, Fransen—like Peter Merylo before him—responded to the seductive lure of Cleveland's infamous string of unsolved butcheries and began delving into the case. "There were times I'd be driving around in the Flats, and I'd feel I was back in the 1930s," he mused in the late 1990s. He had not heard of Marilyn Bardsley's research, and by then she had moved out of the city. The few people directly involved in the case—such as David Cowles, Sam Gerber, and Royal Grossman—with whom she had talked two decades before were all dead. By then, however, the cryptic cards and letter among Eliot Ness's scrapbooks at the Western Reserve Historical Society had come to light.

As a trained investigator, Fransen knew where to look and what strings to pull; as a cop working on an unsolved sixty-year-old case, he enjoyed easy access to some official corridors often off limits to a layman. He quickly covered much of the same ground as Bardsley had twenty years before and within a few months was able to amass an impressive dossier that he handed over to his superiors. Though he could not find any solid proof, Fransen's research left him convinced that Eliot Ness's tale of his secret suspect was true and that the man he had described to Oscar Fraley was, indeed, Dr. Francis Edward Sweeney.

Understandably, the problems that arise in tracing Francis Edward Sweeney's life are compounded by the passage of time and the errors and omissions in public records. Francis Edward Sweeney was born on May 5, 1894, to Martin J. (probably Joseph) and Delia (née O'Mara or perhaps simply Mara) Sweeney, the fifth of six children. Both sets of grandparents had emigrated from Ireland in the mid-nineteenth century. (It is not clear from records whether Martin J. was born in Ireland or the United States.) The families lived close to each other for a while on Cedar Avenue on Cleveland's near east side and even bought a shared plot with more than a dozen grave sites in St. Joseph's Cemetery on Woodland Avenue. Francis's father, Martin J., was a teamster at a time when that term literally meant someone who handles a team of horses. For most of his boyhood, the family lived on Jessie Avenue, now East 79th.

Death and tragedy dogged the family from the beginning. One of Francis's older brothers died at the age of three (certainly not an unusual occurrence in the late nineteenth century), while another died of uremia in 1912 at twenty-five. His sole surviving brother died from injuries sustained from a fall off a house roof in September 1939. Francis's mother, Delia Sweeney, died suddenly at the age of forty or forty-one in 1903 of heart failure. By 1910 his father was confined to Sunny Acres Hospital suffering with tuberculosis (at which point the surviving children dispersed), and by 1920 he was incarcerated in the old state mental hospital on Turney Road. He died in 1923 at the age of sixty-two of "apoplexy," with "psychosis with cerebral arterial sclerosis" listed as contributory causes.

Francis Sweeney was a highly intelligent, ambitious man, and throughout the early years of his adulthood, he worked hard to rise above his blue-collar beginnings. On October 2, 1917, he joined the army and went to Europe, spending most of the next two years working in medical supply. He obtained an honorable discharge in August 1919 but with the potentially ominous notation "25% disabled" attached to his record. Though the exact

Dr. Francis Sweeney at age thirty-four in 1928, the year he graduated from medical school. He did not normally wear a mustache. Courtesy of Andrew Schug, Former Member of Board of Trustees, Cleveland Police Historical Society.

nature of his injury remains unknown (public records indicate it was not combat-related), his disability was severe enough to earn him an adjusted compensation certificate—the contemporary equivalent of VA benefits.

When he returned to Cleveland after the war, he began making solid plans for his future. He served as vice chairman of the County Council of the American Legion, a temporary organization that held its first meeting in the Hotel Hollenden on July 2. Perhaps using his government funds to pay bills, Francis entered the School of Pharmacy at Western Reserve University in 1920 and graduated with his certificate two years later. From 1923 to 1924, he took courses at John Carroll University, apparently to plug the gaps in his scientific background, for on October 1, 1924, he entered the freshman class at St. Louis University's School of Medicine. He finished the prescribed regimen of courses and lectures in four years, distinguishing himself by serving as vice president of his class during his sophomore year.

In the summer of 1927, following his junior year, Francis returned to Cleveland and married Mary Josephine Sokol, a twenty-seven-year-old nurse at St. Vincent's Charity Hospital. The bride's family had come to the city about a decade before from New York State and had settled on East 121st, just off Buckeye in the midst of the huge Hungarian community on Cleveland's east side. The marriage license shaves three years off Francis's age, giving it as thirty: perhaps a lie on his part, perhaps a clerical error but certainly a ghostly echo of his father, whose age also fluctuated on public documents. The couple was married on July 2 by Francis's cousin the Reverend Dominic J. Sweeney at St. Thomas Aquinas Church on Superior Avenue.

After Francis's graduation from medical school in 1928, the couple returned to Cleveland, where he had been accepted as an intern at St. Alexis Hospital on Broadway, and, as a temporary cost-saving measure, moved in with the family of one of Mary's sisters at 13314 Rexwood in Garfield Heights. On January 8, 1929, the state of Ohio formally granted Dr. Francis Edward Sweeney M.D. a certificate to practice medicine and surgery. Their first child, Francis Edward Sweeney Jr. (killed in a 1947 auto accident), was born the same year, and a second son, James Anthony, followed in 1931. The family moved into their own home at 12910 Melgrove, also in Garfield Heights. All the sheer hard work and tenacity had paid off handsomely; the son of working-class Irish parents had achieved success. Now on the threshold of a promising medical career, he was ready to live out the American dream. The few surviving personal accounts of him at this point in his life that Marilyn Bardsley was able to assemble in the early 1970s picture an intelligent, compassionate, highly dedicated physician with a good sense of humor. In 1929 the future, indeed, looked very bright. But the demons began to howl that same year.

According to the petition for divorce filed by Mary Sweeney in 1934, Francis began to drink far more heavily than in the past, and, over the next couple of years, his behavior gradually became more erratic and violent. He started to neglect his medical practice; he would disappear from the family home for days at a time, leaving no word as to where he was going or what he was doing; he became abusive, both physically and mentally, toward his wife and children; he was habitually drunk and began to hallucinate. Finally, Mary had had all she could take. On December 1, 1933, she filed an affidavit in probate court stating that she feared for her husband's sanity. A warrant for his arrest was duly issued and executed. The formal inquest was held in Judge Nelson J. Brewer's court the next day, and Francis Sweeney was committed to City Hospital for observation and treatment, apparently for alcoholism. A month later, on January 3, 1934, the hospital discharged him into his wife's custody. Within a week, she was back in court swearing out a second affidavit, but on January 23, Judge Brewer dismissed the complaint. No doubt growing increasingly desperate, perhaps even concerned for the safety of her children, Mary left the Melgrove residence and, with the boys, again moved in with her sister's family, now on East Boulevard. In September 1934, she sued for divorce, custody of the children, and restoration of her maiden name (all of which the court granted in 1936). After that, Francis Edward Sweeney simply disappeared.

According to the 1936 divorce documents, Francis resided on Kempton Avenue, off of East 105th, but the city directory does not confirm this: none of the several Francis E. Sweeneys listed in Cleveland at that time were living at this address. He surfaced in 1938 when he again passed through the probate court system. On February 11, Dr. Leonard F. Prendergast, a dentist and probable acquaintance, filed an affidavit questioning his sanity, and Francis's older sister followed suit on April 12. On both occasions, court-appointed psychiatrists Stone, West, and Tierney found Francis Sweeney sane, so Judge Brewer dismissed the complaints.

On or about March 17, 1938, a dog belonging to Janet Jones of Bogart, Ohio, a community just south of Sandusky, trotted into the house carrying a severed human lower leg and foot in its jaws. Coroner E. J. Meckstroth identified the limb as female and judged it several months old. "The leg shows as neat a job of amputation as I ever saw," he remarked to the *Plain Dealer* on May 18. With no local missing person reports on his desk to go on and unable to trace the limb to any Sandusky area hospitals, Sheriff William S. Souter contacted Cleveland authorities. For the city's police, any human limb severed with surgical precision served as a stark warning that the shadow of Kingsbury Run was growing: it had moved as far southeast as Pennsylvania and now stretched to western Ohio. David Cowles and Reuben Straus drove to Sandusky to examine the grim find. There is no surviving record, press or otherwise, detailing what conclusions they reached, but according to what Dr. Royal Grossman told Bardsley in the early 1970s, it was the discovery of this leg that drew intensified official attention to Francis Sweeney, a Cleveland doctor who had been in and out of the Soldiers and Sailors Home several times over the last few years.

In September 1983 then eighty-six-year-old David Cowles, the former head of Cleveland's Scientific Investigation Bureau, met with Florence Schwein, first director of the Cleveland Police Historical Society Museum, and Lieutenant Tom Brown. In a recorded oral history covering his long career on the force, Cowles broke a silence on the torso case over four decades old. A typescript was made of the lengthy conversation and then duly filed away. Former museum curator Anne T. Kmieck knew about the interview but had never looked at it closely—until late in 1997 at my request. In this revealing document, Cowles substantiates Grossman's claims by providing an account of the long rumored hotel suite interrogation that covered where it took place, what went on, how long it lasted, and who was there. Though he does not identify Ness's prime suspect by name, there can be no doubt that he is describing Francis Edward Sweeney.

> There was a suspect in those murders [Frank Sweeney]. I won't mention any names. He was born and raised as a boy on the edge of the run [Jessie Avenue, now East 79] He later went into the service; in the service, he was in the Medical Corps. He came back and he went to college [Western Reserve and John Carroll Universities] and went through medical school [the University of St. Louis Medical School] and became an M.D. Married a nurse [Mary Josephine Sokol in 1927]. Came back, did his internship at St. Alexis Hospital out on Broadway and finally kept going down and down and down with the booze. . . . We played on him for a long time. . . . A relative of his was a congressman. [Democratic Congressman Martin L. Sweeney from Cleveland's 20th district was Francis's cousin.] And we had to be very careful how we handled him. However, we had a detail on him, and we picked him up. He had been drinking heavy too. Picked him up. Didn't bring him to jail, but we took him to the Cleveland Hotel [now the Renaissance on Public Square].

Subsequently, according to Cowles, the suspect failed a lie detector test in such grand fashion that polygraph expert Leonard Keeler confidently told Ness he had, indeed, apprehended the infamous Kingsbury Run murderer.

Because there was no evidence other than the polygraph tests, Ness had no choice but to let Sweeney go. Immediately an extraordinary cat-and-mouse game between the doctor and the authorities began that lasted at least into the early months of 1940. On August 16, three months after the May 1938 interrogation, the bodies of victims no. 11 and no. 12 appeared in the East 9th dump. Two days later, Ness led the infamous shantytown raids. A week after that, on August 25, Francis Sweeney formally applied for residency at the Sandusky Soldiers and Sailors Home. (Though the few remaining records suggest that this was the first time Dr. Sweeney had entered the institution, Marilyn Bardsley uncovered documentation forty years ago at the home, now apparently lost, that placed him there at least a couple of years before 1938.) His status at the facility would have allowed him to come and go as he pleased, and according to Bardsley, his records contained a note that Sandusky and Cleveland police were to be notified should he leave. Arnold Sagalyn, special assistant to Eliot Ness, remembers following Frank Sweeney around downtown Cleveland in the summer of 1939.

After his application for residency at the Soldiers and Sailors Home on August 25, Francis Sweeney again virtually disappeared, this time into the Veterans Administration's hospital system. The most concise assessment of his mental and physical condition, as well as his odyssey through the VA system, comes in 1963 from Dr. B. J. Chazin, chief of the Domiciliary Medical Service at the Veterans Administration Center in Dayton.

> Frank Sweeney has been here in the Domiciliary on and off since 1946. In 1956 he was hospitalized. He was in Chillicothe Veterans Administration Hospital and returned from there with the diagnoses of schizoid personality, heart disease and cardiac enlargement. Since then he had numerous admissions to Brown Hospital, mostly with the diagnosis of alcohol intoxication (he is being treated for it now on our Psychiatric Service). He is also a known drug addict with addiction to barbiturates. His most recent diagnoses are: acute brain syndrome due to alcoholism and chronic brain syndrome. He is considered incompetent by the Veterans Administration.

It is not clear whether these incarcerations were voluntary or forced. The freedom to come and go as he pleased would have depended on a host of factors, including the kind of facility and the idiosyncratic nature of its regulations. Records at the Ohio State Medical Board show that he was first judged incompetent in 1956, a finding substantiated by numerous subsequent neuropsychiatric examinations. Certainly from 1956 until his death, his incarceration would have been forced.

According to records, Francis Sweeney was an extremely difficult patient. A 1953 FBI document, which Marilyn Bardsley obtained through the Freedom of Information Act, states that he was "constantly in trouble at the Veterans Administration Center with the courts there, and has been charged ten times out of twenty appearances in court with being drunk."

Up to the time of Sweeney's death in 1964, the director at the Veterans Administration Center in Dayton petitioned the Ohio State Medical Board to remove his license because he got his hands on a steady supply of drugs by writing prescriptions for fictitious individuals.

During his various incarcerations, Frank Sweeney became obsessed with Eliot Ness. When he wasn't bombarding Cleveland's onetime safety director with written taunts and jeers, he railed about him in letters sent to others. In 1948, Sweeney fired off an incoherent four-pager to J. Edgar Hoover at the FBI complaining of "Nessism." His sense of humor twisted though otherwise unimpaired, he closed his rambling epistle with a joke about having "to tolerate His Weak *ness.*"

According to Marilyn Bardsley, Eliot Ness's third wife, Elizabeth, remembered the frightening stream of postcards and letters addressed to her husband, but it is now impossible to ascertain when Frank Sweeney's communications started, how many there were, or when they ended. The six pieces in the library of the Western Reserve Historical Society apparently survived purely by accident. Oddly, Ness told Oscar Fraley that the letters and cards stopped because of the death of the sender, but Frank Sweeney did not die until July 9, 1964, at the age of seventy—seven years after Ness's death—of cerebral edema and pontine hemorrhage with cerebral arteriosclerosis, terminal pneumonia, and hypertensive heart disease as contributing causes.

The name "Gaylord Sundheim" that Ness used to identify his suspect may also have a tenuous connection to Frank Sweeney. If his intention was merely to protect his prime suspect's identity, why would Ness opt for such a strange pseudonym—unless that is the name the suspect gave himself during the interrogation—something that would have a joking personal significance for him; another head game from a mentally deranged man who had already shown how thoroughly he enjoyed taunting and teasing the authorities. The name "Sundheim" could be loosely translated from the German as "house of sin" or "sin's home"—not too much of a reach for a man who joked about "Das Freudiology" in one of his postcards to Ness. Francis Sweeney also spent much of his youth living with his older married sister and her husband on East 64th, just off a street ironically called Francis; a few blocks south, Sweeney Avenue branches off East 55th and leads behind some old industrial buildings to the neighborhood where Jackass Hill used to slope down into Kingsbury Run. And there is also a very short east-west street in Cleveland called "Gaylord" that runs just north of the Turney Road State Mental Hospital where Francis Sweeney's father ended his days in 1923.

None of this, of course, irrefutably puts the Butcher's knife in Francis Sweeney's hand, especially in the legal sense; and Eliot Ness had no hard evidence he could take to court. Arnold Sagalyn, who became special assistant to the safety director fresh out of Oberlin College in the summer of 1939, worked closely with Ness in Cleveland and later in Washington, D.C. As a young bachelor and trusted associate, Sagalyn also socialized with Ness frequently. Andrew Schug, former trustee for the Cleveland Police Historical Society, and I interviewed Sagalyn in October 1997. Then, at the age of seventy-nine, he remained the only person still living who could verify the identity of Ness's prime suspect and testify as to what the safety director actually thought about his guilt. He clearly remembered that day sixty years before when he followed Frank Sweeney around the downtown area. According to Sagalyn, Ness found Sweeney an "interesting" suspect because everything about him, from his profession to the sordid details of his personal life, so closely fit the profile of the killer that had been pieced together so painstakingly over the course of the investigation from the observations of pathologists, police, and those who attended Pearce's conference in September 1936. Sagalyn asserts, however, that Ness continued to be bothered by the complete lack of anything tangible linking him to the murders.

Undoubtedly, the case against Francis Sweeney is even more circumstantial today than it was seventy-five years ago. Ness was surely in possession of information about him that he probably shared only with David Cowles and a few others in his inner circle, and short of sworn testimony about a deathbed confession or some yet-to-be-discovered personal diary or letter, there is no way to tie Francis Sweeney—or anyone else—directly to the crimes. Yet the pieces of circumstantial evidence that can be marshaled against him remain numerous, intriguing, and sometimes compelling—especially the curious case of Emil Fronek.

Clevelanders never know what sort of weather the late fall months are likely to bring. In the good years, the glow of Indian summer October days fades slowly into the silent, cool gray of early winter; but sometimes the arctic winds roar down from Canada, picking up heavy snowfalls from Lake

Erie that can paralyze the city in the space of a few hours. Sometimes the fickle winds quietly blanket the city in dreary cold and dampness—an oppressive dankness that can seemingly pierce the warmest clothes, leaving a man clutching his arms against his chest for warmth and shivering in spite of himself. On this particular winter night in late 1934, Emil Fronek wandered listlessly up Broadway Avenue battling hunger, fatigue, and—just perhaps—inebriation as well. A middle-aged homeless and jobless casualty of the Great Depression, Fronek had slid inexorably into the life of a hobo drifting aimlessly from one transient camp to the next. Desperately in need of a new pair of shoes, his cold, damp feet occasionally made him forget his gnawing hunger as he trudged slowly east on one of Cleveland's major arteries. As he passed East 37th, he glanced up at the towering, dark edifice of St. Wenceslas's Catholic Church; farther up the largely deserted street he passed the huge, sprawling Bethlehem Congregational Church at the corner of Broadway and Fowler. But it also stood dark and silent. (Both churches have since been demolished: St. Wenceslas in 1963 to make way for I-77, Bethlehem Congregational in 1954.) As Fronek neared East 55th, he could see the lighted windows of St. Alexis hospital shining to his left; and suddenly, he was standing in front of a nondescript restaurant or deli called Broadway Lunches. It was closed, of course, but Fronek wandered around to the back of the building, perhaps, in search of some stray scraps of food that had been discarded. The next thing he remembered, however, he was standing on the second floor of a doctor's office—apparently with little idea of how he had gotten there—facing an affable looking, middle-aged man with light-colored graying hair who introduced himself as a doctor. During the ensuing exchange, the doctor offered Fronek a meal and promised him a new pair of shoes. Chances are that Fronek never questioned how a doctor on the second floor of a medical building would have ready access to food; if he thought about it at all, he probably assumed it came from the nearby deli.

When the doctor placed the tempting plate of meat and potatoes in front of him, Fronek ate desperately, literally shoveling the food into his mouth. Occasionally he glanced up at the doctor who regarded him silently with a dispassionate stare. But something was wrong; Fronek began to feel a little light headed. Perhaps, he was eating too quickly, he thought, and his starved digestive system could not handle the sudden influx of so much food! But when the light-headedness began sliding into full-blown wooziness, Fronek panicked. Had he been drugged, he wondered? Suddenly, he lunged for the door, tore out of the building, and began running down Broadway with the doctor behind, calling for him to stop and come back for some more drinks. His wooziness threatening to plunge him into unconsciousness, Fronek managed to lose his pursuer somewhere in the nearby railroad yards—perhaps, in Kingsbury Run; perhaps, along the lines north of Broadway at Track Avenue. He frantically climbed into an empty boxcar; and as he fell exhausted to the floor, he immediately plunged into a deep slumber that lasted until some transients finally managed to rouse him three days later. Now wet, filthy, and still groggy, the angry Fronek returned to the Broadway-East 55th area looking for the office building and the mysterious doctor he was sure had tried to drug him for reasons he couldn't begin to understand; but nothing looked the same in the light of day. After wandering fruitlessly around the neighborhood, Fronek decided that the city of Cleveland was not for him; so he hopped a freight to Chicago where he ultimately landed a job as a longshoreman. Though Emil Fronek never forgot his frightening ordeal of near drugging and lucky escape, he probably never knew that he nearly became the second victim of the Mad Butcher of Kingsbury Run.

Four years later, in August 1938, Emil Fronek's lurid narrative reached the ears of a former Chicago deputy coroner who apparently passed it on to one of the city's newspapers. When someone at the paper dutifully alerted the Cleveland police department, Detectives Musil and Merylo were dispatched to the windy city to bring Fronek back for questioning. Understandably leery about returning to the scene of his ordeal, Fronek bolted from the car and tore down a busy Chicago street with the two startled detectives trailing behind. When they finally caught up with him, Musil and Merylo found themselves surrounded by armed Chicago policemen ready to arrest them on kidnapping charges.

Resigned to returning to Cleveland, Fronek cooperated fully with the police and the press. Basking in the attention the city dailies showered on him, Fronek willingly recalled as many vivid details of his adventure that he could remember. On August 28, Detectives Orley May and Robert Carter drove him slowly up Broadway carefully retracing the path Fronek had walked four years before. The trio cruised past St. Wenceslas on the corner of East 37th and Bethlehem Congregational Church at Fowler, both of which Fronek remembered, and headed east toward East 55th. As the car neared St. Alexis Hospital, Emil Fronek suddenly stared out the window, wide-eyed and alert; the mysterious doctor's office was there, he said, somewhere between

East 50th and East 55th on the north side of the street. The two detectives patiently walked up and down the street with him, but Fronek couldn't find anything that looked like the office he remembered. Everything on the north side of Broadway seemed to be a commercial business, while the south side of the street was lined primarily with homes. St. Alexis, of course, stood close by; so it certainly made sense that a doctor's office would be in the immediate neighborhood. But where was it? The police interviewed him further, and Eliot Ness questioned him for over an hour. Then, having earned his substantial footnote in the annals of Cleveland's most notorious murders, Emil Fronek happily returned to Chicago, vowing to return if the police needed him. Gerber had speculated that the killer could be a doctor, and in his Cleveland days, Fronek certainly had fit the down-on-his-luck profile the Butcher seemed to favor. Fronek's possible drugging could also explain why none of the victims bore any signs of violence other than dismemberment and mutilation. Ness told the press, however, that—interesting as the former transient's story had been—he doubted that this admittedly odd adventure had anything to do with the Kingsbury Run murders. We have to assume that city newspapers were accurately reporting what Ness said; after all, his relationship with the gentlemen of the press corps had always been good, and the as yet unsolved torso killings were still big news in Cleveland. The official explanation for rejecting the relevancy of Fronek's account was that authorities had come to believe that the Butcher's laboratory lay closer to his hunting ground near the heart of the city. The intersection of Broadway and East 55th was just too far east and too far south. The police also continued to be of two minds over whether the Lady of the Lake, pieces of whose body turned up in September 1934, actually belonged in the Butcher's tally; most, therefore, continued to mark the beginning of the murderer's career with the deaths of Edward Andrassy and victim no. 2 on September 23, 1935. Fronek had tangled with this strange doctor a full year before that. But by August 1938, Eliot Ness certainly knew exactly where that elusive "medical office" was; without a doubt he knew precisely who that mysterious physician was. And there can be no doubt that Ness knew that Emil Fronek had escaped the Mad Butcher of Kingsbury Run. The curtain of silence had already begun to descend.

There are admittedly some obvious problems with Fronek's story—nagging questions that arise when his account is examined carefully; but local papers accepted it all without question, treating it as an attention-grabbing sensational story and fascinating chapter in the dreadful saga of murder and dismemberment that had been going on for four years. On the surface, it is a believable and compelling story—the sort of narrative that appeals to the conspiratorially minded and lovers of good cloak-and-dagger mystery. But does it hold up if the "hows and whys" behind some of the details are looked at critically and in depth? How, for example, could Fronek have suddenly found himself on the second floor of a doctor's office with little or no idea of how he got there? How did he manage to bypass the first floor so easily? Did he just stumble in an unlocked door that opened on to the street, or did he make a purposeful entry at some point? Why was he obviously incapable of finding the building four years later? He recognized the general area; why did the specific building elude him? Fronek did not say he had been drinking, but given the dire circumstances of his life, that would see a likely possibility. And how could the affable seeming physician produce a full meal of meat and potatoes so easily late at night?

Emil Fronek's incredible story has been an integral part of the torso murder saga ever since it was reported by Cleveland's eager press establishment in August 1938; but its true significance in unraveling the mystery has gone unrecognized, probably because of Ness's insistence that the strange encounter had nothing to do with Kingsbury Run. But Fronek's compelling narrative provides an important key to unlocking the mystery of who the Mad Butcher was, where and how he incapacitated his victims, where he committed murder and performed decapitation and dismemberment. As he wandered up Broadway with Musil and Carter four years after his ordeal, Fronek was hobbled by faulty memories about the actual nature of the building involved and confusion as to how he had entered it. He insisted it was on the north side of the street; and, no doubt, he was looking for something that could reasonably pass for a doctor's office. But the elusive structure for which he fruitlessly searched was not an office building; it was a former residence. And it was not on the north side of the street; it stood on the south side at 5026 Broadway.

Joseph and Marie Peterka built the large two-story dwelling sometime between 1910 and 1920; and the family, including son Edward, lived in the spacious quarters for several years. After his parents moved out, Edward—now a physician practicing at St. Alexis Hospital—and wife, Libbie, continued to live at the residence until sometime in the early 1930s, at which point the couple moved to Lake Shore Blvd., and Edward converted the downstairs to a medical office complex complete with exam and X-ray rooms, as well as a space at the front of the house (a former bedroom) outfitted for minor

The house at 5026 Broadway where Dr. Edward Peterka, Francis Edward Sweeney, and four other physicians practiced. The building to the immediate right is Broadway Lunches at 5020. Though difficult to tell from the photograph, the deli seems to back up against the Peterka house. The Raus Funeral Home at 5040 is partly visible to the left. Date of photograph unknown. Courtesy of Ted Krejsa.

surgery. Dr. Peterka, along with five other St. Alexis physicians, set up a thriving medical practice on the bottom floor. The upstairs, however, was retained as a living space complete with a functioning kitchen. Presumably any of the six doctors could have stayed there off and on for any number of reasons—heavy work schedules at the hospital, a late afternoon appointment, or even a minor medical procedure. Dr. Francis Edward Sweeney was among the six doctors who practiced in the imposing house at 5026 Broadway. In 1938 Fronek described his would-be assailant as about forty years old with a light complexion, a smooth face, and light hair graying at the temples. He put the man's height at five feet six and the weight at about 150 pounds. Only the height and weight are off. Francis Sweeney was a taller (in the neighborhood of six feet), heavier man. But considering that Fronek was recalling events that had happened at least four years before and that he may have been intoxicated at the time, such discrepancies seem minor.

The only way Emil Fronek could have reached the second floor from the outside was through a door at the back of the building on the northeast side of the house that led to a staircase, bypassing the first floor completely. Both the house at 5026 and the adjacent deli at 5020 were actually closer to intersecting Pershing Avenue than to Broadway. Assuming Fronek went to the rear of the deli in search of discarded food, he would have done so by walking south on Pershing to the back of the building. From there, he would have wandered over to the back of the house, eventually turning the northeast corner at the extreme rear where the sole outside entrance to the second floor stood, thus explaining why he was so confused as to where he had been when he entered the building, why he mistakenly thought it stood on the north side of Broadway, and why he was unable to recognize the structure four years later. Emil Fronek probably never saw the front of the house; the facade would have been hidden by the deli, which extended much farther out toward the street than the former residence, which stood rather far back on the lot. All he had ever seen was the back of the house. Fronek's 1938 account of his adventure to the press and the police does not include an explanation of how he wound up on the second floor. One would have to assume the outside door was open, but once there in the presence

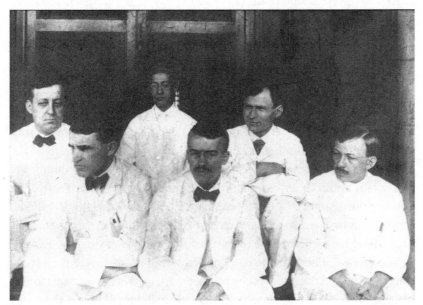

The six physicians who practiced at 5026 Broadway. Dr. Edward Peterka is first on the left in the first row. Dr. Francis Edward Sweeney is in the middle of the second row. The photograph most likely dates from the late 1920s or very early 1930s. Courtesy of Ted Krejsa.

of the doctor—no doubt, Frank Sweeney—it is understandable how he could mistakenly assume he was in a doctor's office. The mystery of where the sumptuous repast Sweeney placed before him came from is now easily solved; it came from the kitchen on the same floor. Sweeney may have even been preparing the meal for himself, and he could have easily drugged the food before placing it in front of the ravenously hungry Emil Fronek.

Fronek's run-in with Frank Sweeney occurred at a crucial time in the doctor's life. His wife, Mary, had taken him to probate court over his alcoholism for the first time in December 1933; by September 1934, she had sued for divorce, custody of their two boys, restoration of her maiden name, and her husband's adjusted compensation certificate from the United States army. By the end of 1934 when Fronek had his fateful encounter with him, Frank Sweeney was spiraling downward into a psychotic state partly brought on by abuse of drugs and alcohol. One of the great mysteries surrounding him has always been where in the city he was living once having left the family residence on Melgrove, presumably in 1934 around the time when Mary filed the divorce papers. The second floor of the house at 5026 would have been the perfect place for him to stay—for at least a while. His colleagues in the office were probably unaware of the full extent of his domestic problems or his unraveling mental state. All they knew was that a fellow physician was going through a rough patch and, in modern day parlance, needed a place to crash. Frank Sweeney would certainly have had a key to the house; undoubtedly all six physicians who practiced at the onetime residence did. (Just how long he enjoyed this privilege, however, is debatable. As his mental state deteriorated, his alcoholism became more pervasive and his behavior more erratic, it is difficult to accept that his colleagues didn't notice and wouldn't intervene in some way.)

The second floor of a house/medical office occupied only during the day, a rear entrance almost entirely hidden from view at the rear of the building, on a street in a mostly commercial part of Cleveland largely deserted at night: it was the ideal secluded spot for a killer to incapacitate his prey. The three earliest of the recognized Kingsbury Run victims—Edward Andrassy, Flo Polillo, and the unidentified victim no. 2— were most likely drugged there just as Emil Fronek had been drugged in the waning months of 1934. Sweeney could have met them virtually anywhere in the seedy neighborhoods surrounding the downtown—on the street, at local bars, in any disreputable dive. Both Andrassy and Polillo were known to hang out at the rundown establishment at East 21st and Central; perhaps, this neighborhood bar served as the hub of Frank Sweeney's murderous activities. Once having met his potential victims, he could easily have lured them to his lair on the second floor of the house on Broadway with a promise of really good booze, food, or, perhaps, even drugs. Though the evidence remains even less than slight, it is possible to believe that Sweeney and Andrassy were already acquainted. Andrassy's working life had been a series of on-again, off-again stints as an orderly in the psychiatric ward of City Hospital beginning around 1925. It is impossible to tell exactly when the hospital terminated his employment for the last time (records have not survived), but he could have certainly been there in December 1933 when Probate Court Judge Nelson J. Brewer responded to Mary Sokol Sweeney's petition and ordered her husband confined at City Hospital for observation. No one would notice two dark figures moving through the gloom at the rear of the house where the view was blocked by an old stable; there was virtually no chance that anyone would see two indistinct shapes slipping through a side door at the rear of the building into an unlighted hall. This scenario clearly explains where potential victims were drugged—at least for the early victims in the cycle. The question that can never be satisfactorily answered is how long did Frank Sweeney enjoy access to the house at 5026 Broadway? Did there come a point when his colleagues began to suspect—not that he was the phantom Butcher—but that there was clearly something wrong with his mental state and deny him use of the building?

Emil Fronek's 1938 recounting of the ordeal he underwent four years earlier provides the key, an extraordinarily significant key, to unlocking a major part of the torso murder mystery. But once drugged into insensibility, where were the unfortunate victims murdered, subsequently decapitated, and dismembered? Certainly not in the residence-cum-medical office! Once again, David Cowles provides the answer in his 1983 taped interview.

> It's a known fact; we had people who testified, who would testify to it that across the street from the hospital [St. Alexis] was an undertaker who buried all of the indigent bodies. And it was a known fact that he'd [Frank Sweeney] go over there and would amputate, or just remove, the way these bodies were found, exactly the same way he would do with unknown bodies in the war [World War I].

The funeral directors Erasmus V. Raus & Sons were not only across the street from St. Alexis Hospital but their establishment stood at 5040 Broadway,

The Raus Funeral Home at 5040 Broadway directly east of the building housing the Peterka-Sweeney medical practice. The picture dates from 1959, and by then, the business had been taken over by the Marek family. Though difficult to be sure from the photograph, it looks as if the house at 5026 had already been demolished. Courtesy of the Cuyahoga County Archives.

next door to 5026 where Francis Sweeney shared offices with five other doctors. Unfortunately, it is not clear what points Cowles is trying to make, and neither of his two interviewers pressed him to straighten out his confusing assertions. He seems to be alleging that as medic Francis Sweeney dismembered unidentified dead soldiers and perhaps secretly performed similar acts of mutilation, or simply practiced his surgical techniques, on unidentified bodies next door to his office. (Did he have a key? Could he come and go as he pleased? Did any of the other doctors enjoy similar privileges?) But how could he do any of this without the undertaker's knowledge? Or was Raus among the mysterious "people who testified"?

The Raus Funeral Home was a large, three-story building that housed family living quarters, undertaking facilities, and—strangely enough—a small foundry and a plating business in the basement. There was a sloping concrete ramp at the back of the building that led down to the lower level

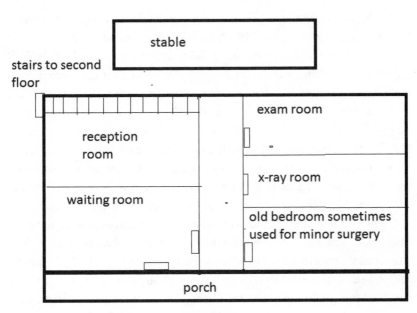

The plan of the bottom floor at 5026 Broadway, as remembered in 2012 by Dr. Edward Peterka's nephew Edward Krejsa. The drawing is not to scale.

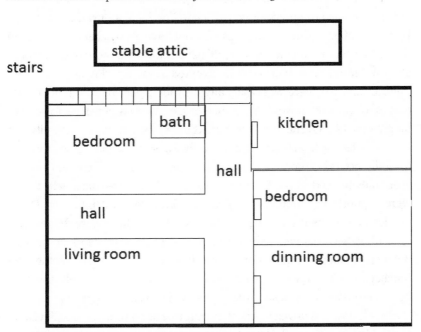

The layout of the second floor at 5026 Broadway, as remembered in 2012 by Edward Krejsa. The drawing is not to scale.

where the bodies would be taken. It's deliciously ghoulish to picture Francis Sweeney lugging or steering his drugged, half-conscious victims through the nighttime darkness, down that hidden concrete ramp to the bowels of a funeral parlor where he committed murder and performed decapitation and dismemberment. He would have had all the room he needed to work, and getting rid of the blood in an undertaking establishment would pose no problem. If the Raus family spent most of their time at night on the top floor, there is little chance they would hear anything in the basement. Such a scenario could, indeed, explain how some of the murder-dismemberments, especially those early on in the cycle, were carried out; but there is another possibility. Raus maintained a second facility reserved exclusively for the indigent and unclaimed dead. The building he employed—long since demolished—was a warehouse-like structure on Mead Avenue, a very short street running north off of Broadway slightly west of the main Raus funeral parlor. Business was probably very brisk. Although there are no surviving statistics, it's more than likely that during the Great Depression there were a lot of unidentified or unclaimed bodies found in back alleys and shanty towns that wound up in the gloomy building to await disposal. Since many of these unfortunates would either be buried in a potter's field or be sent over to the Western Reserve Medical School for the anatomy classes, record keeping and procedural guidelines may not have always been followed all that judiciously. Frank Sweeney would have enjoyed far more working room and run far less chance of being interrupted in the Mead Avenue location. Chances are that there was rarely anyone there; this was, after all, a "side business." How often would Raus, his sons, or his assistants have to go over there? And Jackass Hill and Kingsbury Run stretch out through the city just a few blocks north, just a short car ride away. Now the perplexing mystery of victim no. 11 becomes clear. When the pieces of the unidentified woman eventually arrived at the Western Reserve University Medical School and were properly examined, anatomist T. Windgate Todd informed David Cowles that this was not a legitimate torso victim; these were the remains of an already embalmed body that were passed off as the work of the Mad Butcher. Perhaps, not a Mad Butcher murder victim, but certainly the Mad Butcher's work—Frank Sweeney's sick joke aimed at Eliot Ness, the man he perceived as his nemesis. In May Ness had subjected the doctor to a top-secret ten-day to two-week ordeal in an unspecified room of the Cleveland Hotel. Now three months later Sweeney taunts his tormentor by dumping the pieces of an embalmed body, in clear view of Ness's office window, that he disarticulated in the Mead Avenue establishment belonging to the Raus Funeral Home: the ultimate thumbing his nose at authorities, an arrogant slap in the face of law enforcement, a really defiant challenge. Catch me if you can, Mr. Ness!

Emil Fronek encountered Francis Sweeney that night on Broadway in late 1934 at a crucial time in his life. His wife had petitioned for divorce and custody of the children in September, and St. Alexis seems to have terminated its relationship with him at about the same time (perhaps the necessary "stressors" that trigger a serial killer's crimes?). Dr. Sweeney was on the way down, and from this point on, his slide into drunkenness, drug addiction, and mental illness would accelerate.

In its coverage of the discovery of victim no. 10's leg on April 9, 1938, the *Cleveland News* reported, "A once-prominent Clevelander, described as a physician in disrepute with his profession, is under suspicion in Cleveland's 11 [*sic*] unsolved torso murders." The description in the story is only slightly less specific than Cowles's in his oral history. "The man, said to have discontinued his practice, is middle-aged, has some surgical skill and is described as being a powerfully built, chronic alcoholic with apparent sadistic tendencies." Neither of the other two dailies carried this intriguing lead—the *News* seems to have had its ear closer to the ground than either the *Plain Dealer* or the *Press*—and though both Gerber and Robert Chamberlin verified the *News*'s tip, they refused to divulge the suspect's name. "This man has been a 'hot' suspect for the last two years," Gerber acknowledged, adding that the police had had the renegade doctor under surveillance since the discovery of Edward Andrassy's and victim no. 2's bodies in September 1935. Chamberlin was more evasive. "Yes, we are watching him, as well as two or three others," he admitted.

Gerber's assertions are startling, even astounding. The police did not realize that they were looking for a single killer until the death of victim no. 4 in June 1936. Assuming he had not misspoken or been misquoted, Gerber's statements could only mean that police had somehow linked Francis Sweeney with Edward Andrassy shortly after his murder and continued to regard him as a viable suspect only in Andrassy's and victim no. 2's deaths. In all likelihood, he came under intensified police observation during the summer of 1936, when it became clear that a single individual was responsible for all the murders and, as Dr. Royal Grossman insists, far tighter scrutiny still in mid-March 1938 with the discovery of the severed leg close to the Sandusky Soldiers and Sailors Home.

Suddenly, five months later, on a Sunday night in the middle of October 1938, Clevelanders sitting before their radios were shocked to hear Walter Winchell in New York, with his usual "hold the presses" intensity, announce an imminent break in the torso case.

> Attention, Cleveland, Ohio. The unsolved torso murders, more than a dozen of them in Cleveland, may result one day in the apprehension of one of Cleveland's outstanding citizens. This is the legend brought to New York by a newspaper publisher whose name I promised to withhold. His editors are familiar with the rumors that a fanatic, a medical man with great skill, is allegedly responsible for the gruesome crimes in which all the murdered were dismembered. The Jekyll-Hyde doctor is better described as having a typical movie villain look.

The specifics about the suspect are even more vague than they were in the *News* story back in May, but the details that remain still suggest Dr. Francis Sweeney.

Detective Peter Merylo, Sergeant James Hogan, and other members of the Cleveland police force were among the startled Clevelanders who listened to Winchell's announcement. "We had no such suspect in our books," Merylo asserts in the Otwell manuscript, "although we had questioned plenty of doctors." Ness's interrogation of Frank Sweeney in the hotel suite back in May was obviously a very closely guarded secret.

Ness's assistant, Robert Chamberlin, moved quickly to quash any local excitement raised by Winchell's story. In Otwell, Merylo quotes Chamberlin's denial: "There is only the routine investigation going on. I know of no doctor who is to be arrested." Assuming Merylo is quoting him accurately, Chamberlin picked his words with extraordinary care. "I know of no doctor who *is to be arrested* [my italics]." The previous May, Chamberlin had verified the *News*'s story about a Cleveland doctor who was being closely watched.

Cleveland police traced Winchell's story to Roy Hinkle, chief of detectives in Indianapolis, Indiana. Hinkle had arrested a local steelworker who volunteered information about the Cleveland killings, perhaps as part of some sort of plea bargain arrangement. Merylo quotes Hinkle's words to members of the Indianapolis press in the Otwell manuscript: "The information looks pretty good. The steel worker named a Cleveland doctor. I think the Cleveland police will make some arrests pretty soon." Hogan traveled to Indianapolis to interview both Hinkle and the unnamed steelworker; he returned to Cleveland a disappointed man. The information, he insisted, had been based on supposition, not fact. Had the scrupulous but cautious Hogan missed an extremely important lead?

† † †

Frank Sweeney was not the only medical man to come under suspicion. As Peter Merylo pointed out in the Otwell manuscript, Cleveland police had looked into the backgrounds of many local doctors. The newspapers also carried stories about suspect physicians; and in one intriguing case, the details of the report strongly suggest Sweeney but actually refer to someone else. During the 1950 investigation into Robert Robertson's murder and mutilation, the *Plain Dealer* reported on August 29:

> At the time they learned of the telephone inquiry about Robertson, detectives learned a 58-year-old physician had lived at the Lodge off and on early in 1946. The physician, they were told, spent most of his time with alcoholics, giving them money and exchanging clothes with them.
>
> Authorities were told the man would make friends with a Lodge resident until that resident no longer checked in. Lodge records show the doctor has not been at the place since June 1, 1946. However, because of his medical experience, including service with the army medical corps in World War I, detectives are trying to find him for questioning.

It all sounds like Frank Sweeney, but he is not the doctor referred to. According to the police file on the Robertson killing, which still exists, the elusive physician they hunted was named Kern, perhaps the same Dr. Kern who had briefly come under suspicion twelve years before—a man who had lost his medical license and lived on Fulton Avenue near the Andrassys. (Pages from a telephone book covering the letter K had been found with Robertson's body.)

John Bartlow Martin's *Harper's Magazine* article in November 1949 also contains some tantalizing references to renegade physicians, obviously culled from now missing police reports, and though they could refer to

Francis Sweeney, there is no proof that any of them do. One detective reported, "Made quiet investigation of some information we received about a Physician whose name we cannot mention at this time." Merylo looked into a flophouse resident Martin described as "an aging, once-prominent doctor who had succumbed to narcotics, lost his license, turned to perversion." The most intriguing story concerns the operator of a third-ward beer joint who reported that a well-dressed man who described himself as a physician who had lost his license drank daily in his establishment over a six-month period and often bought drinks for the down-and-outs who made up the bar's usual clientele. He had even bought drinks for Flo Polillo one to two days before her first set of remains turned up. The onetime doctor owned a car and freely advertised his willingness to drive any of the regulars anywhere they needed to go.

According to Arnold Sagalyn, being Ness's prime suspect in the Kingsbury Run murders both excited and amused Frank Sweeney, and he played the role with gusto, relishing his cat-and-mouse games with authorities. The *Plain Dealer* reported an odd incident on April 10, 1938. Someone telephoned Peter Merylo at 4:00 A.M. and teased him with an undisclosed sexual revelation that the caller described as "something for your investigation." By 1950 when Robert Robertson was killed, Sweeney would have matched the admittedly vague description of the elusive sunbather—in his fifties, heavy, thinning gray hair—observed by workmen before police found Robertson's body.

There is not a shred of evidence that Frank Sweeney made the curious phone call, the significance of which Merylo discounted, or that he was the mysterious sun worshiper on the steel girders at Norris Brothers, but, in both cases, it is the sort of behavior one would expect from a man who, according to Arnold Sagalyn, sent Eliot Ness a photograph of a tree in a field with "dig here" written beside it.

† † †

In the same 1984 *Cleveland Magazine* article in which Gerber retracted his 1944 judgment about Willie Johnson's guilt, George Condon confronted the coroner with something he had said to the press at the time of the killings. According to Condon, the papers quoted Gerber's description of the killer as a "broken-down doctor who becomes frenzied with drugs or liquor." "That's nonsense," Gerber snapped. "I never said any such thing. The newspapers made up that stuff." Yet another inexplicable Gerber reversal! His strong denial forty-some years after the fact is startling, especially since his alleged thumbnail sketch of the killer matches Francis Sweeney so perfectly. And in 1955, Howard Beaufait quoted Gerber as having said, "I'm not convinced the butcher is dead. I also do not believe that he has moved to another location. Most likely explanation for his inactivity is that he is locked up in a mental institution."

Francis Sweeney was, indeed, a deeply disturbed man. More than a half dozen mental health professionals have examined his surviving letters and other written communications, including the five postcards and letter to Ness in the possession of the Western Reserve Historical Society. While all recognize the difficulties in basing a diagnosis of a dead man on a small pile of correspondence, most of it dating from the mid-1950s and early 1960s, their tentative assessments are nearly unanimous—that he was a paranoid schizophrenic further hobbled by manic-depressive disorder. Though the crippling disease usually manifests itself in the teen years, occurrences of schizophrenia in later life are not unknown. In the separation and divorce papers Mary Sokol Sweeney filed from 1934 to 1936, she maintains that her husband's heavy drinking began in 1929, when he was thirty-five years old. His condition continued to deteriorate, but he apparently functioned reasonably well until late 1933, when his wife finally had him hauled into court for the first time to probe his sanity. Cleveland psychiatrist Dr. Daniel W. Badal suggests that the symptoms of schizophrenia would have developed slowly over a period of years and that the onset of the disease would have been characterized by vague but persistent bouts of anxiety, which Sweeney probably tried to control with increasing doses of alcohol.

In Frank Dolezal's case, there was a solid connection between him and Flo Polillo and considerably more shaky ones with Edward Andrassy and Rose Wallace. In Francis Sweeney's case, the possible links between him and any of the identified victims are considerably more tenuous. In fact, there is only enough circumstantial evidence to build a plausible relationship between him and Edward Andrassy. Merylo's statement in his memoirs that City Hospital hired and fired Andrassy eleven times over an eight-year period would place him there as an orderly in December 1933, when Sweeney underwent treatment for alcoholism, perhaps providing him with the opportunity to establish the same sort of relationship with Andrassy that he would enjoy with Al Archacki at the Soldiers and Sailors Home three years later. (Suddenly Gus Zukie's story of Peter Merylo's politically connected male nurse at City Hospital rises up like a ghost. Could that shadowy figure—born out of the repetition and ultimate distortion of vague rumors—be a combination of Edward Andrassy and Francis Sweeney?)

† † †

On February 5, 1940, Peter Merylo and Martin Zalewski encountered Francis Sweeney for the first time. Still officially a resident of the Sandusky Soldiers and Sailors Home, he had traveled to Cleveland to stay with his sister on East 65th while his niece underwent surgery at St. Alexis. In his report of February 6, Merylo recounts, "Dr. Sweeney was referred to us by Superintendent Cowles of the Scientific Bureau of Identification for a further check up, as it was believed that Dr. Sweeney might be a good suspect in the Torso Murders." The two detectives immediately noticed his aberrant behavior. "During our questioning," Merylo wrote, "Dr. Sweeney was pacing the floor forward and back, as though he were dictating a business letter." Though Merylo concluded that Francis Sweeney suffered from a "slight ego complex," he discounted him as a viable suspect. "After our conversation with Dr. Sweeney," he wrote, "it is our opinion that Dr. Sweeney had no connection with the Torso Murders."

The most startling aspect of Merylo's report is not his dismissal of Francis Sweeney as a possible suspect. After all, by 1940, Merylo was firmly convinced that the Cleveland Butcher was responsible for all the New Castle murders as well and that he rode the rails mixing with transients in the hobo jungles. On that day in February, however, Merylo confronted a man whom, though he put his weight at 220 pounds, he described as "delicate," "fat and soft," and someone who "could not in our opinion fit into the type of person who would mix with transients around railroad tracks and swamps."

The most illuminating revelation in Merylo's report is that he and Zalewski had not known of Francis Sweeney until February 1940. It is clear from the Otwell manuscript that Merylo did not recognize the subject of Walter Winchell's October 1938 radio announcement as Frank Sweeney or anyone else. Perhaps more than anything else, Merylo and Zalewski's ignorance of Frank Sweeney verifies that there were at least two separate but parallel investigations into the killings going on at the same time.

The press saw and reported on the activities of the police under Sergeant

James Hogan's direction. (Marjorie Merylo Dentz remembers that reporters dogged her father's every step.) Ness obviously used this formal and very public investigation as a screen behind which he directed the activities of two secret and very different groups of handpicked individuals known only to him and probably David Cowles. In the first group were the Unknowns, a few trusted law enforcement personnel controlled by Ness and funded by an anonymous group of business leaders; the second group, composed of carefully chosen low-level hoods, was set up by David Cowles sometime after A. J. Pearce's September 1936 conference and supported financially by the *Press.* Every so often the activities of those closest to Ness would surface in the papers—as in the April, 1938 Chamberlin-Gerber clash over the piece of no. 10's leg—but such instances were rare and treated as isolated events, not part of a highly organized, ongoing, secret investigation. From Merylo's reports it is also clear that Cowles would occasionally direct his and Zalewski's activities without revealing to them the full extent of his information. On that day in early February 1940, Cowles would have known to send the pair of detectives to the East 65th address either because someone had tracked the doctor from Sandusky to Cleveland and reported back to Cowles (or possibly directly to Ness), or someone at the home—following the instructions Marilyn Bardsley says were written in Frank Sweeney's file—had alerted Cleveland authorities when Sweeney disappeared. Exactly why Cowles would alert Merylo and Zalewski to Francis Sweeney when he did is anyone's guess.

The tangle of questions over who knew or believed what about Francis Sweeney now becomes a veritable Gordian knot. From this point in time, it remains extremely difficult to gauge the degree to which Ness and his inner circle actually considered Francis Sweeney a serious suspect; their silence regarding him was virtually total. Ness, Cowles, and Grossman—and, one assumes, the others present during the lengthy hotel suite interrogation in May 1938—continued to participate in the ongoing investigation while maintaining a total public silence that lasted until Ness's converstations with Oscar Fraley two decades later. In May 1940, Cowles was among the contingent of law enforcement personnel who traveled to Pittsburgh to explore a possible connection between the Kingsbury Run murders and the three butchered bodies railroad yardmen had discovered in a string of boxcars slated for demolition. If Ness and Cowles seriously believed in Francis Sweeney's guilt after May 1938, why did they pursue the investigation with such vigor well into the 1940s? Even more perplexing, why did they remain passive and silent in the summer of 1939 when Sheriff O'Donnell arrested and charged Frank Dolezal? Are potential turf issues between O'Donnell and Ness really sufficient to explain away, let alone excuse, the death of an innocent man?

Seventy-five years ago, Eliot Ness no doubt realized that Francis Sweeney's four competency hearings—two in late 1933 and early 1934, two in early 1938—frame the twelve "official" Cleveland killings and the Lady of the Lake almost perfectly and that the details of his melancholy life and the terrible history of the Kingsbury Run murders run like parallel lines—never losing sight of each other but never clearly intersecting. He could have saved his sagging reputation in Cleveland during the early 1940s by shining a very bright spotlight on Francis Sweeney.

The conspiratorially minded will scream cover-up; after all, Francis Sweeney was Congressman Martin L. Sweeney's cousin. But merely keeping confidential the identity of a suspect against whom there was no solid evidence is not the same thing as an organized cover-up. Even if one is not inclined to accept Eliot Ness's straight-arrow reputation, why would he make a hush deal with a Democratic congressman who had pummeled him and the rest of the city's Republican administration unmercifully over their failure to catch the Kingsbury Run murderer? Undoubtedly, Martin L. Sweeney was enraged when he learned—as he surely must have—that his down-and-out cousin had fallen under suspicion, and he would have branded any public move on Francis as a blatant act of political revenge. In this particular context, the only explanation that makes any plausible sense is that the unidentified business leaders, possibly Democrats, who provided the slush fund that supported the Unknowns, may have pressured Ness. Whatever his reasons, Ness, in fact, showed admirable restraint in handling the interrogation affair with such discretion.

But the fate of Frank Dolezal may also have been a factor in Ness's silence. As safety director of the city, he could not exercise any power over the county sheriff's office; he was forced to watch the media hysteria surrounding Dolezal's arrest, incarceration, manhandling, and death from the legal sidelines. In the absence of any hard evidence against Francis Sweeney, he may have kept his silence to avoid seeing another potentially innocent man destroyed.

Those who did know about Francis Sweeney and the May 1938 interrogation guarded their secret well. As late as February 1940, when he officially questioned the doctor at David Cowles's instigation, Peter Merylo seemed unaware of him. Were Eliot Ness and David Cowles purposely keeping Merylo in the dark—not only about Dr. Sweeney but also about everything connected to their behind-the-scenes investigations? Does all this somehow suggest that Ness did not fully trust Peter Merylo?

With regard to keeping Merylo (and Zalewski) out of the loop, conspiracy buffs will revel in the notion of Ness and Cowles putting their heads together in a dark, smoke-filled room, plotting to keep all their really important information on the case away from the lead investigators. A far more likely explanation is that Ness saw and took advantage of a situation that had already developed. The press, the general public, and the police began to realize the city was hunting a lone killer responsible for a series of unspeakably gruesome murder-dismemberments in June 1936 (after the death of the tattooed victim no. 4), a realization that automatically increased the intensity of newspaper coverage. Chief George Matowitz assigned Merylo to the case on September 10, 1936, the very day Jerry Harris saw the first pieces of no. 6 floating in the stagnant waterway; two days later, Mayor Burton told Ness that public pressure dictated that he must get more directly involved in the investigation. An official double appointment and a sixth butchered body within three days! Press scrutiny of the hunt became even more intense and, no doubt, intrusive.

After Coroner Pearce's torso clinic on September 15, 1936, Ness began to realize that extraordinary measures of a decidedly unorthodox nature were needed. If such initiatives were to work, they must be kept secret. What better way to keep his tactics away from the prying eyes of the press than to allow the activities of Merylo, Zalewski, Hogan, and others in the police department to occupy the limelight? After all, a colorful character like Peter Merylo, always ready to speak his mind, was wonderful copy.

And just how far down the chain of command did ignorance of Ness's behind-the-scenes maneuvering extend? Did Chief Matowitz, for example, know about Francis Sweeney? Did Coroner Gerber or Sergeant James Hogan? It is extremely difficult to gauge what Matowitz may or may not have known. His name rarely comes up in newspaper stories and hardly ever appears—if at all—in Peter Merylo's or anyone else's surviving police reports. (Investigating officers reported directly to their superiors, not to the chief.) Both Merylo's memoirs and the Otwell manuscript also suggest that Matowitz was minimally involved in the day-to-day torso investigation.

The evidence strongly indicates that Sergeant Hogan remained ignorant of Francis Sweeney's existence. The head of homicide went to Indianapolis to check the source of Walter Winchell's radio story dealing with the possible arrest of a Cleveland doctor in October 1938. Assuming that Sweeney was, indeed, the subject of Winchell's report, then certainly his name would have come up during Hogan's meetings with Indianapolis authorities. If Hogan had ever heard Francis Sweeney's name in any other context related to the case, he would certainly not have so decisively dismissed Winchell's story when he returned to Cleveland.

Coroner Sam Gerber is a different story. Self-assured, arrogant, and protective of his turf, he seems to have been a rather temperamental man of definite opinions—one who actively sought the publicity spotlight but didn't always behave very well when he had it. On April 9, 1938, the *News* ran its story alleging that police suspected "a once-prominent Clevelander, described as a physician in disrepute with his profession." Gerber not only verified the *News*'s tip, but added that the doctor in question had been under suspicion since September 1935. Surely, he knew that the suspected physician was Francis Sweeney. Yet in George Condon's 1984 *Cleveland Magazine* article, Gerber vigorously denied that he had ever said the Butcher was "a broken-down doctor who becomes frenzied with drugs or liquor." Gerber, of course, was a loyal Democrat and party activist, and his silence about Francis Sweeney, unlike Ness's, could have been politically motivated.

There is no surviving written evidence or rumors to suggest that either George Matowitz or Eliot Ness was dissatisfied with Peter Merylo's work. First and foremost, Eliot Ness valued competence and dedication—as demonstrated by his active support of Democrat Frank Cullitan for county prosecutor in the 1936 fall elections. Chief George Matowitz, a highly respected professional whose working relationship with the safety director seems to have been at least respectful, handpicked Detective Merylo to work the torso murders full-time. Whether or not Matowitz ran his decision by Ness, there was no obvious professional reason for the safety director to question the chief's choice. Granted, Peter Merylo did not particularly care for the safety director, but Ness would not have let that bother him—even if he knew about the tough cop's attitude—as long as Merylo performed well on the job. Ness had always freely employed unorthodox methods, sometimes of questionable legality, and he would have respected, even if grudgingly, a man like Peter Merylo who was also always willing to try anything to get the job done.

At some point, however, between the time he questioned Francis Sweeney in 1940 and his retirement from the force in 1943, Merylo learned of a suspect connected to a politically powerful Cleveland family. There is no way to determine when or how he came by the information, whether others passed it on to him or he developed the lead himself. It is not even clear if he knew the suspect's name, let alone whether he realized it was the same man he and Zalewski had questioned in February 1940. Merylo's daughter Marjorie Merylo Dentz and his nephew Allen P. Pinell chose their words with deliberate care and caution, realizing that their recollections were more than forty years old, but both confirmed that Merylo was aware of a politically connected suspect's existence.

An official silence motivated by any reason would have angered Peter Merylo; one based on politics would have outraged him. He would have insisted that the safety director's suspect was a lead that should be thoroughly explored no matter what the publicity or political fallout. Allen Pinell remembers the bitterness in the Merylo household and recalls his Aunt Sophie explaining that her husband deeply, even vehemently, resented the hands-off policy adopted by unnamed superiors. Pinell remembers the suspect's surname being bandied about in hushed family conversations but is unsure what it was. Although she did not recognize the name Francis Edward Sweeney, Marjorie Merylo Dentz confirmed in a telephone interview of June 9, 1999, that higher-ups in the department told her father to "leave it alone"; even if the suspect was guilty, "his family" had seen to it that he was institutionalized. We will never know exactly to whom "his family" refers, nor can we ever be sure who those higher-ups were. Merylo's professional activities in the three-year period between 1940 and 1943, however, clearly demonstrate that he regarded this secret suspect not as the answer to the riddle of the murders but only as one lead among many to pursue. He doggedly followed trails all over northeastern Ohio and western Pennsylvania, and after he retired in 1943, he still pressed his private investigation forward. Even if he was only minimally convinced that the key to the crimes rested with Eliot Ness's secret suspect, a no-nonsense cop like Peter Merylo never would have wasted his time and energies on such meaningless efforts.

Eliot Ness left Cleveland with the change of administration in 1942. A year later, after twenty-five years of service, Peter Merylo, still maintaining the silence apparently forced on him by his superiors, resigned from the force. He was only forty-eight. And yet, according to David Kerr, who succeeded James Hogan as head of homicide, the rumor of Eliot Ness's secret suspect persisted and grew in the department. *Plain Dealer* staff writer Brian Albrecht interviewed Kerr in late 1988 or early 1989. Then retired and in his eightieth year, Kerr recalled, in Albrecht's words, the stories about a suspected doctor "related to a well-known local political family, who had fallen into disrepute after receiving treatment at an insane asylum." "Late in the investigation," Albrecht went on, "there was a report published that police had focused their search on a once prominent, middle-aged physician said to be powerfully built and a chronic alcoholic with sadistic tendencies. However, no further mention of that suspect appeared again."

After the passage of seventy-five years, does the Mad Butcher of Kingsbury Run finally move out of the darkness and into the light? Does Dr. Francis Edward Sweeney's face now flicker over the phantom's featureless shadow? As my long-time collaborator Mark Wade Stone so often remarks publically: "Everything we find out points to him. Nothing has so far pointed away." He possessed the necessary medical background and skill; he grew up in the area and, therefore, knew the Run well; he fits the profile fashioned by Coroner Pearce's Torso Clinic; he fits more modern FBI serial killer profiles; he was a member of family that wrestled with both mental illness and alcoholism; the papers filed by his wife in probate court chronicle his mental decline and his growing propensity toward violence; he had access to a location where he could immobilize his victims; he enjoyed easy access to an undertaking facility where he could commit murder, decapitate his victims, and easily dispose of the blood; he constantly taunted law enforcement personnel, specifically Eliot Ness with his stream of postcards and letters; he routinely injected himself into the investigation.

Perhaps, the greatest mystery swirling around the Kingsbury Run murders is why Frank Sweeney's name remained hidden for so long. Once identified, his presence clearly hovers over and infiltrates every aspect of the long, difficult history of the investigation like a poisonous mist: the newspaper and other media references to a host of derelict doctors, especially the "powerfully built, chronic alcoholic with apparent sadistic tendencies"; Walter Winchell's radio bulletin dealing with the "Jekyll-Hyde doctor," "a fanatic, a medical man with great skill"; John Bartlow Martin's reference in his *Harper's Magazine* article to "an aging, once-prominent doctor who succumbed to narcotics." Then there are those intriguing stories of leads that constantly popped up but seemed to go nowhere: the well-dressed doctor who fre-quented a local dive, bought drinks for the regulars (including Flo Polillo), and let it be known that he owned a car and would be glad to drive anyone anywhere they needed to go. And, of course, there is Coroner Gerber's asser-tion—later angrily retracted—that the Butcher was a "broken-down doctor who becomes frenzied with drugs or liquor." How was it that the Sweeney name never got attached to any of this seemingly endless proliferation of stories? Some will scream "cover-up", and at first glance that seems a logical explanation for the decades of silence. But Eliot Ness, Mayor Harold Burton, and Chief of Police George Matowitz—all Republicans—would have had no incentive to protect the political reputation of Frank Sweeney's cousin, Martin L. Sweeney, the noisy Democratic congressman from the 20th district. But Frank Sweeney's immediate family may have been another matter: his wife and two young sons, his sisters, his nephews and nieces. The results of Leonard Keeler's polygraph tests were not admissible in court, and there was obviously no hard evidence that authorities could marshal to convict him—no fingerprints, no witnesses, no other pieces of physical evidnece. The opinions of those who knew Ness, Burton, and Matowitz are absolutely unequivocal; neither of them would have ever accepted a "deal" that let a guilty man off the hook. But with no case to take to court, an arrangement that got him off the streets and committed to a mental institution may have been the best option: if Martin L. Sweeney would behave himself on the local political scene and use whatever influence he may have over his seri-ously deranged cousin to render him harmless, then the Cleveland powers that be would keep the name Dr. Francis Edward Sweeney secret. There would be no trial; and even if there were, he would most likely wind up in a mental institution anyway. Martin L. Sweeney could save his reputation, and Frank Sweeney's family would be spared some extraordinarily painful public embarrassment.

There are stories circulating among the descendants of Frank Sweeney's sister Mary that he wrote letters to her from the Dayton VA mental facil-ity, where he was incarcerated and ultimately died, virtually admitting his guilt in the Kingsbury Run murders. Those precious letters, however, seem to have disappeared; no one in the family seems to know who wound up with them and where they might be, assuming they still exist. In only one surviving document does Francis Sweeney slyly admit his guilt. On one of the postcards sent to Eliot Ness and now housed with his papers at the

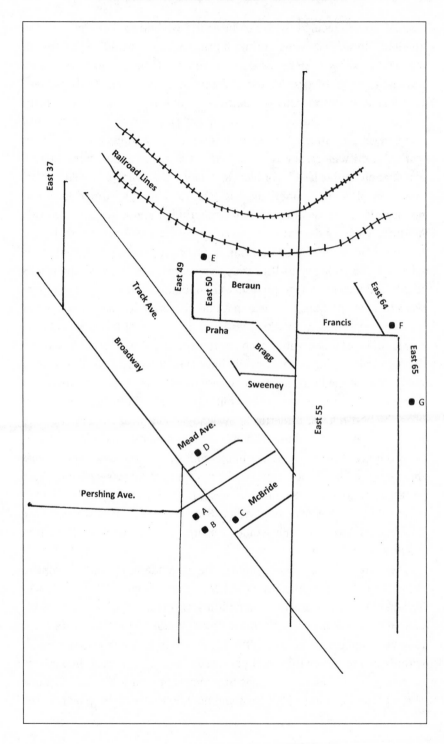

Western Reserve Historical Society, Sweeney obliquely refers to the legendary Sweeney Todd, the demon barber of Fleet Street, who sent his clients
tumbling into his basement where they were summarily killed, cut up, and
baked into meat pies. His greeting to Eliot Ness, his long-time nemesis,
reads simply "Good cheer, the American Sweeney."

NOTES

My conversations and formal interviews with Marilyn Bardsley took place from
1990 to 2000.

Sergeant John Fransen discussed his involvement in the case with me during
a phone interview in 1998.

A marriage license was issued to Frank E. Sweeney and Mary J. Sokol on July
1, 1927, application no. 221378.

Mary Sokol Sweeney describes her husband's behavior from 1929 until 1934
in two separate petitions, case nos. 413785 and 445238.

Francis Sweeney's appearances in probate court over his mental condition are
recorded on Civil Appearance Docket No. 250, case no. 213871

Dates for relevant newspaper articles referred to are given in the text.

David Cowles's discussion of the hotel suite interrogation and his description
of the suspect are from an interview taped in 1983. There are minor differences
in wording between the tape and the transcript. What appears in the text is taken
directly from the tape.

Dr. B. J. Chazin's 1963 evaluation of Francis Sweeney's physical and mental
condition is from a document contained in the dossier compiled by Sergeant John
Fransen now on file at the Cleveland police department.

Facing page: Sites relevant to the murders in the Broadway-East 55 area.

A) The house at 5026 Broadway that served as a medical office for Edward Pe-
terka, Francis Sweeney, and four other physicians.
B) The Raus Funeral Home at 5040 Broadway.
C) St. Alexis Hospital where Francis Sweeney interned.
D) The building on Mead used by Raus for the unclaimed and indigent dead.
E) The spot where Edward Andrassy and the unidentified second victim were
found on September 23, 1935.
F) The home of Francis Sweeney's married older sister at the corner of East 64
and Francis. Frank Sweeney lived there while going to Western Reserve School of
Pharmacology in the early 1920s.
G) The spot where clothes resembling those worn by Flo Polillo (murdered in
January 1936) were discovered in January 1938.

The FBI material on Francis Sweeney is from file no. 62–100340.

As indicated in the text, Andrew Schug (member of the Board of Trustees, Cleveland Police Historical Society) and I interviewed Arnold Sagalyn, former special assistant to Eliot Ness, in October 1997.

Cleveland papers covered Emil Fronek's account of his 1934 run-in with the mysterious physician on August 29, 1938.

Peter Merylo gives an account of Walter Winchell's radio broadcast and subsequent events in the Otwell manuscript.

As stated in the text, some material on physicians checked out by the police is from John Bartlow Martin's "Butcher's Dozen: The Cleveland Torso Murders."

Peter Merylo's police report of February 6, 1940, covering his and Martin's Zalewski's interrogation of Francis Sweeney is in his files.

As stated in the text, Coroner Gerber's denial of alleged previous statements about the Butcher is from George Condon's "The Mad Butcher of Kingsbury Run."

My discussions with psychiatrists and psychologists, all of whom requested anonymity, dealing with a probable diagnosis of Francis Sweeney's mental condition took place from 1996 until 1999.

The information concerning Peter Merylo's knowledge of Eliot Ness's suspect was supplied by his daughter Marjorie Merylo Dentz and his nephew Allen P. Pinell, in a series of phone conversations and personal interviews.

EPILOGUE

"**E**very once in a while we still get a tip on the damn thing," reflected homicide head Lieutenant David Kerr on the Kingsbury Run murders in the late 1940s. The book is never closed on unsolved homicides; after more than seventy-five years, the torso killings are still officially regarded as an open case.

In the summer of 1950, a new generation of police officers answered the call and searched through the steel girders where Robert Robertson's dismembered remains were found. For them, the Kingsbury Run murders were already legend. The men who had worked on the case may have faded from the public's memory as the murders themselves disappeared from the headlines, but in the police department, they enjoyed a reverence previous generations had reserved for Civil War veterans. Only another cop could understand the grinding frustration of working so hard for so long and having virtually nothing to show for it. Orley May left the force in 1944 to become safety director in Berea. He died in January 1968 at the age of seventy. During World War II, Emil Musil worked with federal authorities investigating counterfeit rationing stamps. He retired in 1948, served another twenty years as treasurer of the city's Retired Police Association, and died at age seventy-three in 1970. James T. Hogan resigned in 1941 with thirty-six years of service behind him. He died three years later. Martin Zalewski passed away in November 1958.

Peter Merylo left the force in 1943. No one in the department thought the dedicated Butcher hunter would ever retire, but having put in his twenty-five years, he quietly resigned. Chief Matowitz's support of the torso investigation may have been on-again, off-again, but his public support for his handpicked torso investigator never wavered. In July 1939 the chief had praised Merylo as "the hardest working man on the force." "He doesn't know what it is to be at home," he told the *Press* on July 8. "He has put in hours and hours of overtime and has never asked for a minute of it back. . . . He has crawled through filth and dirt, into cellars and into attics. He has had to deal with bums and perverts and all sorts of repulsive people. He has put more men in jail than any other man on the force."

A detailed examination of the official reports and other papers Merylo took with him on retirement demonstrates that, in spite of his reputation for independence and occasional bull-in-the-china-shop tactics, he was a thorough professional who played by the book and outwardly respected the lines of authority no matter what his personal opinions may have been. He always made sure his superiors wrote official letters of thanks to law enforcement personnel in other states and jurisdictions who had cooperated in the torso investigation and often responded personally to well-intended tip letters from all over the country.

He went on to be chief of plant police at Tinnerman Products after his retirement. But investigative work was truly in his blood, so, after a brief flirtation with a State Department offer to work in the Hawaiian Islands during World War II, he set up his own detective agency. Kingsbury Run, however, never strayed far from his thoughts; he scanned out-of-town newspapers looking for telltale stories and corresponded with law enforcement personnel outside Cleveland. "In my 25 years in the Cleveland Police Department I had never given up on any case that I was ever assigned to," he wrote in his memoirs, "nor did I ever intend to give up the investigation of the Cleveland Torso Murders." His detractors would argue that professional zeal had become personal obsession. He was on his way to his office in the old Arcade when he collapsed and died in May 1958 at the age of sixty-three.

Though largely self-taught in chemistry and the other sciences, David Cowles became a recognized pioneer in law enforcement, bringing the Cleveland Police Department into the modern era by emphasizing the application of science in solving crimes. He became an expert on the polygraph and trained others in its use. Cowles retired from the force in 1957 at the age of sixty-one but kept abreast of developments in the field of scientific investigation. He died at age ninety in 1988.

Dr. Samuel Gerber won reelection as county coroner handily for almost fifty years. He eventually became a highly respected forensic celebrity, coauthoring books and traveling extensively as a lecturer. He grabbed the spotlight again during the infamous Sheppard murder case of the early 1950s. By the time frail health forced his retirement in December 1986, he was a local monument; the man and the office had become one in the public mind. He died less than six months later on May 16, 1987—thirty years to the day after the death of Eliot Ness.

When Ness left law enforcement in the 1940s, his career began a downward spiral from which it never recovered. The ability to lead and inspire, the intelligence and foresight, the sheer imaginative brilliance that propelled him to fame and made the Cleveland police force a model for the entire country deserted him in the business world. He made an ill-advised run for mayor of Cleveland as a Republican in 1947 but suffered a resounding defeat at the hands of the popular Democratic incumbent Tom Burke. Never much of a political animal, Ness even commented publicly that he thought his opponent had been doing a good job. Even after a decade, however, the torso case stalked Ness's public image and blighted his campaign. The specter of his past successes haunted him, and Cleveland simply could not understand why an invincible legend could not crack the city's most notorious case. The Depression-era G-man had lost his glamour.

Eliot Ness's ashes, as well as those of his third wife, Elizabeth, and adopted son, Robert, are scattered on Wade Lake during a formal ceremony at Lake View Cemetery on September 10, 1997. Cleveland Police Historical Society.

When Ness died of a massive heart attack on May 16, 1957, in Coudersport, Pennsylvania, at the age of fifty-four, his family had barely enough money to cremate his remains. The man, his accomplishments, and his fate soon became lost in the gigantic shadows of a reborn legend fashioned by popular fiction, TV, the movies, Robert Stack, and Kevin Costner. Not until Paul W. Heimel authored *Eliot Ness: The Real Story* in 1997 did the public learn that the crime fighter's ashes, as well as those of his third wife, Elizabeth, and adopted son Robert, had never been buried. Rebecca McFarland, Cleveland historian and authority on Ness, and the Cleveland Police Historical Society spearheaded a successful drive to have all the Ness family remains scattered in a formal ceremony.

On September 10, 1997, forty years after his death, more than three hundred people came to Lake View Cemetery and solemnly watched as members of the harbor patrol poured the ashes of Eliot Ness and his family over a wreath in Wade Lake with full police honors. A cordon of officers stood at attention and saluted as pipe bands from Cleveland and Chicago sent the familiar, stirring strains of "Amazing Grace" over the water from the opposite side of the quiet lake; rifle shots rang out, and two police helicopters flew over in tribute; somewhere along the shore a solitary bugler played "taps." A month later, on October 8, a decades-long search for Edward Andrassy's burial site ended; his daughter and granddaughters quietly laid flowers on his grave for the first time.

NOTES

David Kerr's comment is quoted in John Bartlow Martin's "Butcher's Dozen: The Cleveland Torso Murders" (69).

Peter Merylo's memoirs are part of his personal files.

MAPS

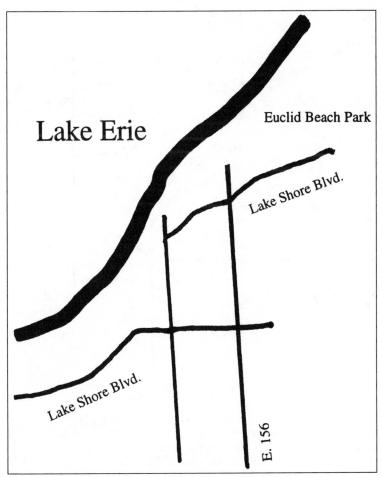

Map 1. A stretch of the Lake Erie shore east of Cleveland.

Frank LaGassie found the first part of the Lady of the Lake on September 5, 1934, at the base of East 156th. Robert Smith discovered the upper half of victim no. 7's torso in the same spot on February 23, 1937. Map by Richard Karberg.

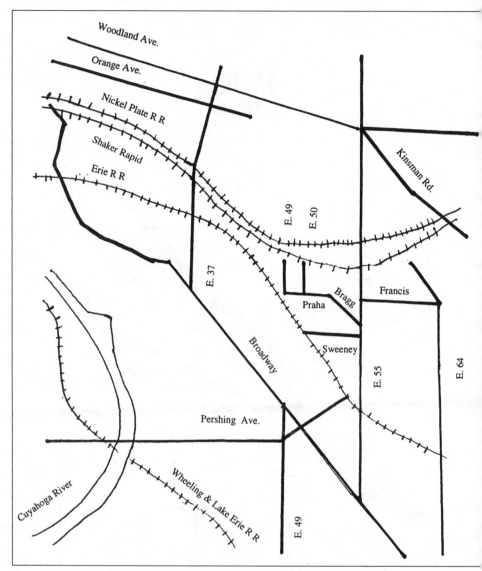

Map 2. Part of the Kingsbury Run bordered by Woodland Avenue and Broadway.

James Wagner and Peter Kostura found the bodies of Edward W. Andrassy and victim no. 2 at the base of Jackass Hill near East 49th on September 23, 1935. Slightly northeast, near the railroad tracks, Louis Cheeley and Gomez Ivey found the pants-wrapped head of victim no. 4 on June 5, 1936; authorities located the body the next day just east of East 55th. The month-long search for parts of victim no. 6 that began on September 10, 1936, took place at a stagnant pool along East 37th in Kingsbury Run.

Dr. Francis Edward Sweeney's office in the early 1930s stood on the southwest corner of Pershing and Broadway. Map by Richard Karberg.

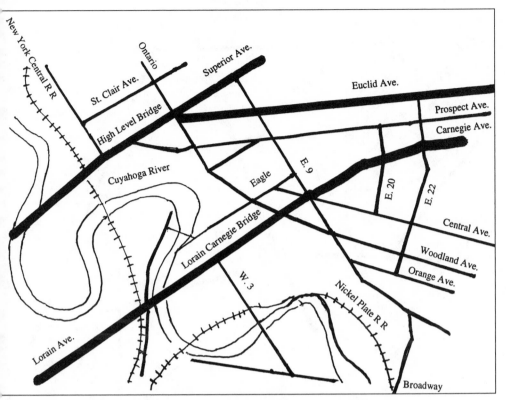

Map 3. A section of the Flats and the near east side.

The first set of Flo Polillo's remains was discovered behind Hart Manufacturing on the east side of Central Avenue close to East 20th on January 26, 1936. The second set turned up on the north side of the Orange Avenue-Broadway intersection on February 7. Russell Lauer found the skeletal remains of victim no. 8 under the Lorain-Carnegie Bridge just west of the Cuyahoga River on June 6, 1937. The weeklong search for pieces of victim no. 9 began in the Cuyahoga River on July 6, 1937, under the West 3rd St. Bridge and extended north to Lake Erie. The first piece of victim no. 10 turned up at the base of Superior Avenue in the Cuyahoga on April 8, 1938; police recovered more of her body from the river on May 2. Eliot Ness led the party of shantytown raiders down Eagle Avenue on August 18, 1938.

In the mid-to-late 1930s, Frank Dolezal lived at a couple of different addresses in the Central Avenue-East 20th area. The bar at the corner of Central Avenue and East 20th became the focus of Pat Lyon's investigation in the summer of 1939 because Edward Andrassy, Flo Polillo, Rose Wallace, and Frank Dolezal supposedly frequented the run-down establishment. Map by Richard Karberg.

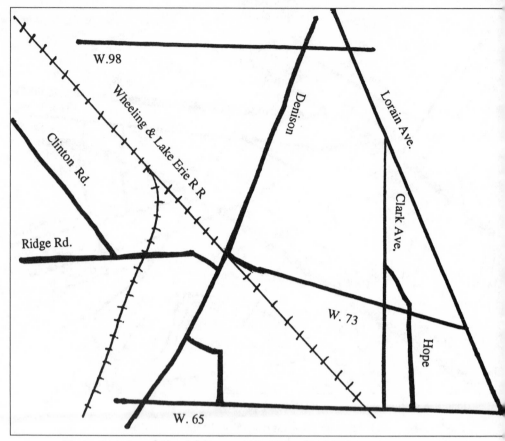

Map 4. A section of Cleveland's west side south of Lorain Avenue.

Marie Barkley of Hope Avenue found the body of victim no. 5 between West 98th and Clinton on July 22, 1936. Map by Richard Karberg.

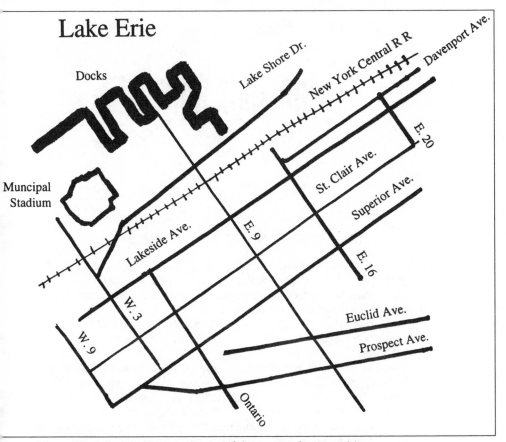

Map 5. The Lake Erie shore at the site of the Great Lakes Exposition.

Victims no. 11 and 12 were discovered in a dump at the corner of East 9th and Lake Shore on August 16, 1938. Twelve years later, on July 22, 1950, Robert Robertson's disarticulated remains were found on the property of Norris Brothers Company at 2138 Davenport Avenue. Map by Richard Karberg.

BIBLIOGRAPHY

MANUSCRIPTS AND ARCHIVAL SOURCES

Allegheny County, Pa., Office of the Coroner. 1923. Cases C-165-23 (Charles Mc-Gregor), Oct. 3. Coroner's Office Records, 1884–1976. AIS.1982.07, Archives Service Center, University of Pittsburgh. Files include autopsy protocols, affidavits, police reports, and various pieces of official correspondence.

———. 1940. Cases C-40-34, C-40-35, C-40-36 (James Nicholson), May 3. Coroner's Office Records, 1884–1976. AIS.1982.07, Archives Service Center, University of Pittsburgh.

———. 1941. Unnumbered case (Wallace L. Brown), Sept. 24. Coroner's Office Records, 1884–1976. AIS.1982.07, Archives Service Center, University of Pittsburgh.

———. 1942. Cases C-42-57 (Ernest Alonzo), June 23. Coroner's Office Records, 1884–1976. AIS.1982.07, Archives Service Center, University of Pittsburgh.

American Civil Liberties Union. Files on Frank Dolezal's arrest, including various correspondence and newspaper clippings. Volumes 2116 and 2136.

Cleveland Police Department. Case file on the murder of Robert Robertson, July 1950. Cleveland Police Department.

Coroner's files. Case nos. 44996, 44997, 45371, 45781, 45960, 46118, 46672, 47022, 47125, 48176, 48621, and 48625. The files contain autopsy protocols (some incomplete), police reports, official and unofficial correspondence, and miscellaneous pieces of other official paperwork amounting to about two hundred pages of material. Cuyahoga County Archives.

Court of Common Pleas, Records.

Andrassy, Lillian (Kardotska). Petition for divorce, case no. 315896.

Dolezal, Charles. Suits against Sheriff Martin L. O'Donnell and others, case nos. 496329 and 496330.

Sweeney, Mary Josephine (Sokol). Petitions for separation and divorce, case nos. 413785 and 445238.

Gerber, Dr. Samuel R. Coroner's Verdict and Testimony on the Body of Frank Dolezal. August 24, 1939. Case no. 49869. Coroner's Office, Cuyahoga County.

"Transcript of Proceedings Commencing at 10:30 A.M., Saturday, August 26, 1939, before Hon. Samuel R. Gerber, County Coroner, in Relation to Death of Frank Dolezal at County Jail, August 24, 1939." Includes depositions taken by Cleveland Police Department's Bureau of Criminal Investigation from individuals in the sheriff's office and others directly involved with Frank Dolezal's death. Coroner's Office, Cuyahoga County.

Cowles, David L. Taped interview conducted by Lieutenant Tom Brown and Florence Schwein. September 6, 1983. Typed manuscript of same interview. Cleveland Police Historical Society.

Federal Bureau of Investigation. Records.

File on Dr. Francis Edward Sweeney, no. 62–100340.

Sweeney, Martin L. File no. 100–32378–1, July 11, 1944. Cuyahoga County Court of Common Pleas.

Fransen, Sergeant John (Cleveland Police Force, retired). Dossier on Dr. Francis Edward Sweeney. 1991–92. Cleveland Police Department.

Johnson, Paul G. 2007. "Murder Swamp." Unpublished manuscript. Private collection of Paul Johnson.

———. N.d. Newspaper clippings, source unknown. Private collection of Paul Johnson.

Lawrence County Historical Society. 2010. "The Black Hand." Lawrence County Historical Society, http://www.lawrencechs.com/museum/collections/the-black-hand/.

Limber, James M. A small collection of photographs related to Kingsbury Run. Cleveland Police Historical Society Museum.

Lyons, Lawrence J. (Pat). Private papers held by his daughter, Carol Fitzgerald, including investigation notes, unpublished manuscripts on Kingsbury Run murders and his role as investigator, and various pieces of offical and personal correspondence.

Merylo, Peter. Papers, 1930–52. The private collection in his family's hands includes the manuscripts for two projected books, Merylo's daily police reports, daily reports from other officers, various pieces of official and unofficial correspondence and paperwork, tip letters, newspaper and magazine articles and clippings from around the country, and photographs amounting to several thousand pages of material.

———. Unpublished Memoirs. Included in his papers.

Merylo, Peter, with Frank Otwell. Unpublished Mansuscript. Included in Merylo's papers.

Probate Court, Records. Actions against Dr. Francis Edward Sweeney. Civil Appearance Docket No. 250, case no. 213871.

Ohio Soldiers' and Sailors' Home, Sandusky, Ohio. Applications for Admission and other documents relevant to Dr. Francis Edward Sweeney's residency at the facility.

PUBLISHED SOURCES

Albrecht, Brian. "The Dirtiest Dozen." *Plain Dealer Sunday Magazine,* July 25, 1993: 8+.

———. "The Terror of Kingsbury Run." *Plain Dealer,* January 8, 1989: Gi+.

Badal, James Jessen. 2013. *Hell's Wasteland.* Kent, Ohio: Kent State Univ. Press.

———. 2001. *In the Wake of the Butcher: Cleveland's Torso Murders.* Kent, Ohio: Kent State Univ. Press.

———. 2010. *Though Murder Has No Tongue: The Lost Victim of Cleveland's Mad Butcher.* Kent, Ohio: Kent State Univ. Press.

Beaufait, Howard. "Kingsbury Run Murders." *Homespun,* November 1955: 32+.

Cleveland Edition. Mar. 9, 1989.

Cleveland News. Articles from 1934 to 1950.

Cleveland Plain Dealer. Articles from 1922 to 1950.

Cleveland Press. Articles from 1934 to 1950.

Condon, George. "The Mad Butcher of Kingsbury Run: A Strange Unsolved Case." *Cleveland Magazine,* March 1984: 76+.

Douglas, John, and Mark Olshaker. *Mind Hunter: Inside the FBI's Elite Serial Crime Unit.* New York: Pocket Star, 1995.

East Liverpool (OH) *Evening Review.* Feb. 12–13, 19, 1924.

Gilmore, John. 2006. *Severed: The True Story of the Black Dahlia Murder.* 2nd ed. Los Angeles, Calif.: Amok Books.

Heimel, Paul W. *Eliot Ness: The Real Story.* Nashville: Cumberland House, 2000.

Martin, John Bartlow. "Butcher's Dozen: The Cleveland Torso Murders," *Harper's Magazine,* November 1949: 55–69.

McClung, Paul. 1952. "The Fiend Has a Thousand Eyes." *Front Page Detective,* July.

Ove, Torsten. 2000. "Mafia Has Long History Here, Growing from Bootlegging Days." *Pittsburgh Post-Gazette,* Nov. 6. Post-gazette.com. http://old.post-gazette.com/regionstate/20001106mobhistory2.asp (accessed Dec. 6, 2010).

Ness, Eliot, and Oscar Fraley. *The Untouchables.* Englewood Cliffs: Prentice-Hall, 1962.

New Castle Herald. Mar. 17–18, 1921.

New Castle News. July 11, Oct. 6, 1923; Jan. 3–8, Oct. 6–10, 14, 19–21, 1925; July 2, 1936; Oct. 16–17, 19–20, 1939; May 3, Nov. 2, 4, 1940.

Nickel, Steven. *Torso: The Story of Eliot Ness and the Search for a Psychopathic Killer.* Winston-Salem, N.C.: John F. Blair, 1989.

Pittsburgh Post-Gazette. Oct. 6–7, 1923; May 4–6, 1940.

Pittsburgh Press. Oct. 3, 1923; May 3–4, 1940; June 1, Sept. 24, 1941; June 23–24, 1942.

Pittsburgh Sun-Telegraph. May 3–5, 1940; May 26, 31, Sept. 25, 1941; June 22, 1942.

Ressler, Robert H., and Tom Shachtman. *Whoever Hunts Monsters.* New York: St. Martin's, 1992.

Ritt, William. "The Head Hunter of Kingsbury Run." In *Cleveland Murders,* edited by Oliver Weld Bayer. New York: Duell, Sloan and Pearce, 1947.

Steubenville (OH) *Herald Star.* Feb. 12–15, 1924.

Van Tassel, David O., and John J. Grabowski, eds. *The Encyclopedia of Cleveland History.* Bloomington: Indiana Universtiy Press, 1987.

Youngstown Vindicator. May 3–4, 8, 1940.

INDEX